M366 Block 4
UNDERGRADUATE COMPUTING

Natural and artificial intelligence

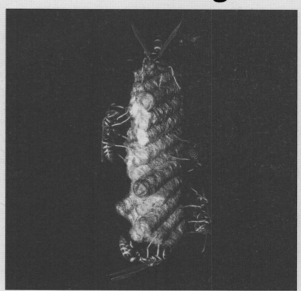

Neural networks

Block

4

Cover image: Daniel H. Janzen. *Polistes* wasps build a relatively simple nest that lasts only a single summer. These New World wasps often site the unenclosed combs under eaves and the other sheltered places where they come into contact with people.

This publication forms part of an Open University course M366 *Natural and artificial intelligence*. Details of this and other Open University courses can be obtained from the Student Registration and Enquiry Service, The Open University, PO Box 197, Milton Keynes MK7 6BJ, United Kingdom: tel. +44 (0)845 300 6090, email general-enquiries@open.ac.uk

Alternatively, you may visit the Open University website at http://www.open.ac.uk where you can learn more about the wide range of courses and packs offered at all levels by The Open University.

To purchase a selection of Open University course materials visit http://www.ouw.co.uk, or contact Open University Worldwide, Michael Young Building, Walton Hall, Milton Keynes MK7 6AA, United Kingdom for a brochure. tel. +44 (0)1908 858793; fax +44 (0)1908 858787; email ouw-cutomer-services@open.ac.uk

The Open University
Walton Hall, Milton Keynes
MK7 6AA

First published 2007, Second edition 2008.

Edited and designed by The Open University.

Typeset by SR Nova Pvt. Ltd, Bangalore, India.

Printed and bound in the United Kingdom by Charlesworth Press, Wakefield.

ISBN 978 0 7492 5070 6

2.1

MIX
Paper from responsible sources
FSC® C016379

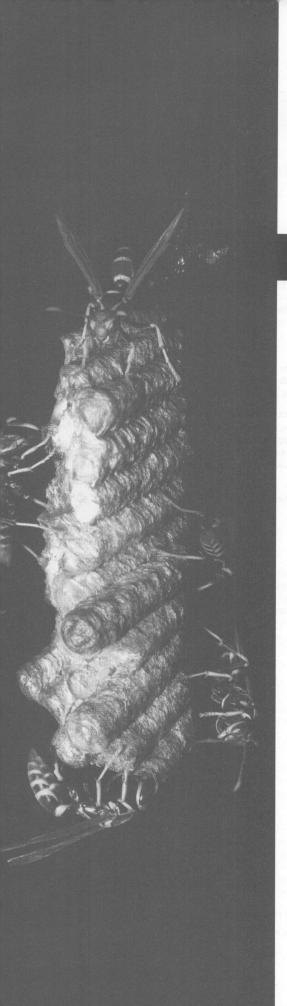

Block 4
Neural networks

Prepared for the course team by Chris Dobbyn
and Patrick Wong

CONTENTS

Introduction to Block 4   5

Unit 1: Mechanisms   9

Unit 2: Layers and learning   61

Unit 3: Unsupervised learning in layers
        and lattices   117

Unit 4: It's about time: recurrence, dynamics
        and chaos   161

Conclusion to Block 4   211

References and further reading   213

Acknowledgements   215

Index for Block 4   216

M366 COURSE TEAM

Chair, author and academic editor

Chris Dobbyn

Authors

Mustafa Ali

Tony Hirst

Mike Richards

Neil Smith

Patrick Wong

External assessor

Nigel Crook, Oxford Brookes University

Course managers

Gaynor Arrowsmith

Linda Landsberg

Media development staff

Andrew Seddon, Media Project Manager

Garry Hammond, Editor

Kate Gentles, Freelance Editor

Callum Lester, Software Developer

Andrew Whitehead, Designer and Graphic Artist

Phillip Howe, Compositor

Sarah Gamman, Contracts Executive

Lydia Eaton, Media Assistant

Critical readers

Frances Chetwynd

John Dyke

Ian Kenny

Paolo Remagnino

Thanks are due to the Desktop Publishing Unit of the Faculty of Mathematics and Computing.

Introduction to Block 4

Block introduction

> It is the entire man that writes and thinks, and not merely the head. His leg often has as much to do with it as his head – the state of his calves, his vitals and his nerves.
>
> Source: Hunt, Leigh (1855) *Stories in Verse*

Block 3 presented you with a general picture of the phenomenon that in M366 we are calling *natural intelligence*. Across the four units of that block, we developed an extended argument around two principal ideas:

► that human intelligence, and the narrow definitions of 'intelligence' that flow from our understanding of it, is not the only form of intelligence in the natural world. Countless other living creatures also display an intelligence of their own – we called it natural intelligence – involving such abilities as perception, classification, learning, communication, and so on. Our own intellectual capacities, we suggested, may, indeed, be based on exactly these abilities – in many areas, human intelligence may be simply a powerful extension of natural intelligence;

► that natural intelligence arises from four mechanisms: *interaction*, *emergence*, *adaptation* and *selection*, the building blocks of both human and animal capacities. Understanding and applying these four mechanisms in computer science and artificial intelligence can lead to new directions of research and more powerful applications.

Block 4 takes a detailed look at one area in which the principles of interaction, emergence and adaptation have led to a wholly novel approach to some of the besetting problems of Symbolic artificial intelligence (AI), and have spawned a whole generation of new computer systems – *neural networks*.

As you learned in Block 1, the early cyberneticists understood that many animal abilities originated in their nervous systems. Applying the principles of nervous interaction in computer systems, they reasoned, would make it possible for such systems to simulate some of those abilities. In this block, we take up this line of reasoning and see how it has developed. The discussion is structured as follows.

Unit 1: Mechanisms

The first unit describes some of the properties of biological nerves and nervous systems, including the electrochemical principles which nerve cells use to signal to one another. The rest of the unit is devoted to computer-simulated nervous systems, or *neural networks*: a little of their history, the elements that go to make them up, their architectures, training rules and some of the mathematical notations that can be used to describe them.

Unit 2: Layers and learning

In Unit 2 you will learn about the most widely used and successful kind of neural network, the layered, feedforward system, or *perceptron*. The discussion will take you through single-layer and multi-layer perceptrons, focusing mainly on the supervised learning algorithms that are used to train them. I will also present various case studies of some of the problems to which perceptrons have been successfully applied.

Unit 3: Unsupervised learning in layers and lattices

This unit deals with another kind of neural architecture, the *self-organising map*. Again, I'll focus principally on how such systems can be trained, through unsupervised learning. The unit concludes with an extended case study.

Unit 4: It's about time: recurrence, dynamics and chaos

The discussion of Unit 4 centres on recurrent networks, in which feedback loops create dynamic behaviour over time. I'll argue that the unpredictable and chaotic characteristics of such networks, while they need new notations to describe them, are powerful properties that can be exploited in artificial neural systems.

You may find Block 4 is more detailed and maybe more demanding than some of its predecessors. However, the theoretical material is backed up by practical exercises and demonstrations in all four units, and I do urge you to work through these.

Block 4 learning outcomes

After studying this block you will be able to:

▶ write an outline explanation of the neurobiological foundations of artificial neural networks (ANNs), illustrating the concepts of dendrite, axon, activation thresholds, spiking, ionic exchange, synaptic gap, neurotransmitters and receptors, and long-term synaptic potentiation;

▶ write a concise account, with diagrams, of the principal elements of an artificial neural system: unit, link, weight, layer and topology;

▶ write a few sentences explaining the concepts associated with the above elements: input function, activation, activation function and learning rule;

▶ name the two principal categories of learning in artificial neural systems, and provide a brief explanation of each;

▶ write an explanation, with supporting diagrams, of the following neural network topologies and systems: single-layer perceptron, multi-layer perceptron, Hopfield and other dynamic recurrent systems, and self-organising map;

▶ explain, with examples, how a neural network topology can be represented mathematically using linear algebraic notation; and how operations such as update and learning can be understood as a series of operations on vectors and matrices;

▶ based in each case on a small concrete example, calculate the weight changes, over a number of steps, in a neural network under the following training regimes: Hebb Rule, perceptron rule, delta rule and vector quantisation;

▶ use a neural network simulation toolkit or spreadsheet to set up, train and analyse single-layer feedforward (SLFF), multi-layer feedforward (MLFF), recurrent and self-organising map (SOM) networks;

▶ write outline descriptions of examples of a number of successful neural network applications;

▶ write a short reflective essay describing how the principles of interaction, emergence and adaptation apply in artificial neural systems, in theory and in practical applications;

▶ write a short reflective essay describing: the relationship between biological systems and ANNs; the shortcomings and strengths of ANNs; and the implications of an understanding of ANNs to the wider problems of AI.

Unit 1: Mechanisms

CONTENTS

1	Introduction to Unit 1	10
	What you need to study this unit	10
	Learning outcomes for Unit 1	11
2	Pulling some threads together	12
3	Recognition, classification and response	14
	3.1 Recognition and completion	14
	3.2 Classification and response	17
4	Biology	19
	4.1 A little history	19
	4.2 The nervous system	20
	4.3 Action potentials – neural firing	22
	4.4 Selection – a note on neural Darwinism	28
5	Computing	29
	5.1 A little history	29
	5.2 Computer models	33
	5.3 Computer models and biological models	48
6	Mathematics	50
	6.1 Networks as directed graphs	50
	6.2 Sigma notation	52
	6.3 Neural networks as vectors and matrices	54
7	Conclusion	57
8	Summary of Unit 1	58
	Solutions to selected exercises	59
	References and further reading	213
	Acknowledgements	215
	Index for Block 4	216

Introduction to Unit 1

Block 4 will take you into completely new areas, so I have a fair amount of work to do in this unit to set up the discussion. Between this introduction and a concluding note, there are five main sections.

In Section 2, I will start by drawing together a few threads from earlier blocks: these are of particular relevance to our theme – neural networks. Next, in Section 3, I'll single out one particular thread which arose in Block 3: the human and animal faculty for recognition, classification and response, one of the key characteristics of natural intelligence. This capacity proves to have a number of curious features that any machine-based intelligence should be able to replicate.

As you learned in Block 1, the pioneers of Cybernetics knew that the ability of organisms to sense their environment, recognise and classify important features of it, and respond to it in a suitable way arises in their nervous systems. Section 4 looks closely at the properties of nerve cells and their networks, as they are currently understood. There will be a bit of biological detail here, but I think that it is the minimum necessary for understanding the computer models of nervous systems that we are going to cover. In Section 5, we move on to investigate the building blocks and possible architectures of such models, along with an important new concept: that of a *learning rule*. Finally, in Section 6, I'll consider how certain types of mathematical notation can be used to describe a neural network concisely and elegantly.

The unit ends with some concluding remarks and a summary.

What you need to study this unit

You will need the following course components, and will need to use your computer and internet connection for some of the exercises.

▶   this Block 4 text

▶   the course DVD.

LEARNING OUTCOMES FOR UNIT 1

After studying this unit, you will be able to:

1.1 write a few sentences describing some of the features of human pattern recognition and classification;

1.2 label diagrams of a neuron and a synapse with the names of some of their constituent parts;

1.3 describe in a paragraph, and with a diagram, the process by which a neuron generates an action potential;

1.4 write a few sentences explaining the action of a synapse and the phenomenon of long-term potentiation;

1.5 write a brief explanation of the workings of each of the following components of an artificial neural network: unit, input function, activation function and weight;

1.6 explain, with diagrams, how units and weights can be combined in various topologies to form an artificial neural network;

1.7 write a paragraph describing, in detail and with an example, the concept of a learning rule;

1.8 explain how neural network concepts can be represented mathematically using signal graphs, sigma notation and vector/matrix notation.

2 Pulling some threads together

Blocks 1 and 3 were mainly concerned with the nature of intelligence. In Block 1, in a general and rather wide-ranging discussion, I looked into history and considered how thinkers of past ages had fixed on certain abilities they believed were fundamental characteristics of human intelligence, and then how the founders of AI took the first steps towards simulating these characteristics on machines. Block 2 took you deep into the details of Symbolic AI. In Block 3, I developed a broader idea of intelligence, which I called *natural intelligence*, and which takes in the abilities of animals as well as those of humans.

SAQ 1.1

Try to recall some of the main features of natural intelligence that were outlined in Block 3, Unit 1.

ANSWER...

Without going into detail, I highlighted six features that I thought were characteristic of the intelligence of animals: *drives*, *recognition*, *classification*, *response*, *communication* and *learning*.

Now we are going to go deep again. Before we do, though, I just want to pick up one or two key points arising from Block 3, as a prelude to the material of this block:

▶ Not all of the six characteristics of natural intelligence will be relevant to Block 4, but I just want to remind you of four of them:

  ▶ *Recognition*. Almost all creatures sense their environments and are able to detect within them features or patterns that are significant for their lives – star patterns, scents, potential mates, and so on.

  ▶ *Classification*. Many animals seem able to classify the patterns they perceive into simple categories – an attack or a breeze, friend or foe, male or female, useful or uninteresting, etc.

  ▶ *Response*. Along with recognition and classification comes an appropriate response. Sometimes such reactions are straightforward, such as just moving away. But you also saw that the responses of even relatively humble creatures can be very complex. Recall from Unit 1 of Block 3 the avoidance strategy of the cockroach or the intricate walking movements of insects. Even running away may not be such a simple matter.

  ▶ *Learning*. Most animals are capable of learning to some degree. Birds or even insects can be taught to recognise and respond to patterns and colours. Higher animals can have remarkable learning abilities, comparable to our own.

  You discovered in Block 2 that these are all areas in which AI has, generally speaking, proved to be weak.

▶ I developed the idea that these, and other, characteristics of natural intelligence could be explained in terms of the operation of four abstract principles: interaction, emergence, adaptation and selection. The first three of these will appear again throughout the coming block.

▶ Finally, a more detailed, but crucial, point: you may recall that in Units 2 and 4 of Block 3 I devoted quite a lot of space to the question of insect walking, looking at various models of this phenomenon. In the discussion of Exercise 2.5 in Unit 2 of Block 3, I argued that such complex behaviours *emerge* from interactions among multitudes of cells in the insects' *nervous systems*. Indeed, although I didn't make the point specifically in that unit, the models of insect walking we discussed were all simplified models of nervous interactions in insects.

Let's start by looking a little more closely at the phenomena of recognition, classification and response. This is an area in which neural networks, the theme of this block, have proved themselves particularly strong. I don't want to repeat anything that I've already covered in Block 3. My aim is to reveal some very surprising features of these capacities, which any computer intelligence would have to duplicate and which present major problems for symbolic models.

<h1>3 Recognition, classification and response</h1>

In Block 3, I revealed these functions of natural intelligence in a number of case studies, pointing out just how common they are in the natural world – cornerstones of intelligence in animals and humans. Not surprisingly, then, the mechanisms of recognition, classification and response have been intensively investigated by ethologists and cognitive psychologists. Their investigations have shown just how strange and remarkable these mechanisms are.

3.1 Recognition and completion

Have a look at Figure 1.1. No problem there: it's a letter R. We recognise it straight away. Animals can be taught to recognise it quite easily. But just *how* do we recognise it?

Suppose we try a symbolic explanation. It's no good saying, 'well, R is a symbol, Unicode H0052, so we recognise it.' That gets us no further at all. We might take the line that the R is a characteristic pattern of pixels as in Figure 1.2(a), with each pixel a symbol (one bit), but this strategy has problems of its own. There's no evidence that when we perceive a pattern there are any cognitive processes at work that scan each pixel, assemble them into a whole and then perform the recognition: for a start, this would be grotesquely slow and inefficient. We could try to take a subtler symbolic line and say, 'OK, the R consists of a combination of three characteristic patterns: a vertical upstroke, a loop closed by the upstroke and a diagonal downstroke', as in Figure 1.2(b). This looks a smart solution, until one realises that exactly the same problem applies to each *component* as to the letter as a whole: how are they symbolically encoded and processed? Symbolic explanations of recognition don't really seem to work here. It appears that the process is one of taking in and recognising a *complete pattern, all at once*.

Figure 1.1 Easy recognition

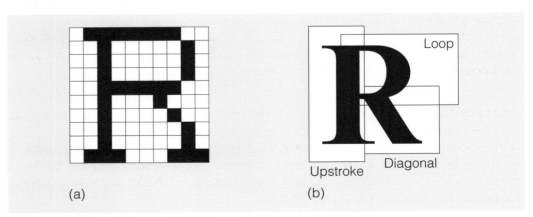

(a)   (b)

Figure 1.2 Possible symbolic representations

There are other curious features of the property of recognition. Look at Figure 1.3. We'd all agree, probably, that every one of these five symbols is an R. But compare them closely, and you can see that they only very loosely resemble one another. How is it that we can see each pattern as an R, without too much difficulty?

Figure 1.3 Variations on the letter R

And what about Figure 1.4(a)? Here certain parts of the letters have been obliterated, yet we have little trouble in recognising the words. And were you conscious of reading each word letter by letter? Almost certainly not. It's much more likely that you took in the word as a single pattern, scarcely noticing the obliterations. In Figure 1.4(b), I've deliberately drawn the letters 'H' and 'A' in such a way as to be ambiguous; but again I doubt if you were aware of it – you just read the sentence correctly. How is this? How are we able to read patterns in which large amounts of information have been withheld, or are ambiguous, without apparent effort?

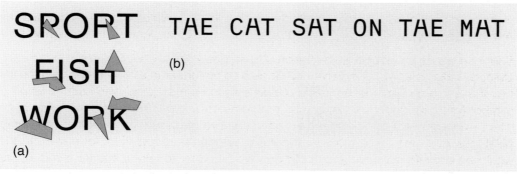

Figure 1.4 Damaged and ambiguous patterns

SAQ 1.2

How are we able to read the damaged patterns in Figure 1.4, avoiding ambiguities?

ANSWER..

We are extracting information from the *context* around the damaged or ambiguous bits, and using this information to build our overall recognition of the pattern. This is particularly true in the case of 1.4(b), I thought, where one is probably not even aware that one is doing it. And so too, in 1.4(a), we know what certain damaged letters must be, because possible alternatives would make nonsense words.

One further point, and then I will sum up. Not only do humans and animals recognise patterns seamlessly and effortlessly. In the case of partially obscured patterns, we unconsciously *complete* them too. Let me illustrate what I mean with two examples. In experiments carried out in 1970 by Richard Warren, subjects were played a tape of a series of polysyllabic words, out of each of which one syllable had been obscured by a loud click. The subjects were required to:

▶ identify the word;

▶ say which syllable had been clicked out.

One might expect, on the basis of our discussion above, that most subjects would identify the words without difficulty – and so they did. What was less predictable was that subjects were generally unable to say which syllable was missing. They reported hearing the *whole word*, with a click somewhere unspecific in the background. Not only had their expectations allowed them to identify the word, their expectations had completed it for them!

As for my second example, have a look at the now famous image in Figure 1.5(a), a photograph of a small region of the Cydonia region of the planet Mars, taken by NASA's 1976 *Viking 1* mission to the planet. What do you see? A human face, I expect – more or less everyone does. Of course, this was enough for many amateur commentators: the 'face' was carved by a Martian civilisation; the structures around it were a Martian city; earlier failed space missions had been shot down by the Martians; and so on. When NASA returned to the planet in 2001 with the superior cameras and computers of the Mars *Global Surveyor*, they were able to reveal that the 'face' is, in fact, an eroded mesa, and does not actually resemble a face at all (see Figure 1.5(b)). The pattern completion abilities of our perceptual systems ensure that we interpret incomplete and muddled sense data as something familiar and significant. And we know that faces are perhaps the most significant images in human mental life. This phenomenon of perceiving a vague or obscure stimulus as something clear and distinct is called **pareidolia**.

Naturally, this has all been denied by true believers, who accuse NASA of faking the image, a cover-up, a massive conspiracy, etc.

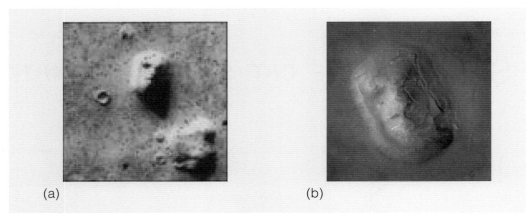

(a)   (b)

Figure 1.5   The 'face' on Mars, taken by: (a) *Viking*, 1976. (b) *Global Surveyor*, 2001

To sum up, consider this question.

SAQ 1.3

Jot down what you think are some of the main features of our recognition abilities.

ANSWER...

I think these are the crucial features:

▶ We perceive *whole patterns* without any conscious processing of their constituent parts. This idea was well known to psychologists of the early twentieth century, and went under the name of the **gestalt effect**.

▶ More or less any small part of a pattern allows us to recognise the whole immediately, a property known as **content addressability**.

▶ We do so seamlessly under conditions of *noise* and *uncertainty*.

▶ We unconsciously *complete* patterns that are noisy, damaged or incomplete.

There is no evidence to suggest that non-human animals are any different from ourselves in these respects. These properties of pattern recognition have presented enormous problems to Symbolic AI.

3.2 Classification and response

You saw in Block 3 that along with the ability to recognise comes the ability to *classify* stimuli into general categories and to select the appropriate *responses*. Even quite humble creatures are capable of this to some degree, although humans seem to be masters of classification and response. On encountering a new situation, we smoothly assign it to a category, activate all sorts of general knowledge about situations of this kind and select flexibly from a huge range of possible responses.

In Symbolic AI, this kind of knowledge is usually represented by *frames* and *scripts*. You will remember from Block 2 that a frame encodes both specific and general knowledge using a slot and filler representation, coupled with mechanisms such as inheritance to handle generalisation (see Figure 1.6). Scripts encapsulate general knowledge about typical human situations – the classic example is the restaurant script – in terms of actors, roles, entry conditions, goals, emotions, and so on. Allegedly, when we enter a new setting we activate the appropriate script, which contains all the knowledge we need to understand the situation and respond appropriately.

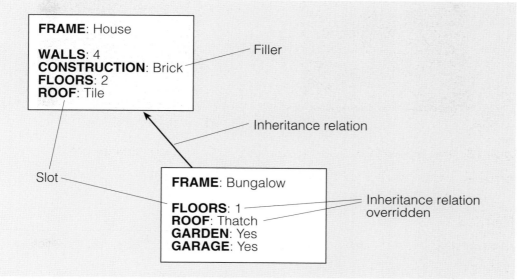

Figure 1.6   Symbolic representation: frames

However, frames and scripts share one of the major drawbacks of Symbolic AI systems. They are *rigid*. Most real-life situations simply cannot be strictly assigned to a single script – they are too complex. In reality, we switch seamlessly between scripts, combine them to find the best response and constantly revise the details of the script we are enacting. New information and cues cause us to draw selectively on immense reserves of general knowledge instantaneously. We make judgements on the possibility of future happenings and select the best reactions on the basis of this knowledge. To put it briefly, our faculties of classification and response have two notable features, both lacking in symbolic models:

▶ *Default assignment*. Small cues enable us automatically to assign a situation or stimulus provisionally to a category. This is constantly revised, with new categories being considered, substituted or combined with the existing assignment.

▶ *Spontaneous generalisation*. Vast amounts of general knowledge about the category are instantaneously activated and can be drawn on selectively. For example, suppose you find out that the author of this unit belongs to the category 'middle-aged male'. Although you have never met me, you can immediately list a number of features that I am very likely to have: two arms, two legs, grey hair, quite tall, deep voice, etc. You could cover several pages with such a list. Naturally, some of these might turn out to be wrong, but that is the point. The general information is constantly revised and updated in the light of particular experience.

Once again, ethological experiments show that animals too have such capacities, although certainly to a lesser degree. The cyberneticists knew that intelligent behaviour of this kind, in humans and animals, arises in the nervous system. For many of these pioneers, the interaction of nerve cells was their special study and the inspiration for their models. For various reasons, as we shall see, their work became eclipsed by the rise of AI. In the 1980s, however, new interest arose; and the study of computational models of nervous interaction, now known as **neural networks**, **artificial neural networks**, **neurocomputing** or **connectionism**, became a major field in its own right. Research and development in neural networks continues to this day. This is the topic of Block 4.

4 Biology

4.1 A little history

The existence of an intricate system of nerves within the bodies of humans and animals has been known since ancient times. Aristotle (384–322 BCE) believed that they were offshoots of the heart, which Greek science imagined to be the centre of life and sensation. He was finally corrected by the Greek physician Galen (131–202 CE) who, by means of dissections, rightly identified their association with the brain and spinal cord. Medieval medical thinkers such as Avicenna (980–1037) connected them with movement and perception, seeing nerve fibres as hollow tubes through which the 'animal spirits' moved around the body. This idea persisted through the Renaissance and into the Enlightenment, despite the very precise anatomical work of Leonardo da Vinci and Vesalius (see, for example, Figure 1.7). Finally, however, in 1620 a Scottish medical student John Moir noted: 'nerves have no perceptible cavity internally, as the veins and arteries have'.

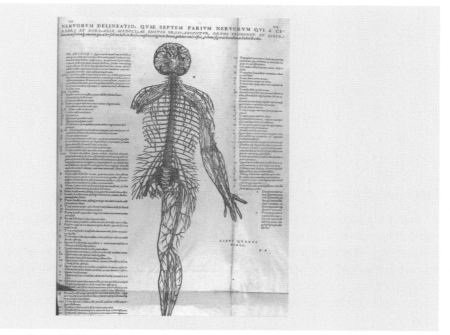

Figure 1.7   A page from *De Humanis Corporis Fabrica* by Anton Vesalius

The modern study of the nervous system was initiated by the Spanish anatomist Santiago Ramon y Cajal (1852–1934). Using a technique of staining cells with silver chromate, originally developed by the Italian physician Camillo Golgi (1843–1926), Cajal was able to confirm Golgi's identification of a special kind of cell, the **neuron**, as the basic unit of the nervous system, and to elucidate its basic structure and properties. He concluded that neurons communicated with one another electrically through special junctions, now known as **synapses**. For this work Cajal and Golgi shared the 1906 Nobel Prize for Medicine.

Figure 1.8   Santiago Ramon y Cajal

Modern biology has confirmed Cajal's hypotheses. Electron microscopy, modern staining techniques and microelectrical recording tools have helped to unravel many of the neuron's secrets. This course is not the place to look at this work in great detail, but we will need to examine a little more closely our current understanding of neurons and their synapses.

4.2 | The nervous system

All vertebrate animals have a **nervous system** responsible for muscular activity, internal monitoring of the body, handling input from the senses and initiating actions. The system can be often divided into:

▶ the brain and spinal chord, known as the **central nervous system** (CNS);

▶ the **peripheral nervous system** (PNS), consisting of all other nerves. The PNS is further subdivided. However, since our concern here is mainly the CNS, and the functions of nerves in general, we need go no further into this.

Turn a microscope on some part of the CNS and what would we see? Figure 1.9 shows a tiny section of the brain under a conventional wide-field light microscope.

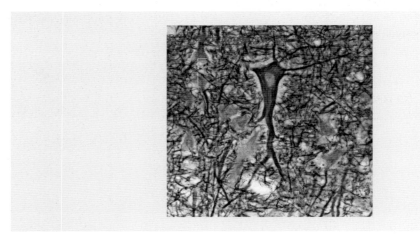

Figure 1.9   Section of the brain under a light microscope

At this magnification, all we can really see is a dense mass of cells and fibres in a rampant jungle of connections. However, the figure does show the general shape of the nerve cells – the neurons – quite clearly. If we now isolate one of these and picture it on its own we would see something like the image in Figure 1.10. The image is of a highly unsymmetrical structure. Like all cells, it has a cell body, but out of this comes a mass of bushy spines. One of these spines, projecting towards the top of the picture, is very long.

If I now draw a diagram of one of these cells (see Figure 1.11), we can put names to some of these parts.

There are a few points I want to reinforce from the diagram:

▶ The arborisation at the end of the **axon** will typically make contact with the somas and dendrites of many other neurons, perhaps as many as 100 000 in some circumstances. The point at which the axon branch makes contact with another neuron is known as the *synapse*.

▶ The axon may be very long: some axons can be centimetres or, in rarer cases, even metres in length.

▶ Some axons are coated in a sheath of myelin (shown in diagram), but this is not always present.

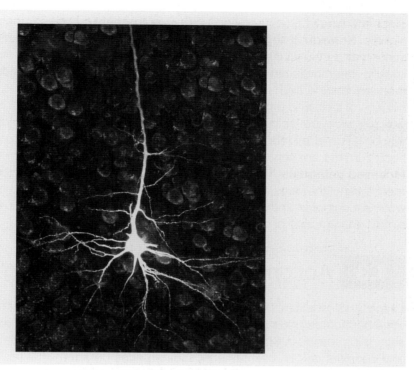

Figure 1.10   Single nerve cell, stained and under high magnification

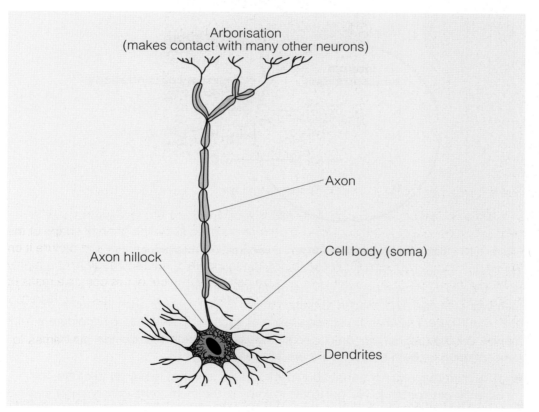

Figure 1.11   Neuron – naming of parts

The average human brain may contain as many as 10^{11} neurons, together with a roughly equal number of **glial cells** that provide nutrition and support. Thus, there may be up to 10^{14} *connections* between neurons in that brain. There are probably as many neurons again in the spinal chord and the PNS. The whole vast array can be seen as one gigantic signalling and switching system. But how *do* neurons communicate with one another?

Since the time of Golgi and Cajal, neurons have been known to be carriers of electric signals. However, it would be a mistake to think of them as conducting electricity in the same way as the wiring in your house or your computer does. In ordinary electrical circuits, the movement of current is caused by a drift of electrons through a metallic medium. But the axon of a neuron has no metals; it is simply a tube filled with a watery solution of salts and proteins. In fact, neurons can and do conduct electricity in a similar way to a wire, but since the resistance of a metre of nerve fibre is roughly the same as that of 10^{10} metres (about the distance from Earth to the planet Saturn) of copper cable, such currents are very weak and can only travel tiny distances: they are known as **localised potentials**. The main way neurons carry electricity is through a quite different mechanism, known as an **action potential**. The precise details of how action potentials work are complex and beyond the scope of this course. What follows is a rather simplified summary of the phenomenon.

4.3 | Action potentials – neural firing

Like any cell, the neuron – its axon, dendrites and soma – is bounded by a *membrane*, a semi-permeable boundary between the cell's internal ingredients and the solution of salts and proteins in which it is bathed. Now let's picture the neuron as a simple sphere and consider certain basic chemical differences between what lies inside and what outside its membrane (see Figure 1.12). I'm focusing particularly on differences in the concentration of **ions** in the solutions within and without.

An ion is an atom that has either *gained* one or more extra electrons, becoming negatively charged (e.g. Cl^-), or *lost* one or more electrons, making it positively charged (e.g. K^+). Dissolving table salt (NaCl) in water, for instance, causes it to split into the ions Na^+ and Cl^-.

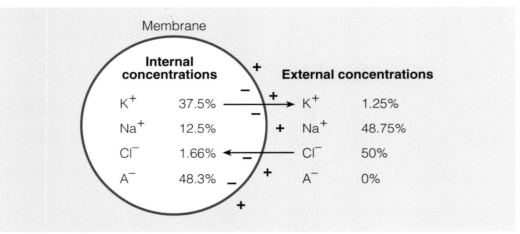

Figure 1.12   Ionic concentrations inside and outside neuron membrane

The basic constituents of the solution inside the cell are ions of chlorine (Cl^-), potassium (K^+), sodium (Na^+) and negatively charged proteins known as anions (A^-). Outside the membrane, the cell is bathed in a solution that is similar, but not quite the same. You can see from Figure 1.12 that the concentration of each ion inside the cell is different from that on the outside. So why don't ions just cross the membrane to even up the concentration on both sides? There are two reasons:

▶ The membrane is not permeable to A^- – these ions are too large to cross. It is slightly permeable to Na^+ but active pumps in the membrane continuously expel these ions from the cell by exchanging them for K^+ ions, thus maintaining the imbalance.

▶ Cl^- and K^+ can cross, but as they start to do so K^+ ions leaving the cell build up a positive charge on the outside of the membrane, and Cl^- ions entering it build up a negative charge on the inside (see arrows on Figure 1.12). Since like charges repel one another, further K^+ ions trying to get out and Cl^- ions trying to get in are pushed back. An equilibrium state results, in which there is a stable difference of electric potential across the membrane, known as the **resting potential**. The actual value of this potential varies, but is usually between –65 mV (millivolts) and –85 mV.

However, the neuron will not remain long at its resting potential. Periodically, disturbances spreading from the dendrites gather at the axon hillock and, when the charge accumulated there rises above a certain threshold, cause a change in the properties of the membrane. It starts to become much more permeable to Na$^+$ as sodium channels in it open. Na$^+$ ions then naturally rush into the cell to even up the imbalance in the sodium concentration. The inside of the membrane rapidly starts to acquire a positive charge. Within a few milliseconds the potential across the membrane completely reverses, to as much as +55 mV – this is termed **depolarisation**. At this point, the situation starts to restore itself. The sodium channels close and potassium channels in the membrane open. K$^+$ ions leave the cell, Cl$^-$ ions enter, and the inside of the cell quickly becomes negatively charged again. This restoration process is called **hyperpolarisation**. The whole sequence of depolarisation followed by hyperpolarisation is over in about 25 milliseconds (ms). After a brief period of undershoot, the ion pumps in the membrane wall eject Na$^+$ and return K$^+$ to the interior, and the original resting potential is restored. Figure 1.13 shows the typical time course of an action potential, with the membrane potential plotted on the vertical axis against time on the horizontal axis.

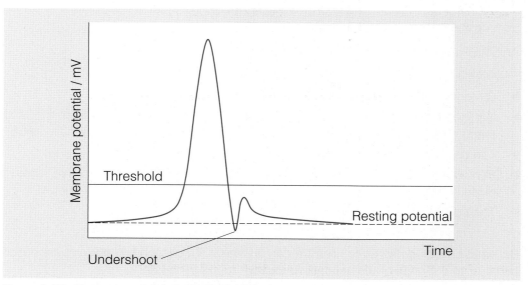

Figure 1.13   Time course of an action potential

The action potential is not an event that occurs just at the axon hillock. The depolarisation of the membrane there causes adjacent areas further along the axon membrane to depolarise in turn and the change spreads rapidly up the axon, with hyperpolarisation following behind it (see Figure 1.14). The pulse of electric charge moves along the axon at speeds of between 5 and 25 metres per second (faster in axons with myelin sheaths), spreading throughout the axonal arborisation all the way to the end points, the **axon terminals**. We say that the neuron emits a **spike** or that it has **fired**.

After firing, the sodium channels are inactivated for about 5 ms, meaning the neuron is unable to fire again during that interval, known as the **refractory period**. However, neurons generally emit whole sequences of spikes, known as **spike trains**, the frequency and amplitude of which will depend on how powerfully the neuron was stimulated to fire in the first place. It is through the *frequencies* of these spikes that neurons encode information to be sent on to other neurons.

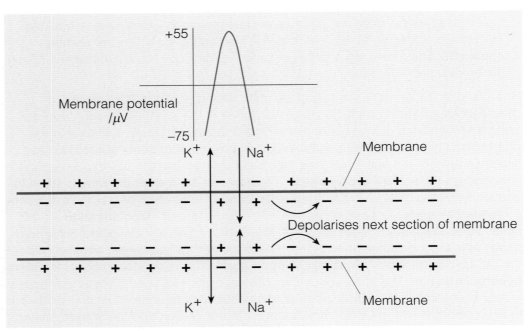

Figure 1.14   Spread of action potential along the axon

SAQ 1.4

Sum up the main events of a neural firing.

ANSWER..

I identified the following main stages:

▶ Changes in the membrane potential reach a threshold.

▶ Na^+ gates open in the membrane and sodium ions flood in; the inside of the membrane depolarises to become positively charged with respect to the outside.

▶ The depolarisation spreads up the axon to the axon terminals.

▶ Behind this wave of depolarisation, the membrane hyperpolarises: the Na^+ gates close, K^+ leaves the cell and Cl^- enters it; ion pumps eject Na^+ from the cell.

▶ The cell returns to its equilibrium state.

But what causes a neuron to fire? We can answer that question by following the action potential to the ends of the axonal arborisation to the synapse.

Ramon y Cajal discovered that neurons made contact with one another across special junctions called *synapses*. A typical axon may form thousands of such junctions on the dendrites and somas of other neurons. A typical synapse is shown in the electron microscope image of Figure 1.15. These junctions are very small, of the order of 2 micrometres (μm, thousandths of a millimetre) across, so they are difficult to study. However, modern techniques have revealed some of their workings, and since these are at least as important as those of the neuron itself I'll now give an account, again rather brief and simplified, of how they work.

At the point where a branch of the axon makes contact with another neuron it swells into a bud-shaped structure within which swim tiny sacs or *vesicles* of special chemicals known as **neurotransmitters**. This structure does not actually make contact with the membrane of the other neuron: there is a tiny gap, about 20 nanometres (nm, millionths of a millimetre) wide, between it (the axon terminal of the **pre-synaptic** cell and the

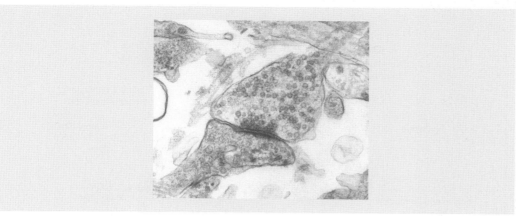

Figure 1.15   A synapse

membrane of the **post-synaptic** cell (see Figure 1.16). An action potential in the pre-synaptic neuron, arriving at this terminal, causes a cascade of events:

1   Action potential arrives.

2   Voltage-controlled calcium channels open in the walls of the pre-synaptic membrane and Ca^{++} ions pour in (Figure 1.16, Stage 1).

3   This causes vesicles to fuse to the pre-synaptic membrane and burst open, releasing neurotransmitters into the synaptic cleft (Figure 1.16, Stage 2).

4   Neurotransmitter molecules bind to receptors in the post-synaptic membrane, causing ion channels in the post-synaptic membrane to open, in turn causing the membrane either to depolarise or to hyperpolarise, depending on the neurotransmitters and receptors involved. Synapses that cause the post-synaptic membrane to depolarise are called **excitatory**, those that hyperpolarise it are called **inhibitory** (Figure 1.16, Stages 3 and 4).

5   Depolarisation of its membrane will spread to the axon hillock of the post-synaptic cell. With sufficient depolarisation this neuron will then generate an action potential of its own, firing in sympathy with the pre-synaptic cell. Hyperpolarisation will make it more difficult for the post-synaptic neuron to fire (Figure 1.16, Stage 5).

6   In the meantime, molecular pumps in the wall of the pre-synaptic membrane shift neurotransmitters back into the pre-synaptic cell. Some neurotransmitters are broken down by enzymes (Figure 1.16, Stage 6).

A few key points to note about synapses before we move on:

▶   The influence of only one excitatory synapse would almost certainly not depolarise a membrane enough to start an action potential. But the post-synaptic neuron will have thousands of other synapses on it, simultaneously transmitting excitatory impulses from thousands of other neurons. Effectively, the post-synaptic neuron *adds* these depolarising effects together and when the sum of the depolarisation reaches the threshold, it fires.

▶   The same idea applies in reverse to inhibitory synapses. If the post-synaptic cell is receiving hyperpolarising impulses from many synapses at the same time, it will enter a depressed state in which it will take a lot of excitation to make it fire.

▶   There are many different neurotransmitters, but no real consensus about exactly how many. About ten 'small-molecule' transmitters (e.g. GABA, acetylcholine, serotonin) are agreed on, and over fifty neuro-active peptides.

▶   The most important point of all: the strength of a synapse can *change* over time, in either the short or long term. To put it another way, excitatory synapses can become more excitatory – an action potential in the pre-synaptic cell can cause greater and greater post-synaptic membrane depolarisation, as time passes. Experiments have shown that if a neuron excites another cell repeatedly over a certain synapse, that

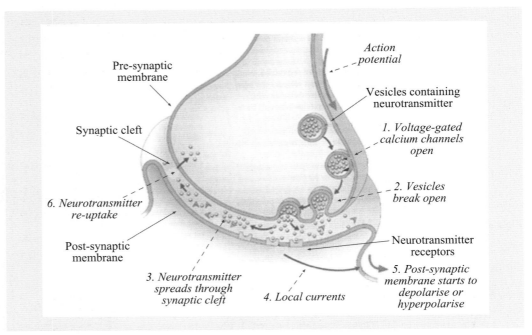

Figure 1.16   Events at the synapse

synapse's excitatory effect will become stronger each time. The same is true, in reverse, of inhibitory synapses – they can become increasingly inhibitory with repeated use. These changes can be semi-permanent, an effect known as **long-term potentiation** (LTP). LTP is thought to be the basis of learning and memory in all animals.

SAQ 1.5

Sum up the main events that take place at the synapse.

ANSWER...

I identified the following main events:

▶ When an action potential arrives at the synapse, Ca^{++} gates in the membrane open and calcium ions enter.

▶ This causes vesicles of neurotransmitter to fuse to the pre-synaptic membrane and burst open.

▶ Neurotransmitters flood into the synaptic cleft.

▶ Molecules of neurotransmitter lock onto receptors in the wall of the post-synaptic membrane; this causes either depolarisation or hyperpolarisation of the membrane, depending on the neurotransmitter and the receptor.

▶ The post-synaptic neuron sums the activities of all the excitatory and inhibitory impulses it receives: sufficient excitation may cause it to fire.

Neurons and synapses are the elementary building blocks of the brain and the nervous system. But what about the larger scale? One particular feature of the brain is the way in which neurons become organised into specialised *groups*, sometimes hundreds of thousands or millions of cells strong, known as **maps**. For example, sense data coming in from the surface of the body, information about the various touches, tickles and pressures the body is experiencing, are handled by a region of the brain known as the **somatosensory strip**. In that region, groups of neurons in one discrete area fire together in response to information from the fingers, in another to information from the face, in another to information from the soles of the feet, and so on. In the same way, the movements of the muscles are controlled by another area of the brain, the **motor strip**. There, the activity of neurons in one clearly defined area controls movements in the muscles of the face, in another the muscles of the hands, and so on. In other words, both regions represent a *map* of the body, in just the same way that in a conventional map – of Canada, say – areas of the paper correspond to areas of the actual country. Figure 1.17 depicts the two maps.

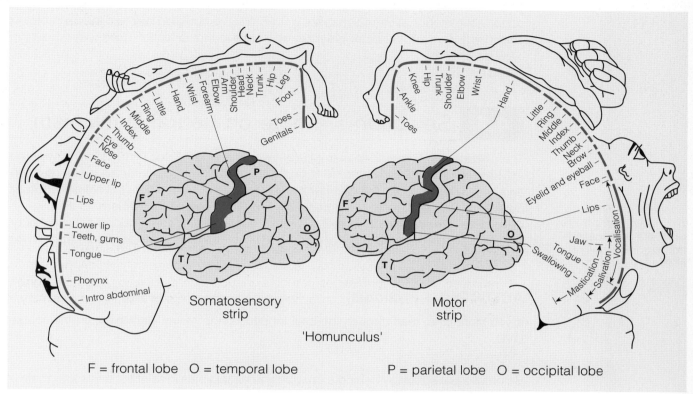

Somatosensory strip

Motor strip

'Homunculus'

F = frontal lobe   O = temporal lobe   P = parietal lobe   O = occipital lobe

Figure 1.17   Somatosensory maps

Note one feature of the brain maps, though: they are *distorted*, giving rise to the rather horrible shapes you can see in the figure, known as **homunculi**. The area of brain mapping certain parts of the body is often much greater (or smaller) as a fraction of the entire area of the map than the surface area of the body part is of the body as a whole. This wouldn't be true of our map of Canada: we would expect the area depicting Alberta to be in exact proportion to Alberta's actual size. So, for example, in the somatosensory strip 14% of the neural area is devoted to the lips. 5% of the motor strip deals with the thumb alone. Neither lips nor thumb are anything like that big a fraction of the whole body area. So why these distortions? The answer should be obvious: the area given over to mapping a certain part of the body reflects its *importance* in our lives, not its actual size. We all know our lips are very sensitive, as opposed to, say, the soles of the feet. Our hands are incredibly delicate tools which we use in every waking moment. It's only natural that a disproportionately large amount of brain tissue should be devoted to them – they matter so much to us.

SAQ 1.6

Our four mechanisms are interaction, emergence, adaptation and selection. How do you think our picture of the nervous system fits in with these?

ANSWER..

I hope you didn't have to ponder too long over this. It's clear that nervous systems are massively *interactive*. The action of one cell will affect thousands of others. One would expect such a system to have *emergent* properties, especially in view of Holland's idea (see Block 3) that the sophistication of an emergent response grows with the number of basic components in the system. You'll see many examples of the emergent properties of neural models in this block. And you've already seen one way in which neural systems *adapt* – the modification of synapses in LTP. You've not seen any explicit examples of *selection*. However, there are theorists who believe that selection does play a part in nervous systems.

4.4   Selection – a note on neural Darwinism

The physiologist Gerald Edelman (1929–) won the Nobel Prize in 1972 for his work on the immune system. However, he is probably best known today for his ideas on brain and consciousness, which go under the general name of the Theory of Neuronal Group Selection (TNGS), but are more popularly known as **neural Darwinism**. In its fully developed form, neural Darwinism is a rather controversial, complex and difficult theory, and it will not be possible to cover it here. However, there is an introductory paper on the theory on the course DVD.

Edelman's 1993 book, *Bright Air, Brilliant Fire*, presents an excellent non-technical summary of the TNGS.

ACTIVITY 1.1 (optional)

If you have time, read through the brief introduction to neural Darwinism on the course DVD.

Before we leave biology behind, I do want you to get some idea of the awesome scale of all this. An action potential is not some isolated event. A typical neuron may fire tens, or even hundreds, of times a second. This in turn will help to cause thousands of other neurons to fire. An average human brain contains billions of neurons, millions of neuronal groups and circuits, thousands of maps, among which whole populations of millions of cells fire together in concert, with floods of activity swirling around the whole arena. At every moment in your life, when you are in the depths of sleep, or even as you read this unit, a ceaseless tumult of neural activity is happening – between your ears.

5 Computing

This is all very well, but our role as computer scientists interested in the potential of natural intelligence is to construct models. We have to engage computers. What would computer models of the nervous system look like?

5.1 A little history

I don't want to present a detailed history of computer modelling of nervous systems here. I'm just going to offer a brief account of what I think were six landmark figures in the development of the connectionist project. Their work should serve as foundation for the next section.

McCulloch and Pitts

You may recall from Block 1 that the cyberneticists of the 1950s were especially interested in the properties of nervous systems. You may even remember the names of two of Cybernetics' most prominent figures in this area: the neurophysiologist Warren McCullough (1899–1969) and the mathematician Walter Pitts (1923–1969).

McCullough was well aware of those physiological properties of the nervous system that were understood in the 1940s. What he and Pitts were interested in, however, was what the nervous system was actually doing. They wanted to know how arrays of simple 'computers' such as neurons were capable of carrying out the complex computation that they were sure must underpin thought. In an enormously influential (and very difficult) paper of 1943, 'A logical calculus of the ideas immanent in nervous activity', they explored this question theoretically using a simplified model of the neuron, which has come to be known as the McCullough–Pitts (MCP) neuron.

Essentially, McCulloch and Pitts' aim was to strip away some of the complexities of real, biological neurons, in order to get at the deep mathematical principles they believed underlay them. In the MCP model:

▶ the intricacies of spikes and spike trains, and the frequency of neural firing, are all ignored: either a neuron fires, or it does not;

▶ networks of MCP neurons operate in **discrete time**. A neuron has a certain fixed time period to accumulate excitation; at the end of this time it either fires or it does not fire. Then a new time period starts afresh, with all previous activity forgotten;

▶ although excitatory input is added up, inhibitory input is not. Inhibition is an all-or-nothing process;

▶ the death of neurons and other changes in the structure of neural connections, such as LTP, are all ignored. The structure of the network is fixed at the start and does not alter.

So the MCP neuron is obviously a highly simplified model. You will meet it again, in more detail, in the next section. But using this simple device as a basis, McCullough and Pitts were able to show by means of intricate mathematical arguments that any finite logical expression could arise from suitable networks of MCP neurons. Thus, they argued, the full complexity of logical thought, which they believed was the basis of human intelligence, could be fully realised in these simple devices.

Hebb

Donald Hebb (1904–1985) was a psychologist, rather than a computer scientist, but his 1946 book, *The Organisation of Behaviour*, plays a key role in the story of neural networks. Hebb was reacting against the rigid behaviourist theories of the time, which – as you learned in Unit 2 of Block 3 – linked sensation directly to action, stimulus to response. In the behaviourist picture there was no place for thought, emotion or mental states. For the behaviourist psychologists of Hebb's era, these were either unobservable, and hence scientifically uninteresting, or simply did not exist at all. Learning and memory were just adaptations of the organism's response to stimuli.

Hebb thought this was absurdly limited. He sought a new picture of psychological life by looking at what might be going on in the nervous systems of humans and animals as they acted and learned. It would take us too far from our main themes to go into the detail of Hebb's work; but his contribution can be summed up in three related themes:

▶ *The Hebbian synapse*. Hebb speculated on what was actually changing in the brains and nervous systems of animals as they adapted. He pointed to the tendency we've already noted of a synapse to increase in strength the more it is used to transmit signals between neurons. An excitatory synapse becomes more excitatory. An inhibitory synapse becomes more inhibitory. In Hebb's words:

> When an axon of a cell A is near enough to excite a cell B and repeatedly or persistently takes part in firing it, some growth process or metabolic change takes place in one or both cells, such that A's efficiency as one of the cells firing B is increased.
>
> Source: Hebb (1946)

For Hebb, then, this form of synaptic modification, which I referred to earlier as *long-term potentiation*, was the basis of learning and memory in all animals.

▶ *Neural circuits and ensembles*. A neuron on its own is only a simple computing device. Hebb was interested in how neurons acted together in groups to spread information about the brain. He presented a picture of ensembles of neurons, each made up of many thousands of cells, spreading activity through mechanisms of convergence and divergence.

▶ *Distributed memory*. It was obvious to Hebb that something as complicated as a specific human memory could hardly be the property of any one neuron. Psychologists call this the idea of the **grandmother cell**. I have clear memories of my grandmother, but the notion that such a rich and diverse memory could be the responsibility of a single brain cell is ridiculous. For a start, every time I swallow a mouthful of beer, neurons in my brain die, and they are not replaced – yet I still remember Granny. Under the grandmother cell hypothesis, it would be quite possible that one day the neuron handling her memory might die and my entire memory of this formidable woman vanish. But this sort of catastrophic forgetting only seems to happen in cases where there is massive degeneration in brain structure, such as in Alzheimer's Disease. It seems clear that our memories are an emergent product of vast numbers of neurons working together. We say that the memory of my grandmother (and all my other memories) are *distributed* over innumerable neurons and synapses.

Now ponder this question for a moment.

Exercise 1.1

Note down what you think might be the advantages of storing memories in this distributed fashion.

Discussion ....

I'll have more to say about this later, but for the moment I thought of two:

▶ *Resistance to damage.* As I mentioned earlier, brain cells die and are not replaced. In a distributed system, the death of a single cell will have little effect, as millions of other neurons are sharing the burden.

▶ *Economy.* If a single memory is stored by thousands of cells, it's also likely that a single cell can participate in the storage of many different memories. This seems to be a way in which the seemingly limitless capacity of human memory becomes possible.

You will be able to see the influence of Hebb's ideas very clearly in the discussion of learning rules in the next section.

Rosenblatt

Frank Rosenblatt (1928–1969) was a colourful computer scientist who did his best work at Cornell University in the late 1950s and early 1960s. Building on the research of McCulloch, Pitts and Hebb, Rosenblatt was the originator of one of the earliest computer-modelled neural networks, the **Perceptron**, also known as the MARK 1 Computer, which he developed at Cornell Aeronautical Laboratory, and reported in his 1958 paper 'The Perceptron: a probabilistic model for information storage and organization in the brain'. The ideas on which the Perceptron was based can be summed up as follows:

▶ Although genetic mechanisms may mean that there is a certain rough uniformity in the way individuals' nervous systems are connected up at birth, they will otherwise be more or less random – and so different from individual to individual.

▶ This initial arrangement of connections and connection strengths will change as a result of the experiences each individual organism undergoes as a result of mechanisms such as LTP – this phenomenon is called **plasticity**.

▶ As the organism experiences more and more stimuli, its nervous system will change so as to respond in roughly the same way to stimuli that are *similar* to one another. Connections between ensembles of neurons will develop in such a way that one group of cells will start to respond exclusively to groups of stimuli that resemble one another. The meaning of 'similarity' depends entirely on the organism. As I pointed out in Block 3, different organisms have widely differing interests and needs, and so will respond to the world in different ways.

▶ The growth and strength of such connections will be reinforced, positively or negatively, by continued experience.

Rosenblatt called his Perceptron 'an intricate switching network, where retention takes the form of new connections'. He believed that it was in such systems that 'the fundamental laws of organization which are common to all information handling systems, machines and men included, may eventually be understood' – an aim typical of the early, optimistic years of Cybernetics.

The study of perceptrons is a central strand in neural networks. I'll introduce their basic principles and architectures in the next section, where I present specific computer models. For the moment, though, all I need to do is point out that perceptrons are used as *classifier* systems. Given a complex stimulus, such as an image or a pattern, the perceptron is able to classify the stimulus into one or another category. As you'll remember, this a key feature of natural intelligence.

For reasons that are now lost in the mists of time, a bitter personal animosity arose between Rosenblatt and the formidable computer scientist Marvin Minsky. Minsky, who was an early advocate of Symbolic AI, intensely disliked Rosenblatt's ideas and did everything he could to discredit his work, especially the Perceptron. As you may recall from Block 1, Minsky's 1969 book *Perceptrons* (co-authored by Seymour Papert) showed mathematically that there were certain kinds of patterns that a perceptron simply could not classify. The effect on neural network research was devastating. The field did not really revive until the psychologists Dave Rumelhart and Jay McClelland found answers to Minsky and Papert's objections in 1986. You'll look at these developments in some detail in the next unit.

Kohonen

The best-known contribution of Teuvo Kohonen, (born 1934), currently Professor Emeritus of the Academy of Finland, to the field of neural networks is probably the **self-organising map** (SOM), the details of which you'll meet later in the block. Kohonen was particularly interested in a phenomenon, which I described earlier, and which has been observed in many parts of the brain, of two-dimensional mapping – specialised groups of neurons firing together in response to stimuli from particular parts of the body, or firing to activate specific muscle groups. He constructed an artificial system organised in just such a way: clusters of geographically adjacent units respond selectively to certain inputs, while other clusters in different regions respond to different stimuli. Moreover, he was interested in how such a system could be made to *self-organise*, to sort *itself* into these areas, without guidance from outside. Using lattice formations of units, he was able to demonstrate these properties in an artificial system. Out of his researches came new theories of **unsupervised learning**, including that of **learning vector quantisation**, both of which we'll explore in detail in Unit 3 of this block.

Kohonen has made many other contributions to the field of neural networks and computer science generally, including theories of optimal mapping, distributed associative memory and algorithms for symbol processing.

Hopfield

John Joseph Hopfield (born 1933) is an American scientist, currently working in the Department of Molecular Biology at Princeton University. By original training a physicist, he has also taught in the physics department at Princeton, as well as at the California Institute of Technology. As a respected physicist, his interest in neural networks in the 1980s lent legitimacy to the field among physical scientists, at a time when most connectionist research was being conducted by psychologists and biologists. His short but enormously influential 1982 paper, 'Neural networks and physical systems with emergent collective computational abilities', outlined a particular kind of neural network, now commonly known as the Hopfield Network.

Hopfield concentrated on a phenomenon identified by Hebb and others, in which computer researchers had hitherto shown little interest: **recurrence**. In the brain, the axons of neurons are often observed to form *cycles*; that is, they send activity back, directly or indirectly, to neurons that have already stimulated them (see Figure 1.18). You can see that this is just a classic example of feedback. Feedback connections like this can be seen everywhere in the brain. Some areas, for example the hippocampus, which is responsible for laying down new memories, are massively recurrent.

Hopfield proposed a model of one kind of recurrent network and provided a deep theoretical analysis of its properties. He noted its analogies with certain other types of physical phenomena, notably systems known as **Ising spin glass** models. Recurrent

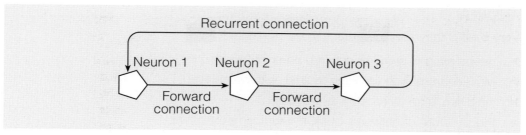

Figure 1.18   Recurrent connections in the brain

networks, as you will see later, are *dynamic*: they change state as time passes, in a manner rather similar to the state searches you looked at in Block 2. Hopfield proposed ways in which such dynamic systems could store a number of memories, along with powerful concepts for analysing the behaviour of the network as its states evolve over time.

5.2   Computer models

You've already seen that McCulloch and Pitts made many simplifying assumptions in their construction of the MCP neuron. But remember from our discussion in Block 1 that *every* computer model is a simplified picture of reality. All neural models are cut down versions of biological fact.

So how do we build computer models of the nervous system? First of all, note that the nervous system is a massively interactive system with billions of cells working in parallel. The computer is a discrete, serial device. So we will have to write programs that *simulate* the distributed and parallel nature of the system in memory and in discrete time. You will be pleased to know that you won't be required to write such programs yourself: you'll be using a software tool that does the work for you. I will ask you to do an exercise with the tool – the Java Neural Network Simulator (JNNS) – slightly later. For now, though, I just want to consider the basic ideas.

I'll start by looking at the first and most basic computer model, which I introduced earlier: the McCulloch–Pitts neuron. You'll find that this is the foundation stone of all future neural models. Then I'll look generally at how we can create neural models by connecting *elements* together in various *topologies* and applying *learning rules* to them. I'll move on to describe these fundamental elements of artificial neural networks – units and weights – then consider the basic topologies into which these can be assembled. Finally, I'll give a couple of examples of learning rules.

The first model – the McCulloch–Pitts neuron

Start by refreshing your memory of McCulloch and Pitts' starting point.

SAQ 1.7

In what ways did McCulloch and Pitts simplify biological nervous systems in their model of the neuron? Write a few bulleted notes.

ANSWER..

Very briefly, they assumed that:

▶ neural firing is an all-or-nothing, on-or-off event;

▶ MCP neurons work in discrete time, with no delays;

▶ inhibition is an all-or-nothing process;

▶ the structure of networks of MCP neurons never alters.

None of these is true of biological systems.

But the best way to appreciate these ideas is in a diagram and an example. An MCP neuron can be pictured as in Figure 1.19.

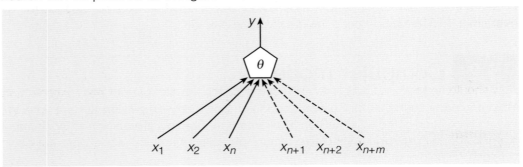

Figure 1.19 A McCulloch–Pitts neuron

The device comprises:

▶ a set of n excitatory inputs $\{x_1, x_2 \ldots x_n\}$;

▶ a set of m inhibitory inputs, $\{x_{n+1}, x_{n+2} \ldots x_{n+m}\}$;

▶ a threshold value θ;

▶ a unit step activation function;

▶ a single output y.

This requires a little further explanation. Since we are dealing with a binary, 'all-or-nothing', device, let's just talk in terms of 1s (all) and 0s (nothing). Suppose that the active excitatory inputs have value 1, and that if there is no activity on the inhibitory input, then its value is 0. Now let's further suppose that there are two excitatory and no inhibitory inputs, and that the threshold θ is 1 (see Figure 1.20). The unit step function works as follows:

▶ Add up the excitatory inputs.

▶ If the sum of the excitatory inputs is greater than or equal to the threshold, then output $y = 1$, otherwise $y = 0$.

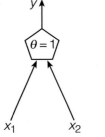

Figure 1.20 An MCP neuron with activations and threshold

So, if x_1 is active (1) and x_2 is inactive you can easily see that the output y is 1, because $x_1 + x_2 \geq \theta$. The result will be the same if both x_1 and x_2 are active.

SAQ 1.8

If the input x_2 in Figure 1.20 were an inhibitory synapse, and both x_1 and x_2 were active, what would be the output?

ANSWER..

You probably weren't tricked into saying that $y = 1$ in this case. On first glance this looks perfectly plausible, as $x_1 + x_2 = 1 \geq \theta$. But then you remembered that in an MCP neuron, *any* inhibitory input will prevent it firing. So in this case $y = 0$.

You can probably see that an MCP neuron, or a group of them, can be used to compute **truth tables**. Consider the truth table for the logical operator OR:

x_1	x_2	x_1 OR x_2
1	1	1
0	1	1
1	0	1
0	0	0

You can see that the MCP neuron in Figure 1.20 responds in exactly this way. When either x_1 or x_2 are active, or when they are both active together, the neuron responds by outputting 1. When both inputs are inactive, the output is 0.

SAQ 1.9

How should an MCP neuron be set up to compute the logical operator AND, whose truth table is:

x_1	x_2	x_1 AND x_2
1	1	1
0	1	0
1	0	0
0	0	0

ANSWER...

There's no trick here. All you need is the neuron depicted in Figure 1.20, but with $\theta = 2$. When both inputs are active $x_1 + x_2 = 2 \geq \theta$. In no other case than this will the neuron fire.

Most subsequent work in neural networks can be seen as a development of McCullough and Pitts' original insights. We can now move on to consider the building blocks of this later work.

The elements – units and weights

There are only two basic building blocks to worry about in any neural network model: neurons (often called **units** or **processing elements** (PEs)) and **weights**. Computer scientists tend to prefer the term *unit* to *neuron*, because they want to avoid the suggestion that they are attempting an accurate model of the biological neuron. I've tended to follow this rule, although I may occasionally slip into referring to a 'neuron' when discussing a computer model of one.

Now let's examine each of these elements.

We can look on the *unit* as a tiny computer that calculates a function. I've depicted a schematic unit in Figure 1.21. It consists of two areas, the *input area* and the *activation area*. Each of these performs a simple calculation:

▶ The input area simply puts together the stimulation it receives from the input lines feeding into the unit. The result is passed to the activation area.

▶ The activation area calculates how active the unit will become on the basis of the total it has received from the input area. This activation is passed out along the output lines flowing out of the unit.

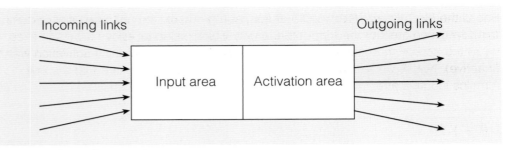

Figure 1.21   Block diagram of neuron

There are several possible functions the unit can use to total up the input it is receiving and to calculate its activation. I'll look at a couple of these in a moment. But you should already be able to see that the McCullough–Pitts neuron has this general pattern.

What about *weights*? Think back to the input and output lines in Figure 1.21. These are links to and from other units. Each link is assigned a *weight*, a real number representing the strength or weakness of that link. Weights may be positive numbers, in which case they will have a positive influence on the unit into which the link feeds, or they may be negative numbers, generally meaning that the influence will be negative.

If this sounds a little cloudy, it should become much clearer if we consider an example of the weights, the input area and the activation area working together. Consider Figure 1.22. You'll see I'm ignoring the outgoing links and concentrating on the three incoming links, which are numbered 1 to 3 from top to bottom of the diagram. The weight on link 1, w_1, is +1.5; that on link 2, w_2, is +0.3; while the weight on link 3, w_3, is quite strongly negative at −1.9. I've also represented the fact that a certain stimulus, in each case also represented by a real number, is being passed along each link. The stimulus on link 1, x_1, is +0.8; x_2 is +0.7; and x_3 is +0.3. Notice that each weighted link and its stimulus is a separate entity – there is no interaction between them until they reach the input area of the target unit. Note also the *subscript* notation I'm using: x_1 is the activity on link 1, w_2 is the weight on link 2, etc.

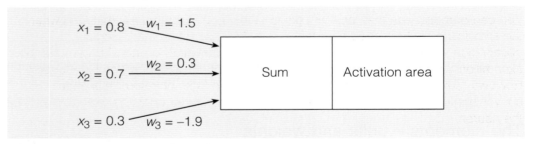

Figure 1.22   Model neuron with weights

The job of the input area is to find the net input stimulation that the unit is receiving. There are basically two ways it can do this. The simplest of these is by far the most common. It simply calculates the *weighted sum* of the inputs it is receiving. What does this mean? Just this: it performs the simple calculation:

$$
\begin{aligned}
netinput &= (x_1 * w_1) + (x_2 * w_2) + (x_3 * w_3) \\
&= (0.8 * 1.5) + (0.7 * 0.3) + (0.3 * -1.9) \\
&= 1.2 + 0.21 - 0.57 \\
&= 0.84
\end{aligned}
$$

You can see that links 1 and 2 have had an overall positive effect on the unit. However, link 3's effect is negative, dragging down the overall input.

Now what about the activation area? The net input (0.84 in this case) is passed to it. Its task is to calculate the activation of the unit. I'll refer to this from now on as the **activation function**. Again, there is a variety of ways in which this can be done.

Recall the McCullough–Pitts model of the neuron. There, the unit used a *threshold function*: when the summed input to the unit was equal to or above a certain fixed value the activation became 1 (active); less than this, and the unit's activation was 0 (inactive). Now if we assume a threshold of 1, then it's easy to see that the unit remains inactive at 0.

SAQ 1.10

What is the activation of the unit depicted in Figure 1.23?

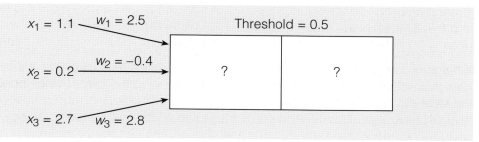

Figure 1.23   Neuron in SAQ 1.10

ANSWER...

The calculation is a straightforward one, as follows:

$$netinput = (x_1 * w_1) + (x_2 * w_2) + (x_3 * w_3)$$
$$= (1.1 * 2.5) + (0.2 * -0.4) + (2.7 * 2.8)$$
$$= 2.75 - 0.08 + 7.56$$
$$= 10.23$$

It's obvious that the net input is way above the threshold, so its activation is 1.

You can probably see that the McCullough–Pitts model of a neuron that fires when the stimulation on it exceeds a certain threshold is based on the biological observation you met earlier – that membrane depolarisation is added up around the axon hillock, resulting in a spike when a certain level of depolarisation is reached. However, computer modellers are not bound by the facts of nature. It is often convenient to use other methods of calculating the net input and the activation of the neuron.

In certain models, the net input is found by *multiplying*, rather than adding, the weighted inputs to the units. So, for instance in the case depicted in Figure 1.22, the net input would be calculated like this:

$$netinput = (x_1 * w_1) * (x_2 * w_2) * (x_3 * w_3)$$
$$= (0.8 * 1.5) * (0.7 * 0.3) * (0.3 * -1.9)$$
$$= 1.2 * 0.21 * -0.57$$
$$= -0.14364$$

The negative effect of link 3 has completely cancelled out the positive stimulus from the other links and made the overall net input negative. Now consider this question for a moment.

SAQ 1.11

What would be the effect of *zero* activity on link 3 when the input calculation is made by multiplication?

ANSWER...

Just applying the same arithmetic we get:

$$\begin{aligned} netinput &= (x_1 * w_1) * (x_2 * w_2) * (x_3 * w_3) \\ &= (0.8 * 1.5) * (0.7 * 0.3) * (0 * -1.9) \\ &= 1.2 * 0.21 * 0 \\ &= 0 \end{aligned}$$

You can easily see that whatever the weight on link 3, and whatever the activity and weights of other links, the net input in this case will always be 0. Link 3 acts as a kind of *gate* that will switch the neuron on or off. Compare this to the effect of inhibitory links in the MCP model.

The use of this multiplicative function for calculating net input is rarely used, however. Much more common are alternative methods of calculating a unit's activation on the basis of the net input. To take one very important example, very frequently the activation *y* is given by the formula:

$$y = \frac{1}{1 + e^{-netinput}} \qquad (1.1)$$

where e is the mathematical constant e, the irrational number beginning 2.7182818284... As it is so widely used in neural networks, it's worth stopping to investigate the properties of this function for the moment. The calculation is straightforward enough. For the neuron example given in Figure 1.23, we know that the weighted sum of the inputs is 0.84. Now, applying Equation 1.1, we get:

$$\begin{aligned} y &= \frac{1}{1 + e^{-0.84}} \\ &= \frac{1}{1 + 0.432} \\ &= \frac{1}{1.432} \\ &= 0.698 \end{aligned}$$

To look a little more closely at the behaviour of Equation 1.1, try this exercise.

Exercise 1.2

Using a calculator, which should have an e^x key on it, calculate the value of *y* for a range of net inputs, starting from large negative values (say –10), all the way up to some very large positive ones (say +10). How does the function behave? If you want, use a spreadsheet or a graphing calculator to plot the graph of the function.

Discussion ....

You should have found that the value of *y* always ranges between 0 and 1, but that no matter now large or how small *netinput* is, the value can never quite reach 1 or 0. For this reason, Equation 1.1 is sometimes called a 'squashing function' as it squeezes its return value between two points.

If you tried plotting a graph, you would have found that it resembled Figure 1.24. You can see that this looks a bit like a threshold function (which is a simple step function), in that there is a point at which the value of *x* climbs steeply towards 1 as the value of *netinput* increases. However, there is not the sharp and discrete jump that one gets with a threshold function. *x* increases smoothly and continuously at all times.

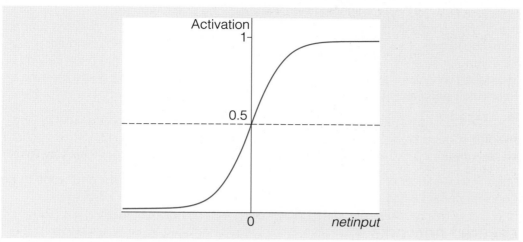

Figure 1.24   Graph of Equation 1.1

Because of the S-shaped profile of their graphs, such functions as these are also sometimes known as **sigmoids**. You will be hearing more about them in the next unit.

Now, to conclude this section and pull the discussion together, consider this question.

SAQ 1.12

What do you think happens to the activation of a unit once it has been calculated?

ANSWER...

Remember from Figure 1.21 that the model unit has a number of outgoing links. The activation of the unit is passed along these as a stimulus to the other units that are connected to it by these links.

A few neural models put the activation through another function, the **output function**, to calculate the proportion of the unit's activity that will be passed on. However, in the vast majority of systems, the activation is simply passed on without amendment. Therefore from now on we will refer to the output of units and networks as their activation, and label it as *x*, or in certain circumstances, where I want to distinguish from some other activation, *y*. For instance, in some cases, to avoid confusion I may represent *inputs* to a network as *x*s and *outputs* as *y*s.

By passing on its activation, then, since units are connected together, a single unit may influence many others. These patterns of connection are known in the jargon as **topologies**.

Topologies

Even with the more elaborate functions, you can see that our model of the neuron is still a pretty simplified one. It would be child's play for a half-way competent programmer to knock up a computer model of one in quick time. But that isn't the point. Neural networks don't derive their power and interest from the computational functions performed by the units in them. As McCullough and Pitts realised, their strengths come from the fact that they are *networks*. Many simple units are connected in patterns, and the interesting computations are made by the network as a whole, in just the same way that many simple ants, acting together, can solve difficult problems in optimisation and transport. To borrow the terminology I developed in Unit 2 of Block 3, the functions of a neural network are an *emergent property* of the interactions between the whole ensemble of units in it.

So, how to connect units together? Looking at the brain is little help. Although brain scientists have identified many functional areas of the brain, and functional areas within these, the complexity found there – involving millions upon millions of neurons and an immense tangle of axons – is simply too overwhelming for a tractable computer model. So computer scientists have tended to follow their own path, using the brain only as an inspiration. We can classify the network models that have been built since the time of Rosenblatt and Hebb into three basic kinds:

▶ layered

▶ lattice

▶ recurrent.

Each of these kinds of structure has its own properties and behaviour, and tends to be good for certain kinds of thing. Let's now look at each of them in a bit of detail.

Layered networks

In layered systems, as their name suggests, the units are organised in layers, with links between the layers. A very simple example of such a network is shown in Figure 1.25. I've depicted each unit as a simple square and the links as arrows, but not indicated the weights on each link.

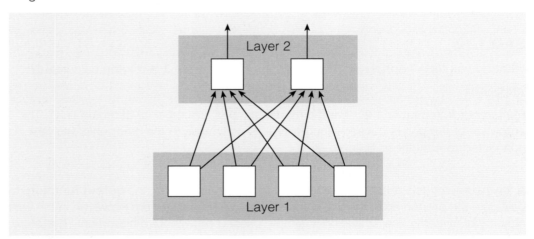

Figure 1.25 Layered network

You can see that the network has the following features:

▶ It consists of a layer of four units connected to a second layer with two units in it.

▶ Every unit in the first layer is connected to every unit in the second layer.

▶ There are no links between units in the same layer.

▶ The connections are *one way only* – stimulus flows from Layer 1 to Layer 2, with no links back from units in Layer 2 to those in Layer 1. This is the reason I've used arrows rather than lines in the diagram: to illustrate the one-way direction of flow of stimulus.

So the activations of the units in Layer 1 stimulate units in Layer 2. You can visualise activity as passing up the diagram from the bottom to the top. The activations of the units in Layer 2 don't feed into any units, so they should be seen as *outputs* from the system. And since the units in Layer 1 do not receive stimulation from any units, they can be seen as *inputs* to the system.

Networks like these can be as complex as you like. Layers can contain as many units as necessary. More interestingly, there can be as many layers as necessary: a very typical set-up is shown in Figure 1.26.

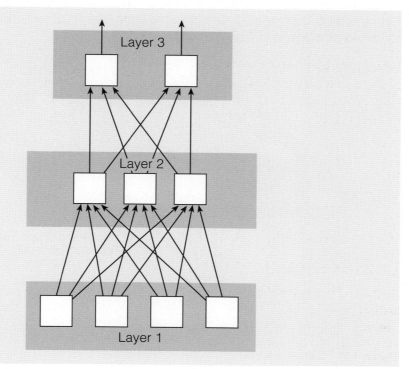

Figure 1.26 Multi-layer network

If you recall that Layer 1 acts an input to the system, receiving information from the world outside it, and that here Layer 3 is an output, pushing back information into the environment around the network, you'll note that Layer 2 has no contact with the world around the system; it is purely internal, and is thus generally called the **hidden layer**. But however many layers there are, or units within each layer, three of the features I noted in the network of Figure 1.25 are almost always present:

▶ complete connection between layers: every unit in a layer is connected to every unit in the next layer, and to no other units;

▶ no connections between units in the same layer;

▶ one-way flow of activation through the network.

For this last reason, such topologies are generally known as **feedforward networks**: activation only flows from input to output. Incidentally, there is often some confusion about how many layers a certain network of this type actually has. Many writers take the line that since the first layer is just a set of inputs to the system, it doesn't count as a real layer. Therefore, for these writers the network in Figure 1.25 would consist of a *single* layer, and that of Figure 1.26 would be a *two*-layer network. I'm going to follow this terminology in the rest of the block.

Before we get on to the two other kinds of network topology, here is your first encounter with a real neural network.

Computer Exercise 1.1

Load up and complete Computer Exercise 1.1 on the course DVD.

Lattice networks

Lattice networks look superficially similar to layered networks, but their principles are rather different. They generally comprise a one-, two- or three-dimensional grid of units fed by a set of dummy input units (like the input layer in a feedforward network). A two-dimensional example is illustrated in Figure 1.27.

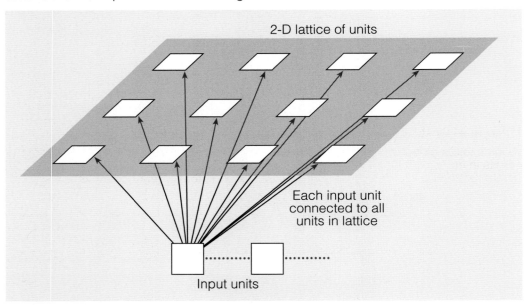

Figure 1.27   Lattice network

This might look to you rather similar to one of the layered feedforward networks you've just looked at. The key difference with this kind of model is that the units in the lattice *interact* with one another. In early lattice models, the interaction took the form of weighted links between the units in the grid. A unit would have a set of excitatory connections (links with positive weights) with its closest neighbours and inhibitory connections (links with negative weights) to units further away in the lattice (see Figure 1.28). Although this set-up is biologically quite realistic – these kinds of **lateral connections** are found in the brains of humans and other mammals – it proved to be difficult to work with computationally, so scientists developed approaches in which these positive and negative interactions among the lattice units were handled in the workings of the learning rule, rather than in the pattern of weights. You will meet such networks in Unit 3.

Recurrent networks

I've already briefly mentioned the concept of recurrence in my account of the work of John Hopfield. I noted that recurrence is found everywhere in the brain and clearly plays a leading part in the neural computation that goes on there. In Block 3 you've seen how important feedback is in nature generally. A recurrent network, then, has at least one feedback connection. However, it's more usual to find that such networks are fully recurrent, with every unit feeding back to every other unit, except itself, as I've illustrated in Figure 1.29.

It should be possible for you to see at once what kind of behaviour recurrent networks are likely to have.

SAQ 1.13

Suppose the three units u_1, u_2 and u_3 depicted in Figure 1.29 have activations x_1, x_2 and x_3. What do you think will happen in the network?

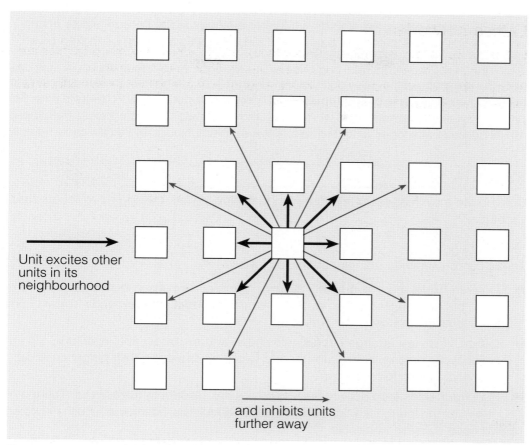

Figure 1.28   Lateral inhibition in lattices

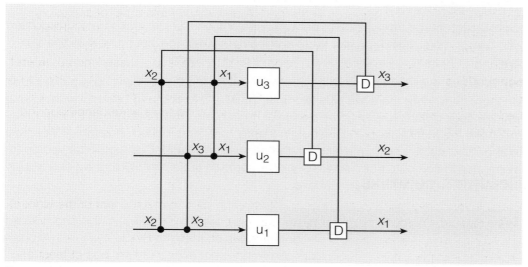

Figure 1.29   Recurrent network with three units

ANSWER..

These activations will each be fed back into the other units: x_1 into u_2 and u_3; x_2 into u_1 and u_3, and so on. These new inputs will cause u_1, u_2 and u_3 to recalculate their activations, and this may change x_1, x_2 and x_3 to new values. These will, in turn, be fed back, and may thus change the activations of u_1, u_2 and u_3 again. This process will continue.

At each change of x_1, x_2 and x_3 we say that the network enters a new *state*. Most network states are unstable, and from these the network switches directly into new states. But some states are stable – no further changes to the network states occur, even with activations being fed back – and these stable states can be looked on as corresponding to learned memories.

Note the presence of the delay calculators in Figure 1.29. Remember that we are trying to simulate neural systems on a computer, and computers operate only in discrete time. So, on each cycle the network waits while u_1, u_2 and u_3 update their activations. Then these are all passed back together to their respective destination units and a new cycle begins.

SAQ 1.14

Sum up the main features of the three fundamental network topologies. What are their properties?

ANSWER...

These can be summed up, very briefly, as follows:

▶ *Layered*. There are *n* layers, with all units in a layer connected to all units in the next layer, but not to units in other layers or in the same layer. Activity feeds forward from the first layer through to the final layer.

▶ *Lattice*. Units are arranged in a single sheet, with excitatory and inhibitory connections among them. Units tend to excite other units in their neighbourhood, and inhibit those further away.

▶ *Recurrent*. Units feed activity back to other units, except to themselves. There are delays on the feedback links, such that all feedback is synchronised. Such networks will have dynamic behaviour.

Learning rules

Finally, each of the three kinds of network topology you've just looked at is associated with one or more *learning rules*. What is a learning rule? The best way to tackle this question is to look at the behaviour of a very basic network.

Figure 1.30 shows an even simpler version of the sort of feedforward network depicted in Figure 1.25. Here there are only two units in Layer 1 and one in Layer 2. In fact, what you are seeing here is Rosenblatt's original Perceptron. You'll notice that it looks pretty much like the McCullough–Pitts set-up in Figure 1.20. And indeed, Rosenblatt was able to show that such a system worked in the same way as a McCullough–Pitts neuron in being able to compute truth tables. Consider the truth table for AND that we looked at in the section on the MCP neuron above:

x_1	x_2	x_1 AND x_2
1	1	1
0	1	0
1	0	0
0	0	0

We can use the perceptron shown in Figure 1.30 to compute this function in much the same way as the McCullough–Pitts neuron does. Here's how.

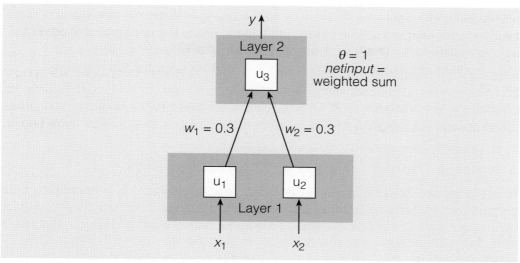

Figure 1.30   Simple feedforward network

Let's say the single unit in Layer 2, u_3, calculates its net input as a weighted sum and has a threshold activation function with the threshold $\theta = 1$. Now look at the truth table. Basically it consists of four two-element input patterns (x_1, x_2), as follows:

Pattern 1	1 1
Pattern 2	1 0
Pattern 3	0 1
Pattern 4	0 0

For each pattern, we would expect a certain response – an activation y – from the unit u_3. Specifically, we want the responses:

Pattern 1	1 1	→	$y = 1$ (active)
Pattern 2	1 0	→	$y = 0$ (inactive)
Pattern 3	0 1	→	$y = 0$ (inactive)
Pattern 4	0 0	→	$y = 0$ (inactive)

from this unit, to match the third column of the truth table. Now, what we can do is force or **clamp** the activations x_1 and x_2 of units u_1 and u_2 to the pattern, so for Pattern 1 the activation x_1 of u_1 would be 1 and the activation x_2 of u_2 would be 1; for Pattern 2, x_1 would be 1 and x_2 would be 0; and so on. (This is why Layer 1 really just consists of dummy units. None of them calculates its activations for itself.) In each case we then want u_3's activation y to be correct, as specified above. Now look again at Figure 1.30 and think about this for a moment.

Exercise 1.3

Does the perceptron as it currently stands produce these responses? If so, why? If not, what would need to be changed to make it do so?

Discussion ....

No, it doesn't. Remember that the net input to the unit is the weighted sum of the input stimulation it is receiving. The activation will depend on whether this net input exceeds or is equal to the threshold 1. Now, taking each pattern in turn we get:

Pattern 1: $netinput = (1 * 0.3) + (1 * 0.3) = 0.6$ so $y \rightarrow 0$

Pattern 2: $netinput = (1 * 0.3) + (0 * 0.3) = 0.3$ so $y \rightarrow 0$

Pattern 3: $netinput = (0 * 0.3) + (1 * 0.3) = 0.3$ so $y \rightarrow 0$

Pattern 4: $netinput = (0 * 0.3) + (0 * 0.3) = 0.0$ so $y \rightarrow 0$

What's gone wrong? It's fairly clear that in the case of Pattern 1, u_3 is not getting sufficient activity from the two input links to bounce it over the threshold. So what can be done about that? One possibility would be to lower the *threshold* to, say, 0.5. This would work, but such an approach often turns out to be rather a crude and inflexible one. Another possibility would be to change the *weights* w_1 and w_2. Setting both w_1 and w_2 to 0.5 would do the trick. But note that there are lots of values of w_1 and w_2 that would do just as well.

So, you can see from the above exercise that changing the weights, or the threshold, or both, will do the business. However, adjusting both is not an approach that is much favoured. It is more straightforward just to work with one set of values, the weights, rather than divide attention between these and the threshold. But in fact, it is possible to provide a perceptron with an adjustable threshold and still work with the weights alone, by altering the topology of the network slightly and incorporating a **bias**. Have a look at Figure 1.31. The perceptron depicted there has two differences from that of Figure 1.30:

▶ The threshold has been set to 0. This new threshold is permanent and unalterable.

▶ A third unit u_b has been added to Layer 1. The activation x_b of this unit is permanently clamped to −1. The same input patterns will still be applied to u_1 and u_2, as in the example above.

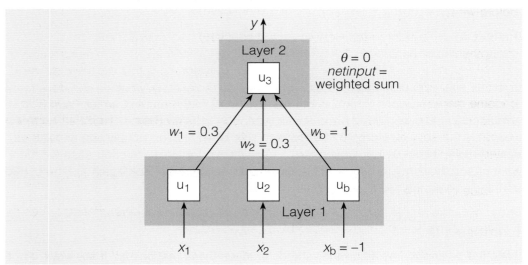

Figure 1.31   Perceptron with bias

It should now be possible to see that this new set-up is equivalent to the one in Figure 1.30, and that changing the weight w_b has exactly the same effect as changing the threshold did in Exercise 1.3.

Exercise 1.4

Show that the networks in Figures 1.30 and 1.31 are equivalent. You can do this by considering the activation function.

Discussion ....

For the network in Figure 1.30 we calculated the activation by applying the formula:

if *netinput* $(x_1 * w_1) + (x_2 * w_2) \geq 1$ then $y \rightarrow 1$, otherwise $y = 0$

Now, for the network of Figure 1.31 the formula becomes:

if *netinput* $(x_1 * w_1) + (x_2 * w_2) + (x_b * w_b) \geq 0$ then $y \rightarrow 1$, otherwise $y = 0$

Since the activation x_b is permanently set to -1 and w_b is 1, then this formula becomes:

if *netinput* $= (x_1 * w_1) + (x_2 * w_2) - 1 \geq 0$ then $y \rightarrow 1$, otherwise $y = 0$

You can see that this is equivalent to the formula for the network in Figure 1.30.

It's also easy to see that changing the weight w_b will have exactly the same effect as altering a threshold.

Essentially, this was Rosenblatt's contribution. He was interested in how humans and animals adapted and learned. The Perceptron was a system designed to explore possible answers to this question. Rosenblatt believed that he had found one possibility in a version of the Hebbian synapse (see above, if you've forgotten what that is) – the idea of *changeable weights*. Now, in the case of the very simple perceptron we've been looking at, it's very easy to adjust the weights by hand to give us the right results. There are only a few weights to consider. But what about a huge network, with maybe thousands of weights? There is no practical way that these can all be set manually. We need an *automated* procedure by means of which the system can learn by adjusting its weights *itself*. What we are looking for is a **learning rule**.

Of course, there are many learning rules. Without them, neural network research could hardly have got very far. And you will hear a great deal about them before you are done with this block. So, for the moment let's just look at one of the simplest of learning rules before we leave this section.

I've just referred back to the Hebbian synapse. Hebb had realised that the strengthening of a synaptic link was directly related to the amount of simultaneous activity on either side of that link. The synapses between cells that are very active together, with a pre-synaptic cell constantly exciting or inhibiting another, tend to become more excitatory or inhibitory. The synapses between cells which have little simultaneous activity tend to decay in strength. So the **Hebb Rule**, or **Hebbian learning**, probably the earliest example of a learning rule in artificial neural networks, can be stated quite simply thus:

▶ If two units at either end of a weighted link are activated *simultaneously*, then the value of the weight is *increased* by some amount.

▶ If two units on either side of a weighted link are activated *at different times*, then the value of the weight is *decreased* by a certain amount.

I hope this is clear enough, although it is a rather cumbersome way of putting it. In the next section I'll look at a more compact means of expressing this, and other, learning rules. You can see, also, that certain facts are missing: how *much* should one increase or decrease the weight, for instance? These details can be left on one side for the moment. The principles of the Hebb Rule are simply these: changes to a weight are:

▶ *time dependent*: the change to the weight depends on the *times* at which the activations of the units on either side of it happen;

- ▶ *local*: the change to the weight depends *only* on the activity of the units at each end of the weight; no other units or weights affect the issue at all;

- ▶ *interactive*: both units are involved together in the decision on how much to modify the weight by.

A final point, but a very important one. In Unit 4 of Block 3, where I discussed adaptive or learning systems, I drew a distinction between *supervised* and *unsupervised* learning. To save you having to look back at that unit now, here is a summary of the difference between these two modes of learning:

- ▶ **Supervised learning** presupposes a bank of *training data*, usually a set of exemplars. Each exemplar will be a *pair*, consisting of an input object and a 'correct' or desired output object. Learning then proceeds through an external *teaching* process presenting each exemplar to the system in turn – usually many times – correcting the system in some way when it outputs a 'wrong' answer (as compared to the 'correct' answer in the training set), and generally doing nothing when the system comes up with the 'correct' answer.

- ▶ **Unsupervised learning** (I called it **reinforcement learning** in Block 3) proceeds without a teacher. Certain actions or outputs of the system are reinforced, others weakened, as time passes, but there is no omniscient access to any 'correct' answer.

Now consider this question.

SAQ 1.15

Is the Hebb Rule an example of supervised or unsupervised learning?

ANSWER...

I expect the distinction between supervised and unsupervised learning to become very clear to you as we deal with concrete examples of learning rules in later units. For now, though, I hope you decided that the Hebb Rule is an example of *unsupervised learning*. There is no external teacher or monitor, and no bank of training data with 'correct' answers. Changes in the system just result from correlations of activity within it.

You will meet many other learning rules in the next unit. To round off this discussion of learning rules, try the following computer exercise.

Computer Exercise 1.2

Load up and complete Computer Exercise 1.2 on the course DVD.

5.3 Computer models and biological models

That, then, is a summary of the building blocks of artificial neural networks: units, weights, topologies and learning rules. I've stressed all along that these are simplifications of the biological systems you studied at the start of the unit. Nevertheless, it should be clear that there are strong correspondences between true nervous systems and the computer models of them. Let's now try to bring biological and computational ideas together in this exercise.

Exercise 1.5

Fill out a table of the correspondences between the computational elements you've learned about and features of biological nervous systems.

Discussion ....

I drew up Table 1.1.

Table 1.1   Correspondences between the computational elements of neurons and features of biological nervous systems

Computational	Biological
unit	neuron
weight	synapse
input area	summation of membrane polarisation around the axon hillock
activation function	spike or frequency of spike train
learning rule	long-term potentiation

Note that these correspondences are quite rough.

Up to now, I've had to rely on verbal descriptions of these computational elements, along with illustrative diagrams. But there is a more compact way of representing the structures and activities of a neural network. It may be slightly intimidating to some at first, but it is very powerful and expressive. It is the language of *mathematical* description.

6 Mathematics

Open any book on neural networks and you will usually find forests of mathematical expressions on every page. All the authors on the M366 team want to avoid this kind of forbidding vista. However, at this stage it's necessary to introduce a few of the mathematical ideas that underlie neural systems.

Exercise 1.6 (optional)

This section introduces some mathematical terminology and notation. If you feel you need some help with this, you may wish to look at the relevant sections in the Maths Guide for this unit now.

In using mathematics as a means of describing neural network systems we are looking for a compact, powerful and expressive means of depicting large and complex systems. Let's now look at three useful ways of representing the components of a neural network and its workings.

6.1 Networks as directed graphs

You may recall our discussions of optimisation problems in Blocks 1–3. There I noted that one particularly useful way of representing an optimisation problem, such as the Travelling Salesman Problem (TSP), is to use notation from *graph theory*. The graph-theoretic representation of a TSP in Figure 3.1 in Block 3, for instance, captured all the essential features of the problem, while leaving out everything that might be irrelevant and clutter up our understanding of it.

Neural networks are not optimisation problems. However, the fact that they are made up of interconnecting components makes graph theory an ideal form of expression for them as well. Simon Haykin has suggested that a neural network can be completely represented in a simple structure known as a **signal graph**. Recall that a graph is essentially a set of *nodes* connected by *edges* (each of which may carry a *weight* or a *cost*). Now, to visualise a neural network as a signal graph, all we need to do is consider such a structure's characteristic nodes and edges:

▶ *Nodes*: each node j has a signal x_j associated with it.

▶ *Edges* are *directed*, meaning that signals flow one way along them. Each edge connects two nodes j and k, starting at j and finishing at k; and each edge has a *transmittance*, which specifies how the signal at node k will depend on that at node j. In a signal graph, there are two kinds of edge:

   ▶ *Weighted edges*. The transmittance of a weighted edge starting at j and finishing at k is given by multiplying the signal x_j at node j by the weight on the edge w_{kj} to give the signal x_k transmitted to node k. This is illustrated in Figure 1.32.

   ▶ *Activation edges*. The transmittance of an activation edge starting at j and finishing at k is given by applying a function $f(x_j)$ to the signal x_j to give the signal x_k at node k (see Figure 1.33). All sorts of functions could be used, but a good example would be the one given in Equation 1.1 earlier.

Figure 1.32   Weighted edge

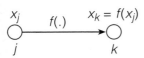

Figure 1.33   Activation edge

Please note that I'm expanding the form of the subscript notation I've been using, which you'll meet time and time again in this block. The weight on the link starting at node j and finishing at node k is represented by w_{kj} (the weight on the link **to** k **from** j). This use of subscripts is standard in neural networks.

All I need to do now is add two further points about signal graphs and then I can put the ideas together into an example. They are:

▶ *convergence*: the signal at a node is calculated by adding all the signals coming into it from converging edges, as in Figure 1.34(a);

▶ *divergence*: the signal at a node is distributed along all its outgoing edges, as in Figure 1.34(b).

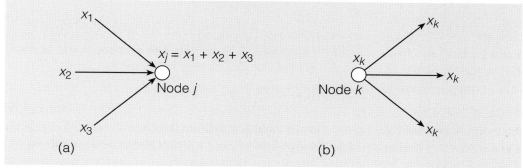

Figure 1.34   (a) Convergence and (b) divergence

Examine Figure 1.35, which puts all the above concepts together. What we have here is a graph-theoretic model of the neuron, corresponding exactly to the one I offered in the block model in Figure 1.21. Then test your understanding of this with this question.

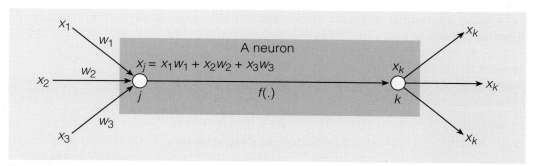

Figure 1.35   Complete graph

SAQ 1.16

Note down the correspondences between the graph in Figure 1.35 and the model neuron in Figure 1.21.

ANSWER..

I summed these up in Table 1.2.

Table 1.2   Correspondences between the graph in Figure 1.35 and the model neuron in Figure 1.21

Figure 1.35	Figure 1.21
incoming signals x_1 to x_n	activations of connected units across incoming links
transmittance of weighted edges	multiplication function carried out in the input area
summation of converging signals $(x_1 * w_1 + x_2 * w_2 + \ldots + x_n * w_n)$	addition function carried out in the input area
transmittance of activation edge	function carried out in the activation area
diverging edges	unit activation distributed to other units across outgoing links

The correspondence is fairly clear.

Although mathematically precise, this is maybe rather a cumbersome representation for the purposes of illustration. For diagrams, Haykin suggests falling back on a more compact model, the **architectural graph**, in which neurons are represented as a single node and weights are omitted. Most of the images of artificial neural networks you've seen in this unit so far have been architectural graphs.

6.2   Sigma notation

Let's recap the special notation I developed above. I came up with the representations given in Table 1.3.

Table 1.3   Mathematical notation used for neurons

Representation	Meaning
x_j (sometimes y_j)	the activation of unit j
w_{kj}	the weight on the link starting at node j and finishing at node k (the weight on the link directed **to** k **from** j)

I don't apologise for repeating this so soon. You will need to get thoroughly used to this notation. Now think about the case of the neuron represented in the architectural graph in Figure 1.36, where the unit u_k has n links converging on it, each with its respective weight w_{kj}, and each link transmitting the activation of a unit x_j.

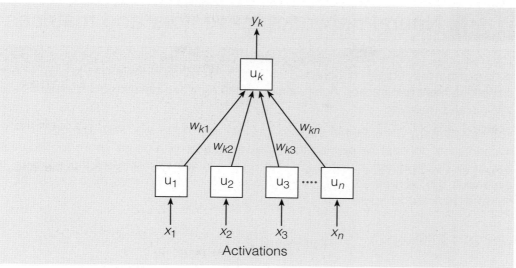

Figure 1.36   Architectural graph of a perceptron

Now we can use mathematical notation to represent the response of u_k, using two equations:

$$netinput_k = \sum_{j=1}^{n} w_{kj} x_j \qquad (1.2)$$

$$y_k = f(netinput_k) \qquad (1.3)$$

Equation 1.2, in *sigma notation*, just represents the weighted sum of the inputs to u_k. Equation 1.3 shows the calculation of the activation of u_k from the activation function, whatever has been chosen for that function (for example, Equation 1.1).

See the Maths Guide for more details on the sigma notation.

We can use a similar notation, *pi notation*, to express the multiplicative formula for calculating the net input that you met in SAQ 1.11, like this:

$$netinput_k = \prod_{j=1}^{n} w_{kj} x_j \qquad (1.4)$$

We can put this scheme of representing units, activations and weights to at least one further use. Remember my earlier account of the Hebb Rule. I won't repeat it here; look back at it if you want. Stated in English, the rule took 51 words to describe. You might even have had to read it twice. Instead of using English, though, we can represent the Hebb Rule quite elegantly using our notation thus:

$$\Delta w_{kj}(t+1) = \eta x_k(t) x_j(t) \qquad (1.5)$$

The expression Δw_{kj} can be interpreted to mean 'the change to be made to the weight on the link between j and k' (Δ is almost always used to mean a *change* to something in mathematical symbolism). η is a constant. t just refers to the time step at which the change is made. To labour the point, you can see that we get the change to the weight at time step $t+1$ by multiplying the activation x_k of unit k (at t) by the activation x_j of unit j (at t) and then multiplying the result by the constant, η, which determines the rate of learning. If you are not a mathematician, it takes a bit of time to get used to this compact way of expressing things, but you can probably see its advantages.

6.3   Neural networks as vectors and matrices

This subscript notation works neatly for individual units and weights, but what about networks that may contain hundreds of units and thousands of weights? We clearly need something more general still. Again, mathematics provides just the right concepts here: *vectors* and *matrices*.

You have already encountered vectors several times in Block 3. How can this mathematical concept be applied to the representation of a neural network? The best way to tackle the question is through a series of examples. First, recall that a vector of dimension *n* is an ordered collection of *n elements* or *components*. Now look at the network depicted in Figure 1.37.

Vectors are always represented with **bold** *lower-case* letters.

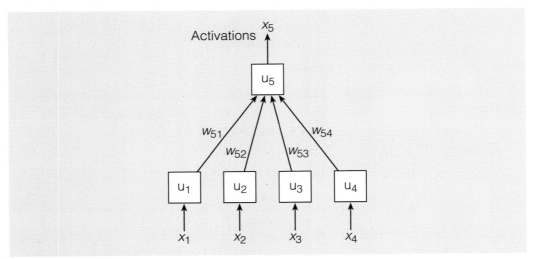

Figure 1.37   Single-layer network

We can take all the activations, x_1 to x_4, of the units u_1 to u_4 and express them as a single vector **x** of four elements:

$$\mathbf{x} = \begin{bmatrix} x_1 \\ x_2 \\ x_3 \\ x_4 \end{bmatrix} \tag{1.6}$$

In the same way, we can treat the four weighted links feeding into u_5 as a vector also, but written – for reasons that should become clearer in a moment – in a slightly different way, as a *row* rather than a *column*:

$$\mathbf{w} = \begin{bmatrix} w_{51} & w_{52} & w_{53} & w_{54} \end{bmatrix} \tag{1.7}$$

Now, as you know already, u_5 will calculate its input as the weighted sum of the activations feeding into it, like this:

$$netinput_5 = \sum_{j=1}^{4} w_{5j} x_j = (w_{51} x_1) + (w_{52} x_2) + (w_{53} x_3) + (w_{54} x_4) \tag{1.8}$$

If we think of this as an operation on the two vectors **x** and **w**, it corresponds to the **dot product** (also known as the **inner product**) of the two:

$$\mathbf{w}^T \cdot \mathbf{x} = \begin{bmatrix} w_{51} \\ w_{52} \\ w_{53} \\ w_{54} \end{bmatrix} \cdot \begin{bmatrix} x_1 \\ x_2 \\ x_3 \\ x_4 \end{bmatrix} = (w_{51}x_1) + (w_{52}x_2) + (w_{53}x_3) + (w_{54}x_4) \tag{1.9}$$

In fact all we are doing here is treating *groups* of numbers as single entities. Note that the dot product of two vectors is not a vector, but a single number, a **scalar**.

This is OK for the simple network in Figure 1.37, but what about something a bit more complicated? Let's think about Figure 1.38.

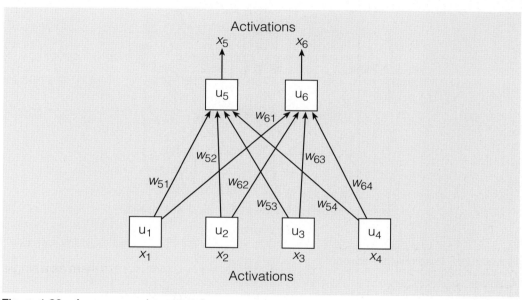

Figure 1.38   A more complex network

Here we have the same input vector **x**, but two weight vectors, one each for u_5 and u_6. Rather than treat these two vectors separately, we can treat them as a single entity, a **matrix**, **W**:

$$\mathbf{W} = \begin{bmatrix} w_{51} & w_{52} & w_{53} & w_{54} \\ w_{61} & w_{62} & w_{63} & w_{64} \end{bmatrix} \tag{1.10}$$

You can see that each weight vector is a single *row* in the matrix. The dimensions of a matrix are given as $m \times n$, where m is the number of rows and n is the number of columns (so **W** above is a 2×4 matrix). Now, as before, each of the output units u_5 and u_6 will calculate its net input using a formula like that of Equation 1.8. In other words, this is equivalent to multiplying the input vector **x** by the weight matrix **W**:

$$\mathbf{Wx} = \begin{bmatrix} w_{51} & w_{52} & w_{53} & w_{54} \\ w_{61} & w_{62} & w_{63} & w_{64} \end{bmatrix} \begin{bmatrix} x_1 \\ x_2 \\ x_3 \\ x_4 \end{bmatrix}$$

$$= \begin{bmatrix} w_{51}x_1 + w_{52}x_2 + w_{53}x_3 + w_{54}x_4 \\ w_{61}x_1 + w_{62}x_2 + w_{63}x_3 + w_{64}x_4 \end{bmatrix} \tag{1.11}$$

$$= \begin{bmatrix} netinput_5 \\ netinput_6 \end{bmatrix}$$

Note the use of the transpose (^{T}) notation here. Since we are representing the weight vector as a *row*, and input vector as *columns*, we need to transpose the weight vector for technical correctness. See the Maths Guide for more details.

Matrices are always represented with **bold** *upper-case* letters.

This is why I represented the weights as a row vector in (1.7) and used its transpose in (1.8).

The result of multiplying a vector by a matrix, then, is another vector. Note the convention that the vector is written after the matrix. It is only possible to multiply an $m \times n$ matrix by a vector of dimension n. For a vector of any other dimension, the multiplication operation is not defined.

Exercise 1.7

Express the network in Figure 1.39 in vector and matrix format and work out the vector of net inputs to units u_4–u_6. What is the vector **y** of activations y_4–y_6 of u_4–u_6 if their activation functions are sigmoids as in Equation 1.1?

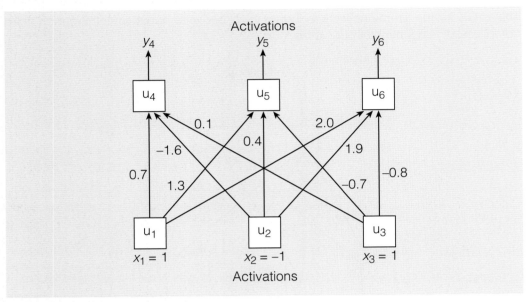

Figure 1.39   Feedforward network

Answer...

The answer to Exercise 1.7 is provided at the end of this unit.

It goes without saying that to have to do such calculations by hand is a very tedious and error-prone business. The good news is that we can leave them to the computers.

That concludes our mathematical business for the time being. Be prepared to meet these notations again in the next unit and throughout the rest of the block.

7 Conclusion

As I promised, we've covered a lot of ground here, from the intricacies of nerve cells and synapses, to the mathematics of artificial neural systems. However, I want to end the unit where I began it: with *pattern recognition* and *classification*. Pattern recognition is of huge importance in natural intelligence, and I think it may underlie many more of the faculties of human intelligence than we give it credit for. Our visual and auditory systems do not perceive discrete, atomic symbols; they pick out complex patterns that have meaning for us, and they recognise, complete and categorise them in the presence of uncertainty and noise. And much of the kind of problem-solving behaviour you met in Block 2 may also depend on pattern recognition. The expert chess player detects characteristic arrangements of pieces on the board and draws unconsciously on a lifetime's memories for responses in these positions, bad and good. Human language itself, the summit of human intelligence, consists of discourses, which are patterns of sentences, which are patterns of words, which are patterns of phonemes, which are patterns of sound waves. And when we utter a sentence, what are we doing but putting together words in patterns that are familiar to us?

Patterns are a major theme of the remainder of the block. As you will see, as you work through the remaining units, artificial neural networks have several capabilities, but pattern recognition is supreme among them.

8 | Summary of Unit 1

In this unit, I've tried to cover four main themes, to prepare you for the discussions that lie ahead. They were:

▶ pattern recognition, completion, classification and response;

▶ biological nervous systems, including the action of the neuron and of the synapse, neural maps and a glance at Edelman's Theory of Neuronal Group Selection;

▶ computer models of nervous systems, their building blocks and topologies, together with the idea of a learning rule;

▶ mathematical models of artificial neural networks: signal graphs, sigma notation and vector/matrix representation.

Armed with these concepts we now move on to explore a range of artificial neural systems. For the moment, though, look back at the learning outcomes for this unit and check these against what you think you can now do. Return to any section of the unit if you need to.

Solutions to selected exercises in Unit 1

Solution to Exercise 1.7

In this network, there are three input and three output units, giving a 3×3 weight matrix, **W**. The vector **n** of net inputs is given by:

$$\mathbf{n} = \mathbf{Wx}$$

$$= \begin{bmatrix} 0.7 & -1.6 & 0.1 \\ 1.3 & 0.4 & -0.7 \\ 2.0 & 1.9 & -0.8 \end{bmatrix} \begin{bmatrix} 1 \\ -1 \\ 1 \end{bmatrix}$$

$$= \begin{bmatrix} 0.7 + 1.6 + 0.1 \\ 1.3 - 0.4 - 0.7 \\ 2.0 - 1.9 - 0.8 \end{bmatrix}$$

$$= \begin{bmatrix} 2.4 \\ 0.2 \\ -0.7 \end{bmatrix}$$

and the vector **y** of activations is calculated as follows:

$$\mathbf{y} = \begin{bmatrix} \dfrac{1}{1+e^{-2.4}} \\ \dfrac{1}{1+e^{-0.2}} \\ \dfrac{1}{1+e^{0.7}} \end{bmatrix}$$

$$= \begin{bmatrix} 0.92 \\ 0.55 \\ 0.33 \end{bmatrix}$$

rounded to two decimal places.

Unit 2: Layers and learning

CONTENTS

1	**Introduction to Unit 2**	**62**
	What you need to study this unit	62
	Learning outcomes for Unit 2	63
2	**Single-layer perceptrons**	**64**
	2.1 Structure	64
	2.2 Geometry – input space	67
	2.3 Geometry – weight space	70
	2.4 Learning	71
	2.5 Learning in perceptrons	72
	2.6 A note on associative memories	86
	2.7 Limitations of single-layer perceptrons	88
3	**Multi-layer perceptrons**	**94**
	3.1 Structure	95
	3.2 Backpropagation – the learning rules	96
	3.3 Backpropagation – the process	100
	3.4 Backpropagation – the error surface	102
	3.5 Factors affecting backpropagation training	103
	3.6 Alternatives to backpropagation	110
4	**Summary of Unit 2**	**112**
	Solutions to selected exercises	113
	References and further reading	213
	Acknowledgements	215
	Index for Block 4	216

Introduction to Unit 2

In this unit, we're going to consider one of the best known of the neural topologies you met in the previous unit: the *layered, feedforward* system. I will follow the example of many writers who also refer to these systems generally as *perceptrons*, after Rosenblatt's original Perceptron, which you met in Unit 1 of this block. In this unit, I want to take you in detail through:

▶ how perceptrons work;

▶ how they can be made to learn;

▶ the mathematical principles that underlie them;

▶ the kinds of problems they can be used for.

We begin with the simplest form of perceptron, the single layer, looking at its structure, how it can be trained, the kinds of problems it can be used for, and its limitations. Much of this discussion will centre on the question of training: I'm going to look in detail at two strategies, known as the *perceptron rule* and the *delta rule*.

As you will learn, single-layer perceptrons have certain serious limitations. Much more powerful and effective is the *multi-layer perceptron*, which I then move on to consider. Again, most of what I want to say about these kinds of system concerns the ways in which they can be made to learn, so there will be a long discussion of the best-known training rule: *error backpropagation*. Many improvements and alternatives to this training strategy have been suggested over the years. You will get a chance to look briefly at two of these: *cascade correlation networks* and *radial basis function networks*.

The perceptron is probably the most common and the most successful of neural network architectures, and is now used in a host of modern applications, from fingerprint recognition to user profiling. I'll try to illustrate its versatility and usefulness with a number of short case studies throughout the unit. These are backed up by a number of longer studies on the course DVD.

What you need to study this unit

You will need the following course components, and will need to use your computer and internet connection for some of the exercises.

▶ this Block 4 text

▶ the course DVD.

LEARNING OUTCOMES FOR UNIT 2

After studying this unit, you will be able to:

2.1 sketch a set of diagrams explaining the topology and geometrical properties of single-layer perceptrons, and illustrating the concepts of input space, weight space and linear separability;

2.2 draw up a set of bullet points laying out the weight adjustment rules and the main steps of supervised perceptron training under the perceptron rule;

2.3 calculate changes to the weight vector of a neuron under perceptron training;

2.4 write a short paragraph explaining the concepts of gradient descent of an error surface;

2.5 draw up a set of bullet points laying out the weight adjustment rules and the main steps of supervised perceptron training under the delta rule;

2.6 calculate changes to the weight vector of a neuron under delta rule training;

2.7 write a sentence defining the concepts of hetero- and auto-associative memories;

2.8 write a paragraph explaining the limitations of single-layer perceptrons;

2.9 draw up a set of bullet points laying out the weight adjustment rules and the main steps of supervised multi-layer perceptron training under error backpropagation;

2.10 calculate changes to the weight vectors of output and hidden neurons under delta rule training;

2.11 draw up a set of bullet points explaining some of the factors that affect the success, speed and efficiency of training under backpropagation, and commenting on their usefulness;

2.12 outline some of the modifications to error backpropagation that have been proposed;

2.13 write a short paragraph explaining the main principles of either cascade correlation networks or radial basis function networks.

2 Single-layer perceptrons

2.1 Structure

You should now know enough from Unit 1 to be able to list the main rules for the architecture of a feedforward network. Test your memory with the following question.

SAQ 2.1

Summarise in a few bullet points the main features of a feedforward network.

ANSWER...

This was just a simple test of memory. The main features were:

▶ units arranged in layers;

▶ all units in a layer connected to all units in the next layer, but not to units in other layers or within the same layer;

▶ activity feeding forward from the first layer through to the final layer.

As you'll see later, perceptrons can have as many units in each layer, and as many layers, as necessary. However, many of their main principles can be appreciated from a study of the simplest kind of perceptron of all: Rosenblatt's original.

Simplifying slightly, Rosenblatt's perceptron consists of a single main unit, into which feed weighted connections from an arbitrary number of dummy units, the activations of which are set, or *clamped*, from outside the system, and which thus act as inputs. The main unit accumulates the weighted sum of the stimulus from the input units and then calculates its activation according to a threshold function. As you saw in Unit 1, this threshold can be set permanently to 0 and a variable threshold incorporated into the model by means of a bias weight. Alternatively, the activation function might simply be a linear one, maybe just the net input itself. Early linear systems of this type were sometimes referred to as **ADALINE**s (ADAptive LInear NEurons). The activation of the main unit is taken to be the output of the system. Figures 2.1 (a) and (b) show a generalised architectural graph and the signal graph for the perceptron.

As you also learned in Unit 1, a perceptron of this kind can be used to compute truth tables, such as AND and OR. But another, perhaps more interesting, way of looking at such systems is as a means of *classifying patterns*. Given the importance of the recognition and classification of patterns in natural intelligence, this is an idea we should follow up. Rosenblatt was, in fact, rather contemptuous of the McCulloch–Pitts approach to neural computation – the view that human thought was a matter of logical inference realised in the structure of the brain. His inspiration for the perceptron came from an understanding of the way animal visual systems work, with the input layer functioning rather like the retina of the human eye, where many thousands of light-sensitive nerve cells respond simultaneously to patterns of light and shade falling upon the retina as a whole. Figure 2.2 shows Rosenblatt's original conception. This looks rather different from

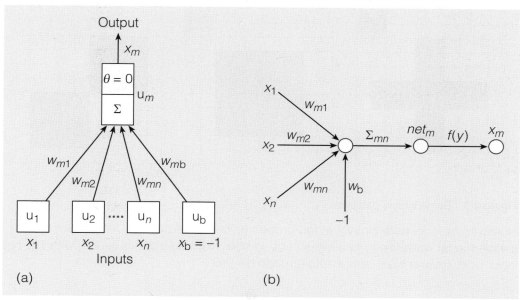

Figure 2.1   Simple perceptron: (a) architecture graph. (b) signal graph

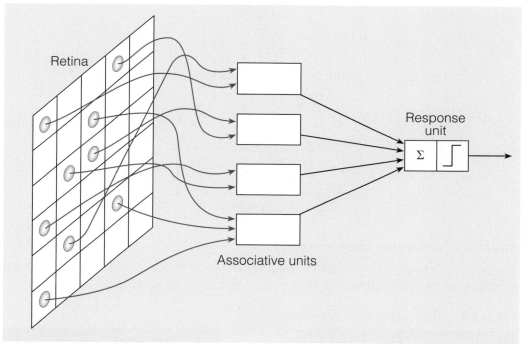

Figure 2.2   Rosenblatt's Perceptron

how I've pictured the perceptron up to now; but since the role of each associative unit in Figure 2.2 is just to sum the activity it receives from the cells in the retina it is connected to, and to pass the result forward, you can see from the signal graph in Figure 2.1(b) that it is equivalent.

If we now consider the retina, you can see that any number of possible patterns can be represented there, as in Figure 2.3, where a black square represents an active cell and a white square an inactive one. And it may be possible to set the weights between the associative units and the response unit in such a way that the response unit will be able to *recognise* and *classify* the patterns, by responding with an activation of 1 to a cross, say, and 0 to a square. Additional response units can be added to the system to give a wider range of possible classifications. This was Rosenblatt's original intention.

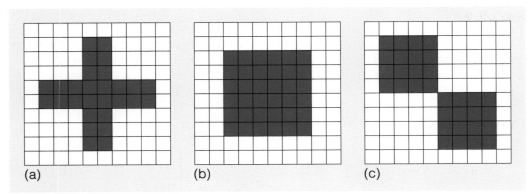

Figure 2.3 Some simple patterns

However, to look more closely at the properties of the perceptron, let's return to the simple model we've been dealing with up to now, illustrated in Figure 2.4, with just two input units (plus a bias) and a single response unit.

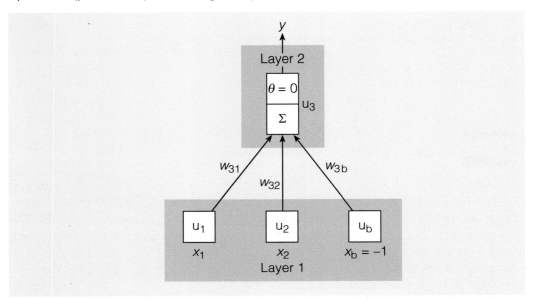

Figure 2.4 Perceptron for simple truth tables

You've already seen in Unit 1 that the weights can be set to ensure that the response unit activates according to either the AND or the OR truth table (see Table 2.1).

Table 2.1　AND and OR truth tables

x_1	x_2	y
1	1	1
1	0	0
0	1	0
0	0	0
AND		

x_1	x_2	y
1	1	1
1	0	1
0	1	1
0	0	0
OR		

In fact, it is obvious that there are *many* values of w_1 and w_2 for which we would get the desired responses.

SAQ 2.2

Assuming $w_b = 1$, find three sets of values for w_1 and w_2 which guarantee the correct response for the AND truth table and three for the OR truth table. Assume that both w_1 and w_2 can take real number values.

ANSWER..

There are, of course, plenty of possibilities. For AND, I came up with:

$w_{31} = 0.99$ and $w_{32} = 0.99$

$w_{31} = 0.6$ and $w_{32} = 0.6$

$w_{31} = 0.55$ and $w_{32} = 0.75$

and for OR, I had:

$w_{31} = 1.0$ and $w_{32} = 1.0$

$w_{31} = 1.6$ and $w_{32} = 1.1$

$w_{31} = 1.05$ and $w_{32} = 1.75$

and so on. Varying w_b would create an even wider range of potential answers. However, the main point is that this very simple perceptron is capable of computing *either* truth table, given the right set of weights.

2.2 Geometry – input space

One of the most enlightening ways of envisaging classifier systems like the perceptron is *geometrically*, by thinking in terms of the *space* of its possible inputs. Mathematicians among you will be completely familiar with the general idea of a space. You've met the concept several times before in earlier units: the state space of a Symbolic AI system (Block 2) or the solution space of a particle swarm optimiser (Block 3), to take two examples. To apply the idea to the perceptron, all we need to do is consider the possible inputs, x_1 and x_2 (ignoring x_b, since this is always fixed at –1). The **input space** can then be very simply depicted, as in Figure 2.5. If x_1 and x_2 can only be the integer values 1 or 0, as they would be in a truth table computation, then the only parts of the space that are available are the four corners of the square labelled in the figure: ($x_1 = 0$, $x_2 = 0$), ($x_1 = 1$, $x_2 = 0$), ($x_1 = 0$, $x_2 = 1$) and ($x_1 = 1$, $x_2 = 1$). The area inside the square is unused. However, if they can take real number values, then a possible input can be any point within the whole of the space depicted, such as the point I've labelled as $x_1 = 0.4$, $x_2 = 0.5$.

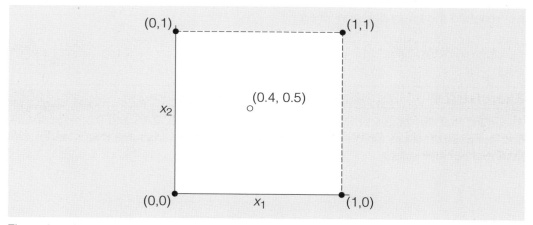

Figure 2.5   Input space for simple perceptron

Now what is happening when the system classifies its inputs, responding 1 to a certain group of them and 0 to others? Geometrically, the answer is clear: it is *dividing* or *partitioning* the space of inputs into two parts, as shown in Figure 2.6. Note that the partitioning line I've drawn is quite arbitrary: there are countless other lines I could have drawn that would do just as well.

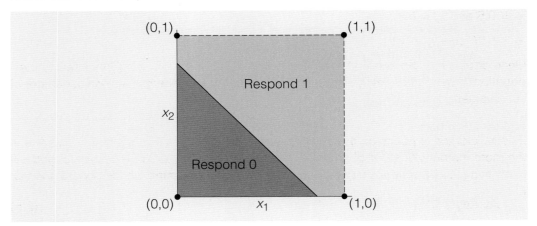

Figure 2.6   Partitioning of the input space

In what sense, then, is our perceptron 'drawing' this line? How is it accomplishing the partitioning? Well, think about the activation function the response unit is using. This is:

$$\begin{cases} x_1w_{31} + x_2w_{32} \geq \theta & y = 1 \\ \text{otherwise} & y = 0 \end{cases} \tag{2.1}$$

which, with the bias weight w_b set to 1 and x_b clamped permanently to −1 can be rewritten as:

$$\begin{cases} x_1w_{31} + x_2w_{32} - w_b \geq 0 & y = 1 \\ \text{otherwise} & y = 0 \end{cases} \tag{2.2}$$

For a perceptron with n input units and a bias the rule is simply:

$$\begin{cases} \sum_{i=1}^{n} x_iw_{3i} - w_b \geq 0 & y = 1 \\ \text{otherwise} & y = 0 \end{cases} \tag{2.3}$$

Let's focus on the point where the response unit is just changing from an inactive 0 response to firing with a response of 1. We call this the **decision boundary**. From Equation 2.2 you can see that this is the exact point at which the net input to the unit has just reached the threshold, and where:

$$x_1w_{31} + x_2w_{32} - w_b = 0 \tag{2.4}$$

Exercise 2.1

Assuming that the values of w_{31}, w_{32} and w_b are set at 0.55, 0.75 and 0.5 respectively, find four pairs of values for x_1 and x_2 that satisfy Equation 2.4. Assume that x_1 and x_2 can take real number values.

Discussion ....

With a bit of tedious calculation, and some rounding, I found:

$x_1 = 0.9$ and $x_2 = 0.006$

$x_1 = 0.3$ and $x_2 = 0.447$

$x_1 = 0.5$ and $x_2 = 0.3$

$x_1 = 0.65$ and $x_2 = 0.19$

Once again, you can see that there are countless values of x_1 and x_2 that satisfy the equation. In fact, since we are allowing real number values, there is an infinite number of such values.

If I now plot these points on the input space, the result looks like Figure 2.7. But again, the more mathematically inclined among you will be way ahead of me here, for you will know that Equation 2.4 is simply a version of the **linear equation** whose general form is:

$$Ax + By + C = 0 \qquad\qquad (2.5)$$

where A and B are not both 0. Plotting the values of A and B that satisfy Equation 2.5 always yields a straight line, whose angle and position is determined by the values of A, B and C. So the border partitioning the input space of a perceptron is always a straight line, and sets of patterns such as those in the OR truth table are said to be **linearly separable**, because it is possible to draw a straight line that will partition the space in the right way. The lines in Figures 2.6 and 2.7 divide the patterns correctly for OR. You can easily draw a different line across one of them to partition for AND.

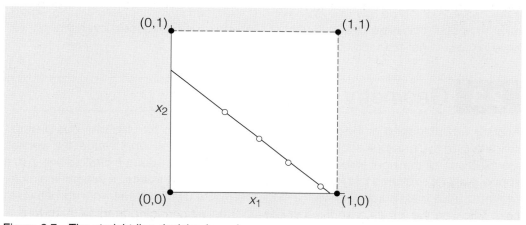

Figure 2.7   The straight-line decision boundary

Up to now, I've only been dealing with a perceptron with two inputs (plus bias). Their geometry is perfectly easy to visualise and to illustrate. However, it should be no trouble to see that all the principles we've identified so far – input space partitioning, linear separability, and so on – can be generalised to perceptrons with any number of inputs and response units. Ignoring the bias from now on, for a perceptron with three inputs, the input space becomes three-dimensional, and thus a *cube*. The partitioning boundary changes from being a line to a two-dimensional *plane* (see Figure 2.8). After three inputs, things proceed exactly as before, but become much more difficult to picture mentally.

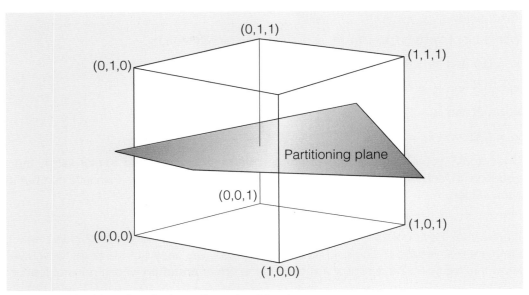

Figure 2.8   Decision plane in three-dimensional input space

For perceptrons with four inputs, the input space is a four-dimensional cube, technically known as a **tesseract** – but mathematicians generally just refer to any cube of more than three dimensions as a **hypercube**. Following the obvious rule that the dimensions of the decision boundary will be one fewer than that of the input space, the boundary is thus a three-dimensional plane, or **hyperplane**. And you can easily see that perceptrons with n inputs have an n dimensional input space and an $n - 1$ dimensional decision boundary. Here, let me repeat a point I made in a different context in Block 3: no human being has the ability actually to visualise such high-dimensional spaces. Mathematicians are no more capable of it than any one else. We are three-dimensional creatures. We simply have to accept that there is a geometry of high-dimensional spaces, even though we have no way, other than through algebra, of thinking about it.

2.3 | Geometry – weight space

Another way of looking at the perceptron geometrically is to turn the previous picture inside out. In the previous section, I developed the idea of an *input space*: the weights are fixed and all the input values that satisfy Equation 2.4 fall along a straight line in this space. Now let's reverse this idea and consider the **weight space** of the same simple, two-input (plus bias) perceptron with a single response unit I've been working with up to now. This time the *inputs* have fixed values and the *weights* can be plotted. To take a simple case, suppose we have three patterns – (0,1) (i.e. $x_1 = 0$, $x_2 = 1$), (1,0) and (1,1) – that we want the perceptron to classify, and that (0,1) and (1,0) belong to class 1 (activation of the response unit = 1) and (1,1) belongs to class 2 (activation of the response unit = 0). Once again, we have decision hyperplanes dividing up the space; but this time all the possible *weights* that satisfy Equation 2.4 for a certain fixed *pattern* lie along this boundary. And since in this example there are three patterns, there are three hyperplanes. The bold arrow on each hyperplane points to the half of the space in which the response unit will activate to 1. I've depicted the weight space and the three hyperplanes in Figure 2.9. The shaded area shows the area within which the two weights must be set in order for the perceptron to respond correctly.

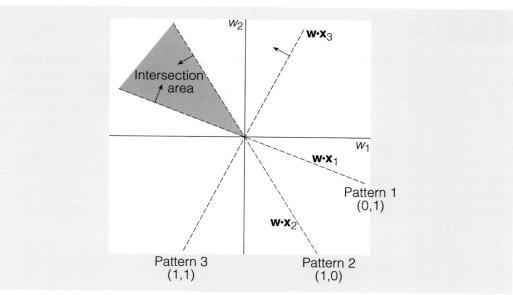

Figure 2.9 Example of two-dimensional weight space

2.4 | Learning

It should also be fairly clear how perceptrons with more than one response unit behave geometrically. If a single response unit draws a single decision hyperplane, then it follows that two response units will create two boundaries and n response units will create n boundaries. This is a lot easier to illustrate: Figure 2.10 shows the example of a system with three response units.

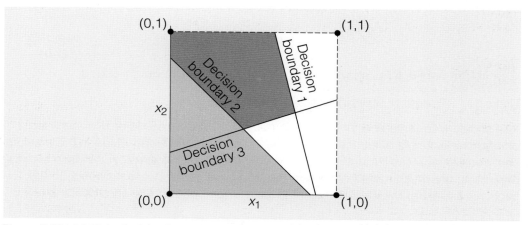

Figure 2.10 Multiple decision boundaries dividing a two-dimensional input space

However, it seems likely that with increasing numbers of inputs, response units and potential classifications it will become increasingly difficult to find the right set of weights to achieve these classifications. Certainly setting the two weights (plus bias) of a two-input, one response unit perceptron is no problem. You did it in SAQ 2.2. But in Rosenblatt's original conception of the system there can be many hundreds of weights; and indeed Rosenblatt himself experienced almost insurmountable difficulties in setting these correctly. But if the process could be automated, then such problems might come to an end. And this is where *learning rules* come in.

2.5 | Learning in perceptrons

Recall from Unit 1 of this block that learning rules (often known also as **training rules** in the neural networks community) are procedures for altering the weights of a neural system towards some desired set of values. In the case of the perceptron, a solution would be a matrix of weights that will correctly classify a set of inputs into two or more sets. In terms of the geometrical picture of the perceptron I presented above, training the system will involve moving the decision hyperplane from some initial orientation in the input space (which will probably cause the perceptron to classify wrongly), step by step to one which divides the space up correctly. The other way of looking at the same process is to see the point in weight space denoting the initial settings of the weights being shifted stepwise into the intersection area. I've tried to illustrate these two ideas in Figure 2.11.

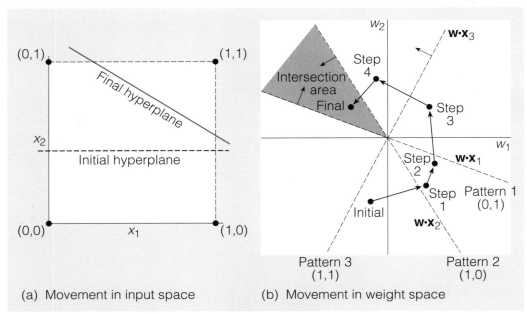

(a) Movement in input space   (b) Movement in weight space

Figure 2.11   Training in: (a) input space. (b) weight space

You should also remember that learning rules can be *supervised* or *unsupervised*. I offered one example of an unsupervised learning rule – the *Hebb Rule* – in the previous unit. You will meet the Hebb Rule again later in this block. However, *supervised* learning algorithms are much more common in the training of feedforward networks. In this section I am going to deal with two of these: the *perceptron rule* and the *delta rule*.

The perceptron rule

First of all, you should bring back to mind the main features of supervised learning with this question.

SAQ 2.3

Jot down a couple of notes outlining the main characteristics of supervised learning.

ANSWER...

I think these are the main features:

▶   a bank of *training data*, usually a set of exemplars;

▶   exemplar *pairs*, comprising an input object and a 'correct' or desired output object;

▶ a *teaching* process in which each exemplar is presented to the system in turn – usually many times – correcting it in some way when it outputs a 'wrong' answer (in contrast with the 'right' answer in the training set), and generally doing nothing when the system comes up with the desired answer.

In the case of the supervised training of a perceptron, each pair of exemplars will consist of:

▶ an input vector $\mathbf{x}$;

▶ a vector $\mathbf{d}$ expressing the activation that the perceptron's response units should give if $\mathbf{x}$ is to be classified correctly.

For a perceptron with n input units (plus bias) and m output units, the dimension of $\mathbf{x}$ and $\mathbf{d}$ must thus be n and m respectively.

The simplest of the learning algorithms for perceptrons originated with Rosenblatt himself – the **perceptron rule**. To illustrate this rule, let's go back to a simple perceptron, the signal graph of which I showed in Figure 2.1(b). Note the following points:

1   Since this network has only one response unit, the weight matrix consists only of a single vector $\mathbf{w}^T$.

2   For any form of supervised learning, we must assume a set of input vectors [$\mathbf{x}_1$, $\mathbf{x}_2$, $\mathbf{x}_3$ ... $\mathbf{x}_n$], each of which is paired with a member of a set of training vectors [$\mathbf{d}_1$, $\mathbf{d}_2$, $\mathbf{d}_3$ ... $\mathbf{d}_n$], each $\mathbf{d}_i$ giving the desired activations of the response neurons for the input vector $\mathbf{x}_i$ it is paired with. In the case of our network, since there is only one response unit, each vector $\mathbf{d}$ will contain only one element d_1.

3   The aim of the training process is to arrive at a set of weights that will correctly assign each of the input vectors $\mathbf{x}_i$ into either class C_1 or class C_2, by activating the response unit to 1 if $\mathbf{x}_i$ is in C_1 or leaving the response unit remaining inactive at 0 if $\mathbf{x}_i$ belongs to C_2.

Recall that $\mathbf{w}^T$ is the *transpose* of the vector. This is because the vector will be the (single) *row vector* in the network's weight matrix.

As with any supervised learning algorithm, the teaching process follows the one outlined in point 3 above: each input $\mathbf{x}_i$ is clamped to the input units in turn, and the perceptron's response is compared with the vector for the desired activation $\mathbf{d}_i$ that is paired with $\mathbf{x}_i$. The aim is to make small corrections to the weights each time an input produces an incorrect classification. The way the algorithm works in detail is as follows.

Perceptron training algorithm

1   Set $\mathbf{w}$ to 0 (set value of all its elements to 0).

2   Set a counter i to 1.

3   Extract $\mathbf{x}_i$ from the training set and clamp the activations of the input units of the perceptron to the values of its elements.

4   Calculate the net input of the response unit, $\mathbf{w}^T \cdot \mathbf{x}_i$.

5   Calculate the activation of the response unit by applying the threshold activation function of the response unit:

if *netinput* $\mathbf{w}^T \cdot \mathbf{x}_i \geq 1$ then **activation** $y \rightarrow 1$, otherwise $y \rightarrow 0$.

6   Apply the perceptron learning rule, as follows:

6.i   if the activation of the response unit is that given by d_i then make no change to the weight matrix, i.e.:

$\mathbf{w}$(new) = $\mathbf{w}$(old)

6.ii if the activation of the response unit is not that given by d_i then alter the weight matrix as follows:

$\mathbf{w}$(new) = $\mathbf{w}$(old) − $\eta\mathbf{x}_i$ if activation is 1 and should be 0;

$\mathbf{w}$(new) = $\mathbf{w}$(old) + $\eta\mathbf{x}_i$ if activation is 0 and should be 1;

where η is a constant. This step is equivalent to calculating an **error signal** e (in this case $(d_i - y_i)$) for the network, multiplying it by the learning constant and by x_i, and then applying the result to the weight vector. If the activation is 1 and should be 0, then $e = (d_i - y_i) = -1$. If the activation is 0 and should be 1, then $e = (d_i - y_i) = 1$.

7   If network has responded correctly throughout then terminate:

elseif $i = n$ then go to step 2   // *reached end of training set*

else $i = i + 1$ and go to step 3   // *more patterns left in the training set*

The algorithm simply repeats the process of applying the members of the training set one by one to the perceptron and making small corrections to the weights each time the activation of the response unit is incorrect. The core of the process is step 6, where the perceptron learning rule is applied. If you look closely at the rule, you can see that what happens is:

▶ if the network is responding when it should not be responding (i.e. it is incorrectly identifying $\mathbf{x}_i$ as belonging to C_1 when in fact it belongs to C_2), $\mathbf{w}$ is given a small nudge in the right direction by *decreasing* the weights by some proportion of the input, thus making the response unit less inclined to activate when it receives that input;

▶ if the network is not responding when it should be responding (i.e. it is incorrectly identifying $\mathbf{x}_i$ as belonging to C_2 when in fact it belongs to C_1), $\mathbf{w}$ is given an opposite nudge by *increasing* the weights by some proportion of the input, thus making the response unit more inclined to activate when it receives that input;

▶ if the network responds correctly no changes are made to $\mathbf{w}$.

η is a constant called the **learning constant**, which governs the rate at which learning takes place. η must be positive. If its value is small then learning takes place slowly: the weights move in small steps towards correct values. If η is large then each change to the weight vector will be larger.

SAQ 2.4

What do you think would be the advantages and disadvantages of small or large values for η?

ANSWER..

If η is large then training will proceed quickly. The number of times the whole training set will have to be presented to the network will be fewer. However, if large changes are being made to the weights at each step, it is quite possible that the values to which the weights are being set will leap over their correct values to other incorrect ones. In the worst cases, the weights will simply oscillate backwards and forwards between two sets of incorrect values.

The converse is true for small values of η. Here, training will be slow, with many repetitions of steps 2–6 of the algorithm. However, it is much more likely that the weights will converge slowly but surely on a correct set of values, with much less chance of overshoot.

The perceptron rule generalises to a perceptron of any shape and size, and to perceptrons that can take real-valued inputs and make real-valued responses. For instance, the perceptron with three inputs and two response units in Figure 2.12 would be trained using exactly the same rule.

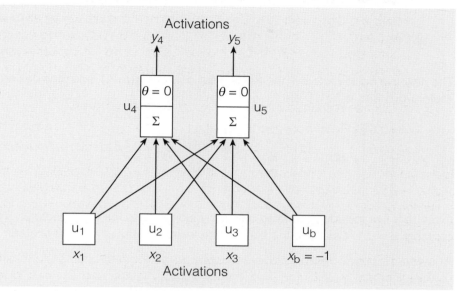

Figure 2.12   Specimen perceptron for perceptron rule training

You know from the previous unit that in this case the weights are expressed as a matrix **W**, such that:

$$\mathbf{W} = \begin{bmatrix} w_{41} & w_{42} & w_{43} & w_{4b} \\ w_{51} & w_{52} & w_{53} & w_{5b} \end{bmatrix}$$

and the dimension of the training vectors $\mathbf{d}_1, \mathbf{d}_2, \mathbf{d}_3 \dots \mathbf{d}_n$ will be two. Each $\mathbf{d}_i$ will have two elements – d_4 and d_5 – representing the desired activations of the units u_4 and u_5 respectively. You can see from the architecture graph in Figure 2.12 that the network really consists of two single-response networks put together, with the weight vectors of each response unit a row vector in the matrix **W**. The training process thus acts on these two row vectors as follows, by calculating a change vector $\Delta\mathbf{w}$ for each row and adding these to **W**:

▶ The error signal e_4, the difference between the desired activation of unit 4 and its actual activation, $d_4 - y_4$, is calculated. Then the change vector $\eta e_4 \mathbf{x}_i$ is added to the first row of the matrix.

▶ The error signal e_5, the difference between the desired activation of unit 5 and its actual activation, $d_5 - y_5$, is calculated. Then the change vector $\eta e_5 \mathbf{x}_i$ is added to the second row of the matrix.

This is equivalent to constructing a change matrix $\Delta\mathbf{W}$ and then adding $\Delta\mathbf{W}$ to **W**. A worked example often helps to clarify things in cases such as this. Have a look at this exercise.

Exercise 2.2

The perceptron shown in Figure 2.12 takes real-valued inputs and its response units activate to 1 or 0 according to a threshold function ($\theta = 0$, as in the above examples). At the start of step t in training under the perceptron rule the weight matrix is:

$$\mathbf{W}(t-1) = \begin{bmatrix} 0.2 & 0.3 & -0.1 & 0.5 \\ 0.7 & -1 & 0.6 & 0.4 \end{bmatrix}$$

The next two input vectors in the training set, $\mathbf{x}(t)$ and $\mathbf{x}(t+1)$, and their desired activation vectors $\mathbf{d}(t)$ and $\mathbf{d}(t+1)$, are:

$$\mathbf{x}(t) = \begin{bmatrix} 0.5 \\ 0.5 \\ 0.3 \\ -1 \end{bmatrix} \quad \mathbf{d}(t) = \begin{bmatrix} 1 \\ 1 \end{bmatrix} \quad \mathbf{x}(t+1) = \begin{bmatrix} -0.4 \\ -0.2 \\ 0.1 \\ -1 \end{bmatrix} \quad \mathbf{d}(t+1) = \begin{bmatrix} 1 \\ 0 \end{bmatrix}$$

(Note that I've included the fixed bias activation in both the input vectors.) The learning constant $\eta = 0.1$. Calculate the state of the weight matrix at the end of steps t and $t+1$.

Answer..

You will find the answer to Exercise 2.2 at the end of this unit.

It goes without saying that this is a very long and tedious calculation to do by hand. We can all agree that it's generally best to leave this kind of thing to the computers, which eat up arithmetic like this. However, I do think it is a useful exercise to demonstrate exactly what is going on inside a perceptron as it trains under the perceptron rule.

The perceptron convergence theorem

But how well does the perceptron rule work? Is it *guaranteed* to arrive at a set of weights capable of making the classifications we want? This is quite a difficult question. There are limitations on perceptrons, as you'll learn shortly, but these are mainly limitations of the perceptron itself, rather than of the perceptron rule. In fact Rosenblatt was able to prove mathematically the **perceptron convergence theorem**. The mathematical proof of the theorem is beyond the scope of this course, so it will be enough just for me to present a simple statement of its main assertion here.

A proof of the perceptron convergence theorem is given on the course DVD. It will form no part of the assessment for this course.

Rosenblatt was able to show in 1962 that if a vector $\mathbf{w}^*$ exists, such that it is a solution vector for two linearly separable patterns, then the series will converge to this vector in a finite number of steps. Since every response unit in a perceptron is independent of the others, this result generalises to perceptrons with any number of response units and input units. But the key words here are 'if $\mathbf{w}^*$ exists' and 'linearly separable patterns'. I'll return to this point after the next section. For the moment, though, I want to look at another learning rule, and a key technique in supervised neural network training – **gradient descent**.

The delta rule – preliminaries

The term **delta rule** really refers to a cluster of specific learning rules, all based on the notion of *minimising* the *error* a network is making. You can see that the perceptron rule contains something of this idea, as at every step it calculates the difference between the expected activations $\mathbf{d}$ of the response units and the actual activations $\mathbf{y}$ – in other words, how far the network response departs from expectations, i.e. its error. It then acts to alter the weights in such a way as to lessen this error. In fact, all supervised learning is based in some way on the idea of minimising error.

The delta rule often appears under other names, most notably the **Widrow–Hoff** rule, or the **least mean square** (LMS) rule. This last name refers to the way the error can be calculated. We can do what we did with the perceptron rule and simply use the usual measure of error e_i for a response unit i, the difference between its desired activation d_i and its actual activation y_i as the measure of the error, i.e.:

$$e_i = d_i - y_i \tag{2.8}$$

However, in LMS systems, the error may often be calculated using an equation such as:

$$e_i = \frac{1}{2}(d_i - y_i)^2 \tag{2.9}$$

Before looking in detail at how the learning rule works to minimise network error, I want to establish a few very important concepts. To do this, let's consider the very simplest network possible, as illustrated in the architectural graph in Figure 2.13. A network as basic as this wouldn't be able to do anything very interesting, of course. However, it will serve to illustrate the concepts of an **error surface** and **steepest descent**.

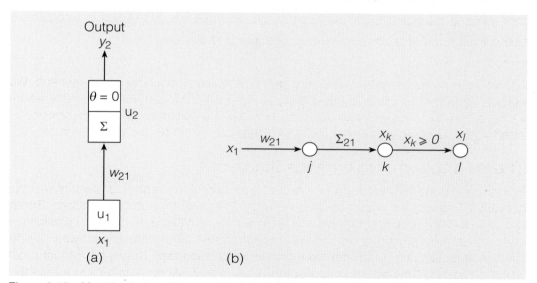

Figure 2.13   Most basic possible network: (a) architecture graph. (b) signal graph

Suppose we have a measure of error, such as the one in Equation 2.9. Suppose further that when the input clamped to u_1 is 1, the expected activation of the single response unit u_2 is 1, and that the initial weight $w_{21} = -1$. In this case, the activation of the response unit will be 0, and its error e_2 will thus be $\frac{1}{2}(0-1)^2 = 0.5$. Now what will be the effect on e_2 of incrementally increasing w_{21}? There's no mystery about that: e_2 will remain constant for a while until w_{21} becomes sufficiently large for the response unit's threshold to be crossed, whereupon it will drop sharply to 0. Figure 2.14 overleaf shows a plot of e_2 against w_{21}. We can term the space in which the error is plotted the **error space**.

Now let's abandon the threshold activation function we've been using up to now and substitute a sigmoid activation function in u_2. You should recall this function from Unit 1 of this block. To remind you, the function is:

$$y = \frac{1}{1 + e^{-netinput}} \tag{2.10}$$

where y is the activation of the unit. Since the value of the function varies between 0 and 1, it is known as a **unipolar function**. Returning to our initial state, with $w_{21} = -1$, the initial error will be about 0.267, if we are using Equation 2.9. If we now again plot e_2

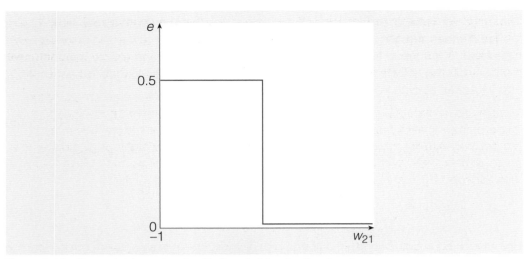

Figure 2.14   Error plot for network with threshold activation function

against changes to w_{21}, this time we get a smooth curve, something like the one I've illustrated in Figure 2.15(a). Note that the desired output of a unit need not always be 1. Consider the case in which it is 0.5. Here the curve drops towards a minimum error and then starts to rise again as the activation of the response unit overshoots its target value (see Figure 2.15(b)).

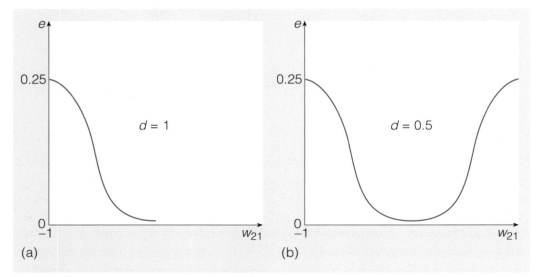

(a)   (b)

Figure 2.15   Error plot for network with continuous activation function for: (a) $d = 1$, (b) $d = 0.5$

SAQ 2.5

Can you explain the difference between the graph shown in Figure 2.14 and those in Figure 2.15?

ANSWER...

Remember from Unit 1 of this block that the sigmoid function in Equation 2.10 is a *continuous* function: its value changes smoothly and continuously, without the sudden step up or down in value that we get with the threshold function. And so we would expect the error also to change smoothly and continuously.

You may also remember that this sigmoid, even though it is a continuous function, looks rather like the threshold in shape. Around the values of *netinput* that are closest to the threshold, when the activation given by the threshold function would be snapping over from 0 to 1, the activation given by Equation 2.10 is climbing most steeply towards 1.

Now what about networks with more than one input unit? Here we are in the same territory as in my earlier discussion of the partitioning of the input space by a hyperplane – that of *high-dimensional spaces*. Suppose we are dealing with a perceptron with two inputs. Now we have to plot e_3 against weights w_{31} and w_{32} in a *three*-dimensional error space, a cube, giving us – instead of an error *curve* – a bowl-shaped error *surface*, as I've tried to illustrate in Figure 2.16.

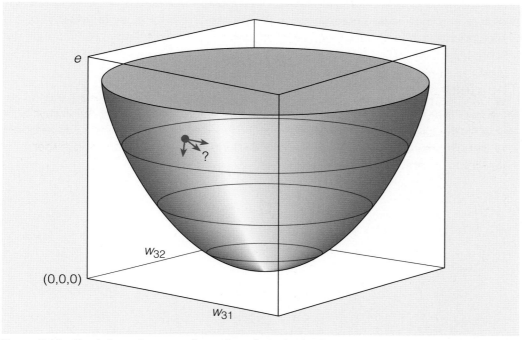

Figure 2.16   Bowl-shaped error surface of two input network

You can guess what's coming next: for a perceptron with three inputs, the changing error describes a three-dimensional surface (a hyperbowl?) in a four-dimensional error space. For four inputs and upwards (and there is no reason why there might not be hundreds of inputs), we get a hyperspace of many dimensions. Yet again, let me stress that it is impossible to truly visualise such spaces; everyone has to devise their own strategies for thinking about them. When I imagine the error surface, I tend to think in terms of a three-dimensional bowl and take on trust the idea that it extends into many dimensions.

The delta rule is a training rule. The purpose of every training rule is to specify which weights should be altered and by how much. In the case of our single-input, single-response perceptron of Figure 2.13, there is hardly much of a choice: there is only one weight, so the options are simply either to increase it by a certain amount, or decrease it by a certain amount. And you can see in this simple case, represented by Figure 2.15 (a), that increasing the weight will tend to lessen the error, moving the present state down the error surface towards the minimum; while decreasing it will move the system up the error surface away from the minimum. As for the slightly more complex situation depicted in Figure 2.15(b), the need is either to increase or decrease the weight depending on which choice takes the error down the slope towards the minimum – this will depend on where you start on the error curve. The position of the system on the error curve is given by the value of the weight.

But what about perceptrons with a single response unit and two or more inputs? Here the situation is slightly more complex. There are two or more weights to be increased or decreased; therefore, at any point on the error surface, there are a number of paths that can be taken. I've tried to illustrate this in Figure 2.16. But which path to take? The best answer is the most obvious one – alter the weights in such a way as to take the *steepest* path downwards, towards the error minimum. But what changes will yield the steepest path down?

As I'm sure you know, the branch of mathematics that deals with continuously changing functions, and the slopes of such functions, is *calculus*. Don't leave immediately, though. The course team have decided to leave out details of the finer mathematics for determining the slope of the error surface. We provide derivations of the delta rule for two-layer and multi-layer perceptrons on the course DVD , for those of you who are interested in the technicalities. However, these will not be assessed – we offer them for interest only.

The delta rule

So, returning once again to the simplest case of a one-dimensional error curve within a two-dimensional error space, illustrated in Figure 2.17, I've already noted that there are only two choices to be made at any position on the error curve: go up or go down.

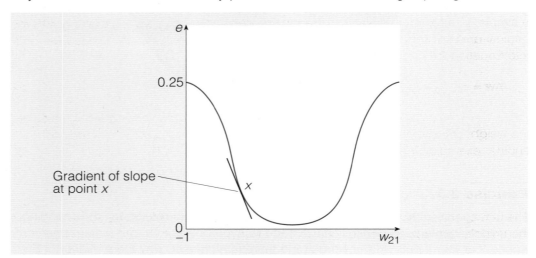

Figure 2.17   One-dimensional error curve with gradient

You can see from the Figure 2.17 that the steepest path here is the *gradient* of the slope at whatever point on the error surface the system currently is. Using calculus, this gradient is given by the **derivative** of the response unit's activation function $f(netinput)$, denoted by $f'(netinput)$. Avoiding mathematical complications, and using the simplest possible calculation of the error signal on an output unit (see Equation 2.8), the delta rule specifies the change to the weight vector of response unit i as follows:

$$\Delta \mathbf{w} = \eta(d_i - y_i)f'(netinput)\mathbf{x} \tag{2.11}$$

The changes to each individual weight in the weight vector are given in the related expression:

$$\Delta w_{ij} = \eta(d_i - y_i)f'(netinput)x_j \tag{2.12}$$

You will note the similarity between this and the perceptron rule we looked at above. Both rules rely on calculating weight changes on the basis of an *error signal* calculated by subtracting the actual output of the response unit from the desired activation. The difference is in the inclusion of a term for the gradient of the error surface. The actual value of $f'(netinput)$ will depend on the activation function being used. As you've learned, this must be a continuously varying function that is differentiable. In all the examples I've presented up to now, this has been the sigmoid in Equation 2.10, the derivative of which is given by:

$$f'(netinput) = y(1-y) \tag{2.13}$$

where y is the activation of the unit. However, a variation on this function is often used, which is:

$$f(netinput) = \frac{2}{1+e^{-netinput}} - 1 \tag{2.14}$$

and which has the derivative:

$$f'(netinput) = \frac{1}{2}(1-y^2) \tag{2.15}$$

The graph of this function has exactly the same S-shape as Equation 2.10. However, instead of being bounded by 0 and 1, as in the case of Equation 2.10, Equation 2.14 varies between –1 and 1, and so is known as a **bipolar** function.

Because I've left the calculus aside, the weight calculation itself really just boils down to a simple, if rather monotonous, matter of arithmetic. Assuming we are working with my original unipolar sigmoid function, as in Equation 2.10, and substituting Equation 2.13 into Equation 2.11, the formula just emerges as:

$$\Delta \mathbf{w} = \eta(d_i - y_i)y_i(1-y_i)\mathbf{x} \tag{2.16}$$

and all we, or the computer, have to do is plug actual values into this equation, calculate the weight adjustment and apply it to the original weight vector. Working through another example would be instructive. Try this exercise.

Exercise 2.3

The perceptron shown in Figure 2.18 takes real-valued inputs and its response unit uses the unipolar activation function given in Equation 2.10.

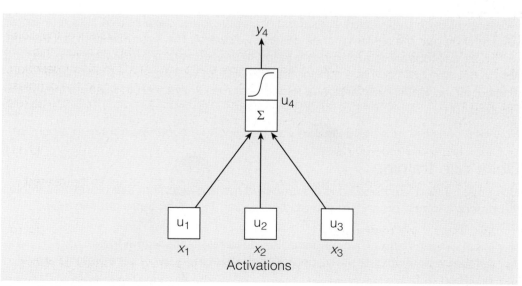

Figure 2.18   Network for Exercise 2.3

At the start of step t in training under the delta rule, its weight vector is:

$$\mathbf{w}(t-1) = \begin{bmatrix} 0.32 & -1.61 & 0.77 \end{bmatrix}$$

The next input vector $\mathbf{x}(t)$ in the training set and the desired activation $d(t)$ of the response unit are:

$$\mathbf{x}(t) = \begin{bmatrix} 0.5 \\ 0.5 \\ 0.3 \end{bmatrix} \quad d(t) = 1$$

For simplicity, we are going to ignore bias units and weights from now on. The learning constant $\eta = 0.1$. Calculate the state of the weight vector at the end of step t.

Answer...

You will find the answer to Exercise 2.3 at the end of this unit.

The state of the system, as defined by its weight vector, has been shifted slightly towards the error minimum. As I've already said, calculations like these are dull and error prone. There will be fewer of them in future discussions. However, before we leave the subject, think about this question for a moment.

SAQ 2.6

Think about the geometry of the delta rule for a moment, as I illustrated it in Figures 2.15 and 2.16. What role does the learning constant η play in this picture?

ANSWER...

The adjustments to the weight vectors determine the *direction* in which the system will move. The delta rule is designed to ensure that the direction is always along the steepest path down towards the error minimum. However, remember that the actual adjustments made are multiplied by the learning constant. So η governs the *distance* the system moves along this path at each step.

In SAQ 2.4, I asked you about the advantages and disadvantages of small and large values of η. Exactly the same considerations apply in the case of the delta rule. Small values mean that the system inches cautiously towards the error minimum, so training will be slow, probably requiring many steps. However, with a large value of η, training will be quicker, but there is a danger that the system will overshoot the minimum and, worst of all, oscillate backwards and forwards across it. I've tried to illustrate the idea in Figure 2.19.

Now let's consider how the delta rule can be used in a supervised training algorithm.

Delta rule training

Delta rule training is embodied in a supervised training algorithm that closely resembles the perceptron rule procedure you studied earlier. However, there are two main differences:

▶ *Initial weight matrix.* Training under the delta rule starts with a matrix of *random* weight values, unlike perceptron rule training, where the weights are all initialised to 0.

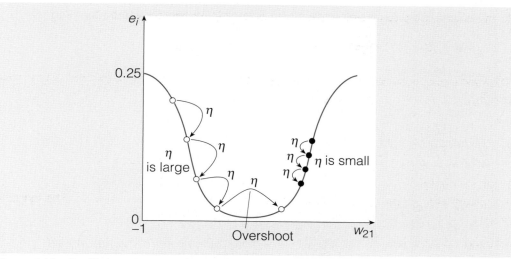

Figure 2.19 Oscillation of error with large value of η

▶ *Stopping condition.* Ideally, the training process would stop at the point at which the response units respond with exactly the right activations for all the patterns in the training set. This is what happens with the perceptron rule. However, with the delta rule the situation is somewhat different: here the response units use a continuous activation function, which squashes the activation between 0 and 1 (or −1 and 1). This means it is quite likely that these units will never be able to give an absolutely perfect response, only one that is reasonably close to perfect. So, in delta rule training, the stopping condition is made to depend on the error that the training process is trying to minimise. As the training proceeds, as each pattern $\mathbf{x}_1$, $\mathbf{x}_2$, $\mathbf{x}_3$ ... $\mathbf{x}_n$ is presented, the network's response will be erroneous to some degree. At the end of each round of n patterns, these errors are added together to give the cumulative network error E_{net} for the entire training set. Then after all n patterns have been applied, E_{net} is compared to a certain pre-decided maximum acceptable error E_{max}: if E_{net} has fallen below E_{max} then training stops; if not, then the patterns $\mathbf{x}_1$, $\mathbf{x}_2$, $\mathbf{x}_3$ ... $\mathbf{x}_n$ are presented again.

For a perceptron with a single response unit, the algorithm for delta rule training can be summed up as follows.

Delta rule training algorithm

1 Set all the elements of $\mathbf{w}$ to random values.

2 Set a counter i to 1; set E_{net} to 0.

3 Extract $\mathbf{x}_i$ from the training set and clamp the activations of the input units of the perceptron to the values of its elements.

4 Calculate the net input of the response unit, $\mathbf{w}^T\mathbf{x}_i$.

5 Calculate the activation of the response unit y_i by applying the sigmoid activation function of the response unit, either:

$$y_i = \frac{1}{1+e^{-netinput}}$$

or:

$$y_i = \frac{2}{1+e^{-netinput}} - 1$$

6   Calculate the weight adjustment vector $\Delta\mathbf{w}$ by applying the delta learning rule:

$$\Delta\mathbf{w} = \eta(d_i - y_i)f'(netinput)\mathbf{x}$$

7   Calculate the error and add it to the cumulative network error:

$$E_{net} = E_{net} + \frac{1}{2}(d_i - y_i)^2$$

8   Update the weight vector, as follows:

$\mathbf{w}$(new) = $\mathbf{w}$(old) + $\Delta\mathbf{w}$

9   If $i = n$ then: *// reached end of training set*

if $E_{net} < E_{max}$ then terminate

else go to step 2

else $i = i + 1$ and go to step 3   *// more patterns left in the training set*

As you've seen already, this algorithm generalises easily to perceptrons with many response units.

Now that you have a grasp of the minutiae of delta rule training, we can introduce the computer again and build a more substantial example of this learning algorithm.

Computer Exercise 2.1

Load up and complete Computer Exercise 2.1 on the course DVD.

No doubt this all seems rather technical and remote from our original goal – creating intelligent systems capable of solving practical problems. But even quite simple single-layer perceptrons are capable of interesting feats, and have been applied successfully to real-world systems, as well as in theoretical experiments. Here is a brief case study of such an early system, applied to a common problem in signal processing.

Case Study 2.1: Signal processing

As we all know from our own experience, a major problem in telecommunications networks is the various kinds of distortions that signals are subject to – 'smearing', background noise, echoes, and so on. So a significant task for telecommunications engineers is to devise and install *filters* that will scrub distortion and noise from the line. Fairly obviously, the function of any filter is to take an input signal and produce an output signal that is a cleaned-up version of the original input. An *adaptive filter* will make continuous changes to its internal algorithms in response to new information appearing in the input signal. Adaptive filters have been used in communications networks for many decades. In Figure 2.20, I've illustrated the most general form of such a system.

See Widrow and Winter (1988) for a much fuller account.

You can see from Figure 2.20 that the kind of corrective feedback process illustrated there is, in a general way, quite similar to the one I've been presenting for the perceptron; and, indeed, many adaptive filters are based on the principles of the ADALINE (the simple perceptron I illustrated in Figure 2.1 at the start of this unit). Figure 2.21 shows a signal graph of this system, together with its corrective feedback.

Up to now, we've been thinking about perceptrons as systems that handle visual patterns of some kind – squares, crosses, alphabetic characters, etc. – in other words, patterns of pixels distributed in *space*. However, there is no reason why a

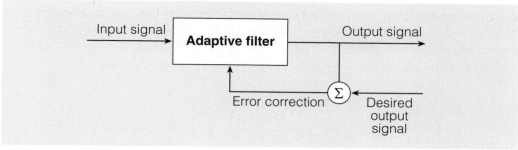

Figure 2.20 An adaptive filter

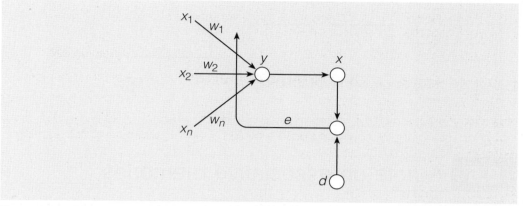

Figure 2.21 Signal graph of ADALINE used as adaptive filter

perceptron can't deal with inputs that are distributed in *time* also. Here's how.
Figure 2.22 shows a diagram of a simple perceptron used as an adaptive digital filter.
The input is a series of samples taken at fixed time intervals (the sampling interval) by a
digital-to-analogue converter from a signal passing down a communications line.
Each sample is fed into a chain of delay units. A delay unit holds the sample for one
sampling interval and then passes it down to the next unit. Thus every input to the
system is a snapshot of the present state of the signal, together with the set of n
past states that led up to this state. These samples are passed through weighted
connections to a response unit, which produces the filtered signal for that time step.
The network is generally trained using a version of the Widrow–Hoff rule, based on
an error signal that is calculated by subtracting the actual response from a desired
response.

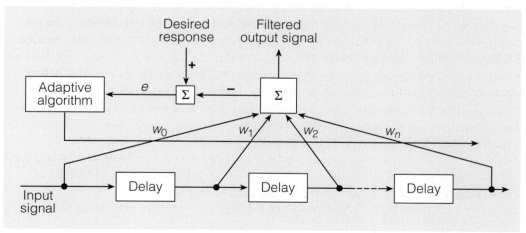

Figure 2.22 ADALINE used as an adaptive filter

Once trained, adaptive filters based on the perceptron can be used for a variety of applications, such as noise cancellation (see Figure 2.23) and even taking cardiac measurements from the heart of a foetus, filtering out interference from the mother's own heartbeat. Other applications include echo removal and signal prediction.

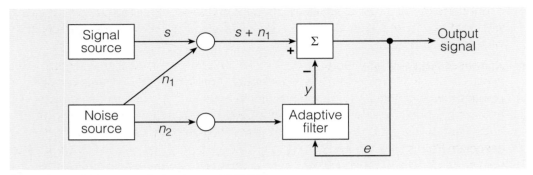

Figure 2.23   Noise cancellation by an ADALINE

2.6 A note on associative memories

An **associative network**, or **associative memory**, is a special form of perceptron, with general topology like the one illustrated in Figure 2.24.

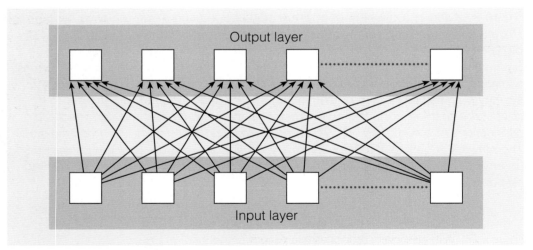

Figure 2.24   Generic associative network

As with all the perceptrons you've studied so far, there are two layers (one of which is a dummy), which are fully connected, with any number of units in either layer. Units can have sigmoid activation functions, threshold activation functions, or their activation may simply be identical to the net input they receive. Training is usually with some version of the delta rule, or may be by means of Hebbian learning.

The idea of associative memories is to store *pairs* of patterns that are related to one another, so that if one pattern is clamped to the input, the associated pattern appears at the output. You can see that we are now firmly back in the context of pattern recognition that I discussed in Unit 1 of this block.

There are two kinds of associative network: **hetero-associators** and **auto-associators**.

► *Hetero-associators*. These networks associate one pattern with another, different, pattern. The two patterns may be of equal size, but this is not necessarily the rule: the input and output patterns may well be of different size. To relate this to my discussion of pattern recognition in Unit 1, you can see that this sort of memory might correspond to our association of one complex cluster of ideas or sensations with another: an image with its name, for instance; or a tune with the memory of when we first heard it.

► *Auto-associators*. In an auto-associative memory, each pattern is associated with *itself*, so the input and output sizes are equal. At first sight, this seems rather pointless: why associate a pattern with itself? However, the usefulness of auto-associators becomes clear when we note their power to reconstruct damaged or noisy patterns. Figure 2.25 illustrates the idea. The network there has been trained to associate Pattern A, represented as a string of 1s (+) and –1s (–), with itself. If, after training, a *damaged* version of Pattern A is presented at the network input, then the full and correct version of A is reconstructed at the output. Once again, you can see the similarity to the human psychological characteristic – our effortless capacity for pattern completion. And there are obvious practical applications to such systems, in the area of signal filtration, image recognition, and so on.

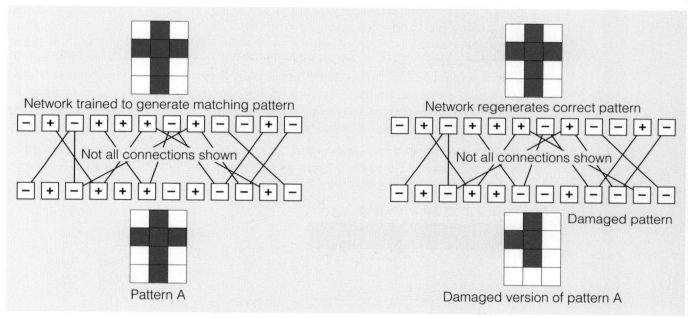

Figure 2.25   Auto-associator reconstructs a pattern

But there is one theoretical question to be answered: how many patterns can a typical associative memory store? The answer is not entirely straightforward. Technically, associative memories can only distinguish *perfectly* between vectors that are orthonormal. Since in a set of vectors of dimension n only a maximum of n can be orthogonal, so an associative network with n inputs will technically be restricted to storing only n patterns. However, in practice matters are not quite as bad as this. Associative memories can generally store more patterns. If the set of pairs of patterns are strongly related to one another by a rule of some kind, then it is possible for a network to store many more patterns than this. The psychologists Rumelhart and McClelland were able to exploit this fact in a classic early experiment. Their theme was a certain aspect of human language.

See the Maths Guide for an explanation of orthogonality and orthonormality.

ACTIVITY 2.1 (optional)

On the course DVD there is a fairly lengthy case study based on Rumelhart and McClelland's original paper. Spend about fifteen minutes reading over this.

Finally, try this reasonably straightforward practical exercise with associative memories.

Computer Exercise 2.2

Load up and complete Computer Exercise 2.2 on the course DVD.

2.7 | Limitations of single-layer perceptrons

I hope I've been able to show that simple two-layer perceptrons can have interesting properties and can be used to solve significant computational problems. But the melancholy truth is that they are just *too* simple. They have severe limitations, and there is a large and very significant range of problems that they simply cannot be applied to. Now is the time to look at those limitations.

Earlier in the unit, in my discussion of the perceptron convergence theorem, I claimed that a perceptron under a suitable form of training will always converge to a weight matrix that can discriminate between *linearly separable patterns*. I left the point there; but the implication was that perceptrons could not cope with patterns that are *not* linearly separable. Now, many of you may already know what I mean by the term 'linearly separable'. However, for others, it's a term that I can easily illustrate by returning to our basic two input (plus bias), single output perceptron, illustrated earlier in Figure 2.4. One single, classic example illustrates the point about linear separability.

You've already seen that networks like the one in Figure 2.4 can compute basic truth tables, such as AND and OR. But now let's consider another truth table, XOR (eXclusive OR), which is illustrated in Table 2.2.

Table 2.2   XOR truth table

x_1	x_2	x_3
1	1	0
1	0	1
0	1	1
0	0	0
XOR		

Expressing this in terms of our perceptron's behaviour, the response unit should activate when either of the inputs are active, but not when both or neither are active. On the face of it, this doesn't seem any more difficult a problem than AND or OR, but in fact it is very easy to show that it is *insoluble* using this kind of perceptron. All we have to do is to look again at the geometrical properties of such systems. You'll remember that the two-layer perceptron works by forming a straight-line decision boundary across the input space, dividing it into regions corresponding to classifications of the input patterns. To remind you, Figure 2.26(a) shows possible decision boundaries for the AND and OR truth tables. Now try to draw any straight line that will divide the space into two separate regions, one containing (1,1) and (0,0), the other containing (1,0) and (0,1) – as I've tried to do in Figure 2.26(b). You can't: the two sets of patterns are not *linearly separable*. No set of weights exists that would allow the perceptron to discriminate between them.

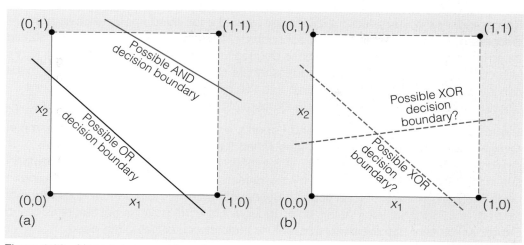

Figure 2.26   Linearly inseparable patterns

Maybe this sounds a trivial result, but in reality it strikes right at the heart of early claims made for perceptrons: that they were analogues of human and animal perceptual systems, capable of the kind of pattern recognition and classification that I've already identified as being at the heart of natural intelligence. Computer scientists Marvin Minsky and Seymour Papert, who have already made several brief appearances in M366, took the argument much further in their 1969 book *Perceptrons*, a concerted assault on the foundations of perceptron theory. They were able to show that XOR was only one member of a large class of problems not computable by two-layer systems. Among the other properties of patterns that the two scientists were able to show could not be detected by a standard perceptron were **parity** and **connectedness**. I've illustrated these in Figures 2.27 and 2.28. Parity is the property of the image in Figure 2.27, of having an odd or an even number of patterns in the image.

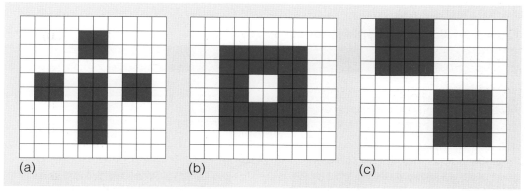

Figure 2.27   Parity

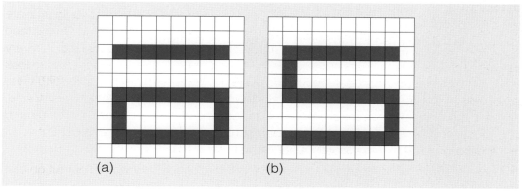

Figure 2.28   Connectedness

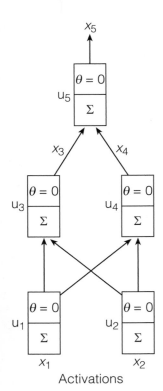

Figure 2.29   Extension of the single-layer perceptron

Connectedness is illustrated in 2.28: to our eyes, the left-hand image is obviously disconnected, the right-hand image connected. At first sight, one would think it should be possible for a two-layer perceptron to deduce from local information whether a figure was connected or not. But Minsky and Papert were able to show mathematically that it cannot. Simple perceptrons of the kind that I've been discussing up to now cannot effectively distinguish connected from unconnected images.

The traditional story is that Minsky and Papert's work dealt a body blow to research in neural networks. Interest in the field languished thereafter, research money went elsewhere, and the long ascendancy of Symbolic AI began. Moreover, the accepted tale is that *Perceptrons* was fuelled by the personal hostility of the authors to various neural network researchers, particularly Rosenblatt. Such a story can be questioned or revised, as I'll suggest later. At this point, though, it is worth pointing out that Minsky and Papert's argument has not always been fully understood, or has often been misrepresented. They did not actually argue that *no* perceptron could classify such patterns as XOR and connectedness. Rather, their view was that perceptrons could not produce an *efficient* solution. To understand what they meant by this, we need to return to Rosenblatt's original conception of the perceptron, as I illustrated it in Figure 2.2. Have a look back at that diagram. In my earlier discussion, I downplayed the role of the associative units, which are wired up in some pattern to the pixels in the retina, and feed their inputs into the response unit. But if these can be brought into play, a classification problem like XOR can easily be solved. Consider the network I've depicted in Figure 2.29. The two associative units, u_3 and u_4, now intervene between the input units u_1 and u_2 and the response unit u_5. Essentially, the associative units are MCP neurons set up to respond by activating with a 1 when a certain specific pattern of activity is present at the input, and to remain inactive at 0 in the presence of all other possible patterns.

Now suppose the two associative units u_3 and u_4 are wired in such a way as to respond as in Table 2.3.

Table 2.3   Activation settings for associative units

x_1	x_2	x_3		x_1	x_2	x_4
1	1	0		1	1	0
1	0	1		1	0	0
0	1	0		0	1	1
0	0	0		0	0	0
u_3 response				u_4 response		

One useful way of looking at this is that the two associative units are tuned to be **feature detectors**. They respond by activating in the presence of crucial features in the input: in the case of our example here, u_3 responds to the presence of x_1's activity and x_2's inactivity in the input, and u_4 to x_2's activity and x_1's inactivity.

Finally, we tune the weight vector feeding into u_5 so that u_5 responds according to Table 2.4.

Table 2.4   Activation settings for response unit

x_3	x_4	x_5
1	1	1
1	0	1
0	1	1
0	0	0

And of course it is perfectly possible to find weights for this response pattern. It is simply the linearly separable OR. Now, to bring all of the five units together, try this question.

SAQ 2.7

Draw up a table showing the activations of all five units in the network for each of the four possible input patterns (x_1, x_2).

ANSWER..

My table looked like this:

x_1	x_2	x_3	x_4	x_5
1	1	0	0	0
1	0	1	0	1
0	1	0	1	1
0	0	0	0	0

Focusing just on columns x_1, x_2 and x_5, you can see that the network computes XOR perfectly satisfactorily.

So it is possible, in theory, to construct a perceptron that can handle the kinds of difficult classification tasks that Minsky and Papert identified, given suitably tuned associative units. The two authors acknowledged this. But their argument was, as I've claimed already, that in many important cases it is impossible to do so *efficiently*. To illustrate exactly what this means, let's consider another, only slightly more complex, example. Suppose we are trying to devise a perceptron for alphabetic character recognition and we want our system to respond 1 to the little 'T' pattern on a nine-unit input grid, as shown in Figure 2.30.

Figure 2.30   Specimen pattern – 'T'

Exercise 2.4

What do you think would be the minimum number of associative units needed for the perceptron to detect the 'T' shape in Figure 2.30. Only consider the 'T' pattern; forget about any other characters.

Discussion ....

There are nine units in the input pattern, and each input unit can be set to 1 or 0, so the *maximum* number of associative units – one for each possible combination of nine 1s and 0s – would be $2^9 = 512$! How inefficient is that? But of course, we don't need nearly that many. In fact, the minimum number we need is *three*, the first wired to the three units in the top row of the input, the second to the inputs in the middle row, and the third to the bottom row. Then, the first associative unit is wired to respond 1 to the pattern (1,1,1), and 0 to any other pattern; the second responds 1 to (0,1,0) and 0 otherwise; the third responds in exactly the same way as the second. The weight vector into the response unit can then be set, or trained, to ensure that the response unit activates only if it receives the stimulus (1,1,1) from the associative units.

The maximum number of connections between the input layer and any associative unit is termed the **order** of the perceptron. In our example above, each associative unit receives three connections, so the order of this particular perceptron is 3. In the super-inefficient perceptron I proposed before that, each of the 512 associative units is wired to all nine input units, so the order there is 9. However, there is no rule that says that all associative units must receive the same number of connections. So, for example, it is perfectly possible to have a perceptron with three associative units, the first receiving five inputs, the second two and the third three: the order of such a system would thus be 5. We can take the order of a perceptron as being related to its *efficiency* – the higher the order, the lower the efficiency.

The order 3 perceptron in Exercise 2.4 seems efficient enough, although its purposes are obviously extremely limited. But what about other sorts of pattern discrimination? Let's return to the problem of *parity* that I illustrated in Figure 2.27. Consider the patterns in Figure 2.31: (a) is a pattern of six activations, (b) of five, (c) of four and (d) of three. A parity detector would be required to respond 1 to pattern (a); 0 to pattern (b); 1 to pattern (c); and 0 to pattern (d).

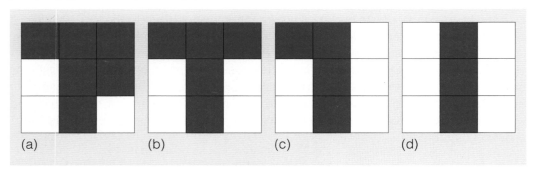

(a)   (b)   (c)   (d)

Figure 2.31   Pattern demonstrating parity calculations

Minsky and Papert used elegant mathematical arguments to show that only a perceptron of order 9 could compute parity in this way. This is obviously a disappointing result, but their news was even more dispiriting than this. A further proof demonstrated that for an input pattern grid of n rows and n columns, the order of any perceptron that can detect parity on such a grid must always be n^2. Any system that grows in such a way with the number of inputs is terminally inefficient. Minsky and Papert concluded that although perceptrons were 'interesting' systems to study, as an area of research they would ultimately prove to be 'sterile'.

It is certainly true that after the publication of *Perceptrons* research into neural networks faded away. But the traditional account of the matter, revolving around feuds and personal hostility, may be overstated. Some revisionist historians of technology have pointed out that both Minsky and Papert had themselves at one time made important contributions to neural network theory. Although Papert did confirm his adversarial attitude to neural computing and its practitioners in the interview I quoted in Block 1, Minsky himself always denied any such stance. In 1990 he remarked:

> Why is there so much excitement about Neural Networks today, and how is this related to research on Artificial Intelligence? Much has been said in the popular press as though these were conflicting activities. This seems exceedingly strange to me, because both are parts of the same enterprise.

Source: Minsky (1991)

Figure 2.32 Dave Rumelhart

And although research into neural networks slackened, it did not cease altogether. Work continued, new algorithms were evolved and the field renewed itself in the 1980s.

The source of this renaissance can be traced to the publication in 1986 of the monumental, two-volume *Parallel Distributed Processing: Explorations in the microstructure of cognition* (generally just referred to as *The PDP Papers*, or simply *PDP*), a collection of research papers authored by psychologists Dave Rumelhart and Jay McClelland, together with other members of their PDP Research Group. *The PDP Papers* covers a huge amount of ground, describing many new techniques and applications in neural networks. I referred to one of these in the case study in Activity 2.1. However, at the core of the work is a solution to the key limitation of perceptrons that I have just been discussing, one which opened up a vast new arena of theory and application. Let's enter this now.

Figure 2.33 Jay McClelland

3 Multi-layer perceptrons

Minsky and Papert had acknowledged all along that a solution to the problem of linear separability in perceptrons could exist. They admitted that if perceptrons could be chained together in the kind of topology I've portrayed in Figure 2.34(a) then much more sophisticated classification might be possible. However, to see such a network as a bundle of two-layer perceptrons is rather confusing. It's more straightforward to envisage such a system as a single perceptron with multiple layers – a **multi-layer perceptron**, as in Figure 2.34(b).

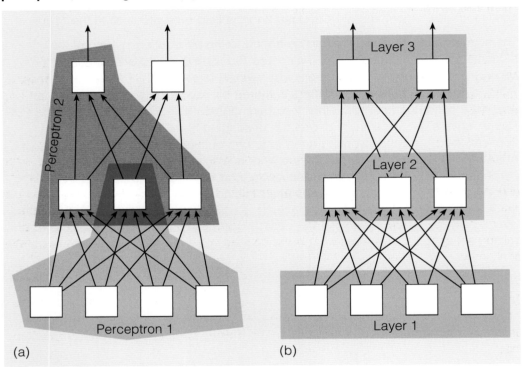

Figure 2.34   Multi-layer perceptrons

The possible advantages of such a system were obvious to Minsky and Papert, as well as to other theorists of the time. In rather the same way as Rosenblatt's associative units (see our discussion above), the units of the intermediate layers can act as *feature detectors*; and the geometry of the way in which a multi-layer system can partition the input space becomes much richer and more complex. I've illustrated this in Figure 2.35, which compares the simple partitioning carried out by a two-layer perceptron (a) with that of a multi-layer system (b). You can see at a glance the additional complexity that is possible. In fact, it can be shown that – given the right number of layers and units – *any* partitioning of the input space is possible. Obviously this opens the door to much more powerful perceptron classifiers.

But Minsky and Papert dismissed the idea of multi-layer perceptrons as a promising field of research. This was partly because they claimed an 'intuitive' sense that these would be as limited as their two-layer predecessors. But their main objection was that the *training* of multi-layer systems would not be possible. Consider this rather tricky question for a moment.

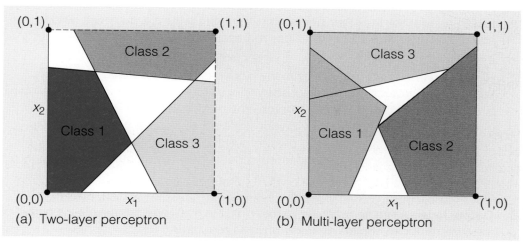

Figure 2.35   Multiple partitioning of the input space

SAQ 2.8

Why do you think training a multi-layer perceptron would be a problem? Think back to the two supervised training rules, the perceptron rule and the delta rule, that you looked at earlier.

ANSWER...

In both cases the training algorithm was a *supervised* one. And in both cases the error signal was calculated by comparing the *actual* activation of the units in the final layer with the *desired* activation. Up to a point, this is still OK for a multi-layer perceptron – it has a final output layer too – but we have the added complication of the units in the intermediate layer. We know what the desired activation for the output units is – the training set specifies this – but what is the desired output of the intermediate units? We don't know. So we have no basis for calculating an error signal for them.

The units in the intermediate layers of a multi-layer system are not directly part of the input or the output of the system: they are purely internal. For this reason, they are usually referred to as the **hidden units** or the **hidden layers**. I'll continue to call them that.

It was many years before this problem was cracked. But in 1986 Rumelhart, Hinton and Williams presented a new algorithm, published in *The PDP Papers*, known as **error backpropagation** or the **generalised delta rule** for the training of multi-layer perceptrons. Popular history generally credits these three authors with the discovery of the process, but more purist historians of science point out that very similar discoveries had been made by Werbos in 1975, Parker in 1985 and LeCun, also in 1985. However, it was the immense popularity and influence of *The PDP Papers* that really brought error backpropagation to the attention of the research community, and it is now firmly associated with the names of the authors. Such are the fortunes and misfortunes of a research career.

3.1 | Structure

The structure of a multi-layer perceptron is simply a generalisation of the two-layer perceptrons we've been looking at up to now. I illustrated a typical one in Figure 2.34. To clarify a few points:

1   **Input layer**. This can contain as many units as are necessary to represent the input pattern. In some practical applications, inputs of many thousands of units can be

found. As with the two-layer perceptron, the input units are dummies, whose activations are clamped to the values representing each element of the input pattern.

2   **Hidden layers**. There may be as many hidden layers as required. Practically speaking, however, it is never necessary to use more than two, and one hidden layer is generally sufficient for nearly all problems. And in 1957 the Russian mathematician A.N. Kolmogorov demonstrated that a neural network with one hidden layer only can, in theory, perform any mapping. In this block, I'll only be considering multi-layer perceptrons with one hidden layer. The rules that apply to them can be generalised to networks with any number of hidden layers. Hidden layers may contain any number of units.

3   **Output layer**. As in the two-layer perceptron, the final layer represents the output of the system. It can contain as many units as required.

4   **Units**. The learning rule we use for training multi-layer perceptrons is, as one of its names suggests, a generalisation of the delta rule. Therefore all the units in the hidden and output layers are required to have continuous activation functions, such as the unipolar sigmoid of Equation 2.10, or the bipolar version of Equation 2.14. Unless I say otherwise, from now on I'll be dealing with the unipolar sigmoid in the examples I discuss. The units of the input layer, being only dummies, do not strictly require an activation function.

5   **Weights and connections**. Like the single-layer perceptron, multi-layer systems invariably have a fully connected topology: all the units of a layer are connected to all the units in the succeeding layer, with no recurrent connections or links between units within a layer.

Now let's consider how multi-layer perceptrons can be trained.

3.2   Backpropagation – the learning rules

As you've already learned, the regime most commonly used to train multi-layer perceptrons is *error backpropagation*, a version of the delta rule, which we've already covered in some detail. Therefore, some of what you've learned already is applicable to multi-layer systems. To base the following discussion on a concrete example, let's consider the perceptron illustrated in Figure 2.36, which has o output units, m hidden units and n input units. All the hidden and output units have the same activation function, the unipolar sigmoid of Equation 2.10.

Now recall that the purpose of a supervised training rule, as in all perceptrons, is to alter the network weights so as to bring the *actual* output closer and closer to the *desired* output, for each pair of patterns in the training set. In vector-matrix terms each step of the process has to calculate a new matrix by building a matrix $\Delta\mathbf{W}$ of the changes to the weight matrix $\mathbf{W}$ and then applying these changes by adding $\Delta\mathbf{W}$ to $\mathbf{W}$.

But instead of a single weight matrix $\mathbf{W}$, as in all the perceptrons you've seen so far, the network in Figure 2.34 has two: $\mathbf{W}_1$, an $m \times n$ matrix containing the weights connecting the input layer with the hidden layer, and $\mathbf{W}_2$, an $o \times m$ matrix of the weights between the hidden and output layers. Training these two matrices requires somewhat different rules, so I'll consider each separately, starting with $\mathbf{W}_2$.

Training $\mathbf{W}_2$

Rather than consider all the units in the output layer of our model network, let's first just consider one, unit u_i, along with the vector of weights $\mathbf{w}_i$ that feed into it – row i in $\mathbf{W}_2$. I've illustrated this in Figure 2.37. The training rule has to calculate a vector $\Delta\mathbf{w}_i$ of changes to this set of weights and then apply them to $\mathbf{w}_i$. How?

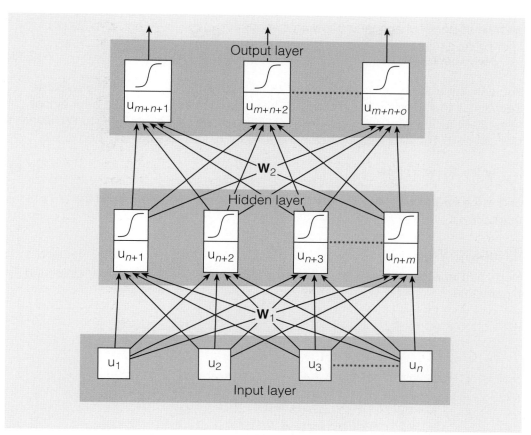

Figure 2.36   Multi-layer perceptron for backpropagation

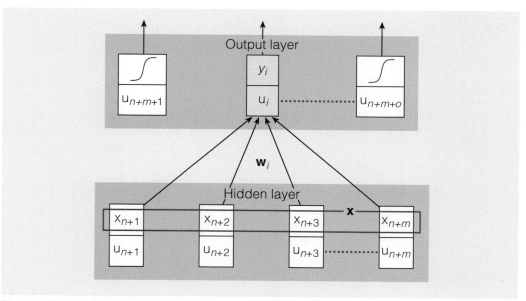

Figure 2.37   Backpropagation – training the weights of an output unit

Easy. All we have to do is apply the delta rule in exactly the same way as we did with the single-layer perceptrons above. u_i is a member of the output layer, so we know what its desired output is supposed to be – it is given as part of the training set. So the error signal e_i on u_i is simply:

$$e_i = (d_i - y_i)y_i(1 - y_i) \tag{2.17}$$

and the vector of changes to u_i's weight vector is:

$$\Delta \mathbf{w}_i = \eta e_i \mathbf{x} \qquad (2.18)$$

You can see that Equations 2.17 and 2.18 taken together are exactly the same as Equation 2.16 in Section 2.5 above. However, here I'm calculating the error signal separately, as it will be needed in the calculation of the weight changes to $\mathbf{W}_1$ which I'll discuss next. The new weight vector $\mathbf{w}_i(t + 1)$ for u_i after this training step is just:

$$\mathbf{w}_i(t+1) = \mathbf{w}_i(t) + \Delta \mathbf{w}_i \qquad (2.19)$$

and is the new row i in $\mathbf{W}_2$. Exactly the same procedure is applied to all the units in the output layer.

Training $\mathbf{W}_1$

Here, as I've noted already, the problem is different. Consider the unit u_j illustrated in Figure 2.38.

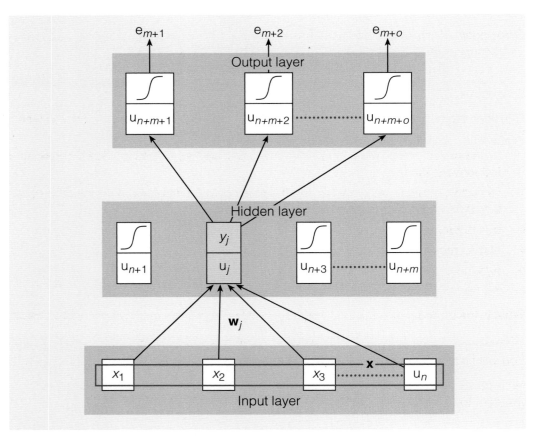

Figure 2.38   Backpropagation – training the weights of a hidden unit

Assume that the error signals on the output units have already been calculated, using Equation 2.17. But u_j is a *hidden* unit, so we have no ready way of calculating the error signal on it. However, Rumelhart, Hinton and Williams were able to show mathematically that the error signal e_j on a unit u_j in the hidden layer is given by:

$$e_j = y_j(1 - y_j)\sum_{i}^{o} e_i w_{ij} \qquad (2.20)$$

where y_j is the activation of the unit and where o is the number of units in the layer above u_j to which u_j sends feed-forward connections. Think about this for a minute and it becomes quite logical. We can reason it like this:

1 u_j will almost certainly be in error to some degree, given by its error signal e_j.

2 Because u_j feeds into all the units in the output layer, e_j must contribute to the error signal of each of *these* units.

3 Each connection between u_j and a unit u_i in the output layer has a weight which is a measure of the strength of its influence on that unit.

4 Therefore each weight determines how much influence e_j has on the output unit u_i's error signal.

5 Therefore e_j must be related to the *sum* of the error signals on each u_i, multiplied by the weight between u_i and u_j.

This last is exactly what the Σ term in Equation 2.20 expresses.

Once the error signal on u_j has been determined, $\Delta\mathbf{w}_i$ and $\mathbf{w}_i(t + 1)$ follow in exactly the same way as in the calculations I used for the output layer's training above, from Equation 2.18.

Once again, if you are uncertain of the algebra a straightforward numerical calculation might help to reinforce the point.

Exercise 2.5

Consider the network in Figure 2.39, which is just a variation on Figure 2.38. Assume that:

▶ the input vector $\mathbf{x}^T = [0.5, 0.1, 0, -1.4]$ has been applied to the input units and activity fed forward through to the output;

▶ the error signals e_9, e_{10} and e_{11} on the three output units have been calculated as 0.1, 0.32 and 0.46 respectively;

▶ u_6's outgoing weight vector $\mathbf{w}_{6out}^T$ is $[-0.77, 0.21, 1.6]$;

▶ unit u_6 receives a *netinput* stimulus of $+3.22$;

▶ u_6's incoming weight vector $\mathbf{w}_{6in}$ is $[-0.5, 0.78, 1.2, -0.9]$;

▶ the learning constant η is 0.5.

What is the error signal on u_6 and the change to that unit's incoming weight vector $\Delta\mathbf{w}_{6in}$?

Answer...

You will find the answer to Exercise 2.5 at the end of this unit.

Note how very small the weight adjustments are. The system inches down the error gradient towards the minimum.

This is how error signals are calculated for hidden units under backpropagation. These basic calculations and adjustments are applied to all the units in the hidden layers. And the same rules generalise to all hidden layers, if the network has more than one.

Let's now put this all together and spell out the full algorithm for backpropagation.

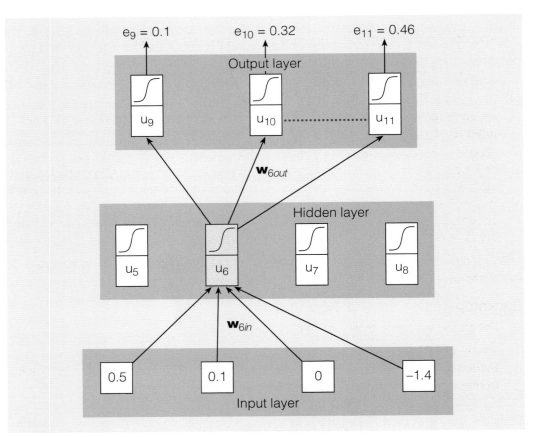

Figure 2.39   Backpropagation – training example for Exercise 2.5

3.3   Backpropagation – the process

As with its parent, the delta rule, training under backpropagation just consists of applying the learning rules over and over again, until the error in the system reaches an acceptable level. Considering a network with just one hidden layer, and with unipolar sigmoid activation functions, here are a few initial points:

▶ *Initial weight matrices.* As with the delta rule, training begins with matrices $\mathbf{W}_1$ and $\mathbf{W}_2$ set to *random* weight values. These random values are usually confined within certain limits, such as between –2 and +2.

▶ *Feedforward and feedback phases.* Each cycle of training consists of a feedforward phase and a feedback phase. In the feedforward phase, the next input vector in the training set is clamped to the input layer and the activations of the hidden and output units calculated. In the feedback phase, the error signals on the output and the hidden units are calculated and the weight adjustments computed and applied.

▶ *Network error.* In my discussion of the delta rule earlier in this unit, I introduced the concept of the *cumulative network error*. For each pattern in a training set presented to the network, the error made by the output units is calculated. In the case of a network with only a single response unit, such as the one I worked with in my discussion of the delta rule, this will be a single signal, which can be calculated by using either Equation 2.8 or Equation 2.9. For a network with many response units, there will be a vector of such error signals. For a network with n output units, calculating the network error E_p for the pth pattern in a training set, Equation 2.8 becomes:

The vertical lines indicate the *length* or *norm* of the vector. See the Maths Guide for details.

$$E_p = \sum_{i=1}^{n} d_{pi} - y_{pi} \qquad (2.21)$$

and, for the same network and pattern, Equation 2.9 becomes:

$$E_p = \frac{1}{2}\sum_{i=1}^{n}(d_{pi} - y_{pi})^2 = \frac{1}{2}\|\mathbf{d}_p - \mathbf{y}_p\|^2 \qquad (2.22)$$

As each pattern is presented, the errors the network makes for each are added together to give a cumulative error for the entire set E_{net}.

4 *Stopping condition.* Again as with the delta rule, the network will almost certainly never be able to give an absolutely perfect response, so in backpropagation the stopping condition also depends on the cumulative network error E_{net} for the entire training set. After each cycle, E_{net} is compared to a certain pre-decided maximum acceptable error E_{max}: if E_{net} has fallen below E_{max} then training stops; if not, then the patterns $\mathbf{x}_1$, $\mathbf{x}_2$, $\mathbf{x}_3$ ... $\mathbf{x}_n$ are presented again.

The algorithm for backpropagation training, for a set of n patterns, can be summed up as follows.

Backpropagation training algorithm

1 Set all the elements of $\mathbf{W}_1$ and $\mathbf{W}_2$ to random values.

2 Set a counter j to 1; set E_{net} to 0.

3 Extract $\mathbf{x}_j$ from the training set and clamp the activations of the input units of the perceptron to the values of its elements.

4 Feedforward phase:

   4.i calculate the net inputs of all the hidden units;

   4.ii calculate the vector $\mathbf{x}_h$ of activations of all the hidden units by applying Equation 2.10 to each unit;

   4.iii calculate the net inputs of all the output units;

   4.iv calculate the vector $\mathbf{x}_o$ of activations of all the output units by applying Equation 2.10 to each unit.

5 Calculate the network error E_j for this cycle, using either Equation 2.21 or 2.22. Add it to the cumulative network error E_{net}.

6 Feedback phase:

   6.i calculate the error signal on each output unit using Equation 2.17;

   6.ii calculate the error signal on each hidden unit using Equation 2.20;

   6.iii calculate the weight adjustment vector $\Delta\mathbf{w}_{jin}$ for the incoming weight vectors of each unit in the output layer by applying Equation 2.18;

   6.iv adjust the weight matrix $\mathbf{W}_2$ by adding each vector $\Delta\mathbf{w}_{jout}$ to the appropriate row in $\mathbf{W}_2$ as in Equation 2.19;

   6.v calculate the weight adjustment vector $\Delta\mathbf{w}_{jin}$ for the incoming weight vectors of each unit in the hidden layer by applying Equation 2.18;

   6.vi adjust the weight matrix $\mathbf{W}_1$ by adding each vector $\Delta\mathbf{w}_{jout}$ to the appropriate row in $\mathbf{W}_1$ as in Equation 2.19.

7 If $j = n$ then   // reached end of training set

   if $E_{net} < E_{max}$ then terminate

   else go to step 2

   else $j = j + 1$ and go to step 3   // more patterns left in the training set

This algorithm generalises easily to perceptrons with several hidden layers.

As you can probably guess even from the algorithm and from the small calculation you did in Exercise 2.5 above, training under error backpropagation can be quite slow, even on speedy computers. There may have to be many hundreds of cycles through the training set, so in a substantially sized network, the sheer number of calculations to be carried out will be immense. Since Rumelhart et al.'s original work an intense research effort has gone into improving on the original algorithm. I'll look at some of these slightly later in the unit. As a prelude, let's think about one important aspect of backpropagation training.

3.4 | Backpropagation – the error surface

You will recall that backpropagation is a generalised form of the delta rule, and that the delta rule is an example of a *gradient descent* learning strategy. The idea is to minimise the overall error as rapidly as possible by taking the steepest path down the *error surface* towards the *error minimum* at every training step. Equations 2.17 to 2.20 give the steepest path in a multi-layer perceptron. In Figure 2.16 in Section 2.5, I depicted the error surface of a single-layer perceptron with two inputs and one response unit (and thus two weights), a bowl-shaped configuration in a three-dimensional error space. Perceptrons with greater numbers of weights have higher-dimensional error surfaces that cannot be visualised, but have the same bowl-shaped character. In the case of single-layer perceptrons, the contour of the surface is perfectly smooth, just like a real bowl. However, for multi-layer perceptrons, the picture is a lot more complicated. The error surface here is far from smooth; it is rough, irregular and jagged, as I've tried to show for just one weight in Figure 2.40(b). For a multi-layer perceptron with n weights there will be an error surface in $n + 1$ dimensions. So try to generalise the picture in Figure 2.40(b) in your mind to many dimensions. Instead of skiing smoothly straight down the error surface, as one does in a single-layer perceptron, learning in a multi-layer perceptron is more like stumbling down a boulder-strewn hillside, pitted with canyons, hillocks, cavities and fissures – in total darkness.

Does this matter? Yes it does, because it presents us with the problem that bedevils so many optimisation systems, that of **local minima**. The backpropagation algorithm always seeks the steepest path down. But it is quite possible for the training process to arrive at the state I've illustrated in Figure 2.40(c), which is far from the error minimum, but where there is *no* path down – all the paths are up. The system is trapped. In such cases, there may be little remedy but to start again.

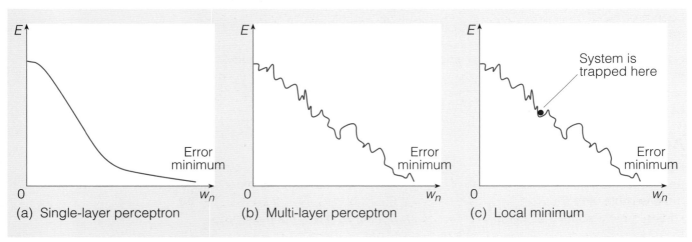

(a) Single-layer perceptron   (b) Multi-layer perceptron   (c) Local minimum

Figure 2.40   Complex error surfaces

SAQ 2.9

Where do you think the network will start on the error surface, before the first cycle of training?

ANSWER..

As you probably said: it all depends. But what does it depend on? Well, if you look back at my outline of the backpropagation algorithm above, you'll note that the process starts with all the weights being set to random values. The actual set of weights that comes out of this determines the point from which the system will start its descent down the error surface. An unlucky outcome might mean that the system begins training far from the error minimum, or even in a local minimum. However, the random initialisation might result in a much better starting point on the error surface. Possibly – though wildly improbably for a network of any size – training might even start at the error minimum itself.

Now let's leave the theory for the time being and try a practical exercise.

Computer Exercise 2.3

Load up and complete Computer Exercise 2.3 on the course DVD.

3.5 | Factors affecting backpropagation training

I hope you were able to conclude from Computer Exercise 2.3 that error backpropagation works and works well. Although you may have experienced the phenomenon of your network's sticking in a local minimum, in practice, in larger networks, this seldom seems to happen. Nevertheless, as I mentioned earlier, since Rumelhart and McClelland's original work much intellectual effort has gone into improving on the original training process. A lot of this centres on the *speed* and *efficiency* of the training process. Researchers have been concerned about the length of time it can take to train large networks, with perhaps hundreds of thousands of weights, on huge training sets. Many improvements on the original algorithm, now sometimes called (rather contemptuously, perhaps) **vanilla backpropagation**, have been proposed; and there has been intensive research into the factors that affect training.

I don't have a great deal of space in which to discuss this work. In this subsection and the next, I am just going to deal in outline with some of the factors that influence the speed and efficiency of training. I'll then deal very briefly with two alternatives to backpropagation training that have been proposed since 1986.

Architecture

Perhaps the most obvious factor affecting backpropagation training, or any other form of training for that matter, is the number of units present in the network: the more units, the more weights, and thus the more calculations that will be required at each cycle. So, finding a compact and efficient architecture for a network is an important issue. Consider a problem to be solved by a multi-layer perceptron trained under backpropagation, in which the network is to classify P training patterns, each of dimension N, into M categories. The perceptron will have one hidden layer of J units, an input layer of I units and output layer of K units. What are the optimum values of I, J and K?

Up to now, I've taken the line that the number of units in the input layer is equal to the dimension of the input patterns, $I = N$. However, it may be possible to encode the inputs in such a way that the number of units in the input layer can be reduced. For example, the three patterns in Figure 2.41(a) would conventionally be encoded as vectors of dimension 9 (one for each square in the pattern), like this:

$\mathbf{x}_1$ = [1, 1, 1, 0, 1, 0, 0, 1, 0] → T

$\mathbf{x}_2$ = [0, 1, 0, 0, 1, 0, 0, 1, 0] → I

$\mathbf{x}_3$ = [1, 0, 1, 0, 1, 0, 1, 0, 1] → X

However it would be quite possible to reduce this to 2 if we assign a two-number unique code to each square, as in Figure 2.41(b), and encode each vector in this way:

$\mathbf{x}_1$ = [1, 1] → T, X

$\mathbf{x}_2$ = [1, 2] → T, I

$\mathbf{x}_5$ = [2, 2] → T, I, X

and so on. This reduces N (and thus I) to 2, but with the downside of increasing P to 9, since there will need to be one input vector for every square on the grid. There is always going to be a trade-off between these two values.

(a)   (b)

Figure 2.41   Encoding input patterns: (a) specimen patterns. (b) one approach to encoding

Things are rather more straightforward with K. Hitherto, I've assumed that the number of output units will be equal to the number of categories: $K = M$. But there's no reason why a more efficient means of expression cannot be found. A common way of expressing the category of an input is in binary notation, so for our little example here, where $M = 3$, we can simply represent each category as a binary number:

T = 00

I = 01

X = 10

giving $K = 2$. This requires just two output units (one for each column of the binary number) and with one number (11) left spare if we want to add another category later. For large numbers of categories, this can radically cut down the number of output units required.

Hidden units

So, how many hidden units? As you will have noticed, I didn't mention anything about this number, J, in the section above. This is partly because it is a much less clear-cut issue. There is no good *theory* to guide the correct choice of the number of hidden units; and clearly the number chosen must depend to a large extent on the problem being tackled. For example, for a problem with $N = 2$ and $M = 2$, a layer of 200 hidden units is hardly likely to be necessary. Some theorists argue that the only way to decide is experimentally, on a problem-by-problem basis. However, there is work to suggest that:

$$J = \log_2 M \tag{2.23}$$

is a good basis for an initial decision.

Initial weights

I've already re-emphasised the important point that backpropagation training starts with weights set to random values. Beginning with weights all set to 0, as happens with the perceptron rule, generally means that a network training under backpropagation, will not train at all. However, there is no point in randomising values within a huge range, e.g. −100 to +100. This will simply prolong training unnecessarily. Randomising within the range −2 to +2 is usually quite sufficient.

Learning constant

This issue came up in my earlier discussion of the delta rule. Exactly the same considerations apply here. Remember that the value of the learning constant governs the *size* of the steps taken down the error surface (look back at Figure 2.19 in Section 2.5 for an illustration of this). It's worth pointing out that only very small values of η are likely to give true steepest-path descent, as larger values will make it probable that the state of the system will hop to a higher part of the error surface, as I've illustrated in the Figure 2.42, since the surface is so jagged in multi-layer perceptrons.

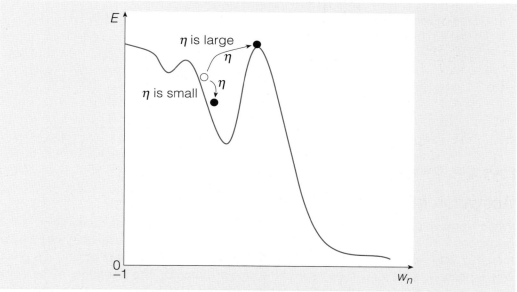

Figure 2.42   Effect of the learning constant on progress down the error surface

Learning constants of anything between 0.001 and 10 have been reported as working successfully.

Momentum term

Most of the problems of training under backpropagation stem from the irregularity of the error surface. In any particular state, the steepest path down the surface may not actually be in the overall direction of the minimum at all. It is possible to compensate for this by adding a **momentum term** to the calculation of the changes to the weight vectors of each unit in Equation 2.18, like this:

$$\Delta \mathbf{w}_i(t) = \eta e_i \mathbf{x}(t) + \alpha \Delta \mathbf{w}_i(t-1) \tag{2.24}$$

where α is a constant known as the **momentum constant**, and e_i is the error signal on the unit i, calculated by either Equation 2.17 or 2.20. The t indicates the training step at which the change is being made. The best way of looking at this is to see the change made to the weight at step t as a *compromise* between the change that will move the system down the steepest path at step t and the change that was made at the previous training step, $t-1$. This helps to keep the system moving in a roughly consistent direction. I've tried to illustrate this in Figure 2.43: imagine you are looking down on the error surface from above and the ellipses are contour lines. Setting α to 0 obviously removes the term completely from the calculation.

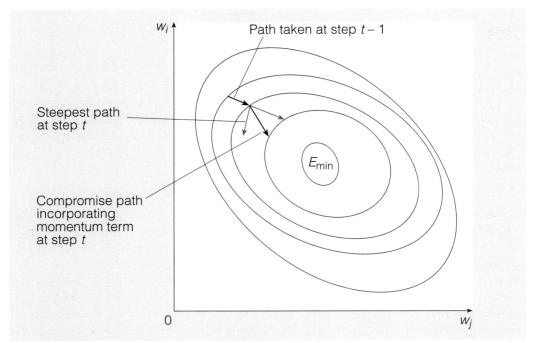

Figure 2.43   Gradient descent using a momentum term

Activation function

When I presented the sigmoid activation function in the previous unit (see also Equations 2.10 and 2.14), I remarked that it looked rather like a threshold function, even though it was a continuous curve. The slope of the curve is steepest around the point where *netinput* is 0.5 (or 0 in the case of the bipolar sigmoid). The steepness of the slope around this point can be affected by adding another term λ to the equation, changing Equation 2.10, for example, into:

$$y = \frac{1}{1 + e^{-\lambda \, netinput}} \tag{2.25}$$

Or you can look on Equation 2.10 as Equation 2.25 with λ set to 1. Figure 2.44 shows the effect of λ on the steepness of the function.

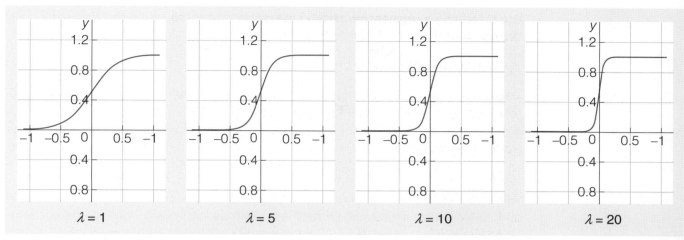

Figure 2.44   Unipolar sigmoid with varying values of λ

Order of presentation of patterns

Throughout my account of both perceptron rule and delta rule training, the assumption was that the input vectors were simply presented in the order in which they occur in the set. However, experiments show that this is not necessarily the best strategy, as the network tends to become biased towards certain patterns as it trains. Often better is to present the patterns in *random order* on each cycle though the set. This adds a certain amount of noise into the training process, helps prevent the network weights becoming skewed towards certain patterns and can speed up training.

Error minimum

Another phenomenon that the neural network specialist has to beware of is **overtraining** or **overfitting**. Forcing the network further and further towards the error minimum by training for more and more cycles is not necessarily an advantage. The network can become locked into a final state where it is difficult for it to generalise from the information it has learned. Suppose we were to train a network on P patterns down to a very low error. Having done so, suppose further that we want to test it out on a set of patterns that are similar to those in the training set, but not quite the same (these would sometimes be called a **validation set**). An overtrained network may respond incorrectly to these new patterns with the weights it already has, as these bias it strongly towards producing a very low error with the original set of patterns. The network has learned the training examples perfectly, but nothing else. It may be necessary to reinitialise the weights and start all over again.

SAQ 2.10

Can a multi-layer perceptron, training on patterns of 1s and 0s, ever produce an error of 0? If not, why not?

ANSWER..

No, almost certainly not. The reason for this lies in the sigmoid activation functions we've been using. Remember that that these are *squashing functions*: that is, they return values between 0 and 1 (or −1 and 1). But if you examine their graphs, you'll note that although the curve approaches 0 and 1 at either end, it never quite reaches it. So an output unit required to respond 1, say, may get to 0.9999, but never quite have an activation of 1. Hence, the error will never be quite 0.

With continuous valued training sets an error of 0 might become possible. Another possibility is to substitute threshold units for sigmoid output units after training has been completed. Some researchers have adopted this tactic. However, for most of the time, 0.9999 is far too near to 1 to matter.

Batch update

Look back quickly at the backpropagation algorithm. You'll note that the general sequence of instructions in a training cycle is:

1   present a pattern;

2   feed forward;

3   feed weight changes backwards;

4   present the next pattern ...

and so on. You've already seen that this works reasonably well. However, there can be problems with such a strategy – making weight changes after the presentation of each pattern can lead to wild oscillations in the weights from pattern to pattern. The network will almost certainly stabilise eventually, as you have witnessed in Computer Exercise 2.3, though training may be slowed down. But many of these changes might well cancel each other out over the course of presenting *all* the patterns in the set. A more efficient strategy, then, might be to *batch up* the changes in a temporary store and then apply the combined changes only at the end of the training cycle, all in one go. This is equivalent to creating a temporary weight matrix $\Delta\mathbf{W}$ for each layer and accumulating the weight change for each pattern in it:

$$\Delta\mathbf{W} = \Delta\mathbf{W}_1 + \Delta\mathbf{W}_2 + \Delta\mathbf{W}_3 ... + \Delta\mathbf{W}_n \tag{2.26}$$

for all n patterns. At the end of the training cycle $\Delta\mathbf{W}$ is added to the weight matrix for that layer.

Now here is a chance to test some of this out.

Computer Exercise 2.4

Load up and complete Computer Exercise 2.4 on the course DVD.

Case Study 2.2: Multi-layer perceptrons for prediction

The number of applications of multi-layer perceptrons to be found in the literature is astronomical. They have been applied to problems as diverse as fingerprint recognition, pathology and laboratory medicine, explosives detection, financial analysis, data mining, fault diagnosis, robotic control ... I could go on. Trying to pick a single, typical application for illustration seems doomed to failure. So, in the end I chose one recent application more or less at random, in an area that is maybe a little less explored than others: prediction.

Crucially important to city planners is the question of the reliability of public transport. Bus journeys within a city are subject to random delays due to local traffic conditions, road works, passenger load, etc. Predicting accurate arrival times at stops can be a headache for bus companies; historic data is not of much use in such fluid situations: what is really needed is real-time data and reliable dynamic prediction models.

See Chen et al. (2002) for a much fuller account.

One group of researchers has addressed the problem by conducting a number of studies of arrival time prediction using neural networks, basing their work on a segment of the transit system of New Jersey, USA. They created two basic models of the data they were working with: a *link-based* model and a *stop-based* model. In the link-based model, the route between two stops is divided into sectors, or links, between traffic intersections, as in Figure 2.45(a): data concerning each link such as traffic volume, traffic speed and known delays is collected in real time. A stop-based model concentrates on mean speeds, volumes and delays on the entire route between two stops (see Figure 2.45(b)). Both models incorporate a separate mechanism for calculating the likely amount of time the bus will spend, or dwell, at the previous stop, based on passenger demand, arrival time and other factors.

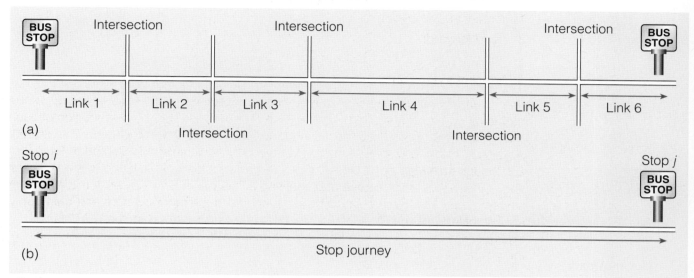

Figure 2.45   (a) Link-based and (b) stop-based traffic models

The neural network for the link-based data resembles Figure 2.46(a). Data for each link along the route between stops i and j is fed into a separate multi-layer perceptron. The activations of all these are summed and combined with the calculation of the dwell time at the previous stop i to reach a predicted arrival time at the next stop j. The stop-based model is simpler and is illustrated in Figure 2.46(b). Averages of traffic speed, volume and other delay factors, along with the number of intersections between stops i and j are input to a single perceptron, the output of which is again combined with the dwell time at stop i to give an estimated arrival time at j.

The researchers evaluated their model by comparing its performance with data generated by a discrete event simulator and with real transport data. They found that both models performed well, but could be improved further by adding a *prediction error* term to the estimated arrival times, the value of which is worked out at each stop by statistical means, based on discrepancies between real and predicted arrival times.

ACTIVITY 2.2 (Optional)

The course DVD and/or the course website contain a number of longer case studies of backpropagation applied to real-world problems. If you have time, you may wish to study some of these.

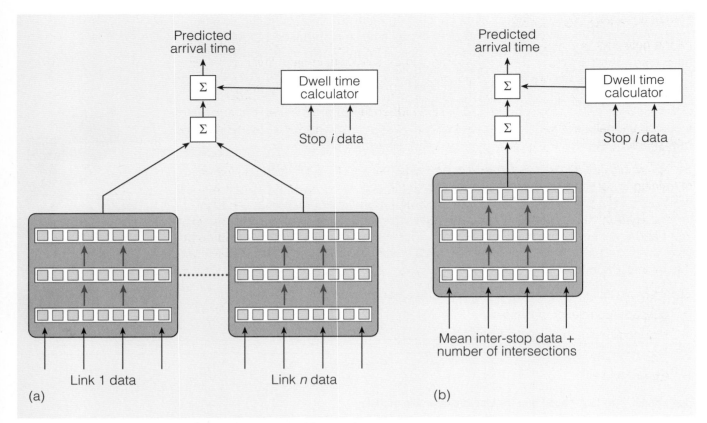

Figure 2.46   (a) Link-based and (b) stop-based neural forecasting systems

3.6   Alternatives to backpropagation

Since 1986, researchers working with feedforward networks have never left backpropagation alone. Innumerable improvements and alternatives to it have been devised. These are far too many and various for any kind of detailed treatment here; so all I want to do here is point you towards two alternatives, both of which preserve the multi-layer, feedforward architecture we are looking at in this unit, but offer rather different approaches to training.

Radial basis function networks

Radial basis function (RBF) networks are feedforward systems, their architecture very like that of the multi-layer perceptrons with one hidden layer that you've been studying. The input and output units are similar to those of a conventional perceptron: input neurons do not perform any processing, but simply feed the input vectors into the next layer; and the units in the output layer simply produce the weighted sum of their inputs, which is usually passed through a linear activation function.

The key difference between perceptrons and RBFs is in the properties of units in the hidden layer. In this layer, the units have a special kind of activation function known as a **Gaussian**. The weight vectors of these units are subjected to a special kind of unsupervised training, the aim of which is to enable these units to detect and respond to certain categories of input. This kind of unsupervised approach is known as cluster discovery, and is covered in more detail in the next unit. For the present, though, the course DVD contains a short technical account of RBFs, which you can opt to study in Activity 2.3 below.

Self-growing networks

All the networks you've met so far, and most of those that you will meet in future units, have had a fixed topology. Their layers, the numbers of units in each layer and their patterns of connectivity are set up in advance by the designer and do not change. And as you've already learned, there are no hard-and-fast rules for what that precise structure should be: the number of units in the hidden layer, in particular, depends very much on the nature of the problem, and on the intuition of the designer. Sometimes the best topology can only be reached by trial and error.

Self-growing networks do not start with a fixed topology. With such systems, the object of training is not just to find a suitable set of weights, but also to build a network with the optimum number of *units*. Since most self-growing systems are based on our now-familiar layered model, and since these will generally need a specific, known number of input and output units, the training process will generally start with an input and output layer only, and then gradually add hidden units, setting their weights appropriately, until the minimum number needed to solve the problem efficiently is reached.

Self-growing networks come in many flavours, among them:

► cascade-correlation networks

► reduced coulomb energy networks

► pyramid networks

► tower networks

► upstart networks.

Obviously, it's not going to be possible for you to study all of these in sufficient detail to make sense. The next activity invites you to look a little more closely at one of them: the **cascade-correlation** (CC) network.

ACTIVITY 2.3

The course DVD contains two very short technical papers, one on RBF and one on CC networks. Choose *one* of these and study it carefully. You might wish to look briefly at the other, if you have time.

Computer Exercise 2.5

Load up and complete Computer Exercise 2.5 on the course DVD.

4 Summary of Unit 2

This has been a long and complex unit – so much so that you may have felt you lost the main thread among the details. But my major line of argument should be fairly clear. We've been dealing exclusively with layered networks, with a particular pattern of connectivity, whose activity feeds forward in one direction only. In discussing these, I've focused on:

▶ ways in which the behaviour and limitations of such systems can be visualised and analysed *geometrically*, by considering their input and weight spaces;

▶ means by which feedforward systems can be made to *learn*, by convergence or by gradient descent;

▶ the *limitations* of feedforward systems, especially those with a single layer only, based on a geometrical analysis;

▶ *applications*: I've tried to illustrate the properties and potential of feedforward systems through a number of case studies.

Learning rules and algorithms have tended to dominate the discussion, as they do most treatments of neural networks. Almost exclusively, we have been considering forms of supervised learning. However, as you know, another pattern of learning – unsupervised – exists, and other forms of neural topology than layering can be created. It is to these quite different forms of system and training that we turn in the next unit.

Before moving on, look back at the learning outcomes for this unit and check these against what you think you can now do. Return to any section of the unit if you feel you need to.

Solutions to selected exercises in Unit 2

Solution to Exercise 2.2

First of all, at step t, calculate the vector of net inputs to u_4 and u_5:

$$\begin{bmatrix} netinput_{u4} \\ netinput_{u5} \end{bmatrix} = \mathbf{W}(t-1)\mathbf{x}(t) = \begin{bmatrix} 0.2 & 0.3 & -0.1 & 0.5 \\ 0.7 & -1 & 0.6 & 0.4 \end{bmatrix} \begin{bmatrix} 0.5 \\ 0.5 \\ 0.3 \\ -1 \end{bmatrix}$$

$$= \begin{bmatrix} (0.2*0.5)+(0.3*0.5)+(-0.1*0.3)+(0.5*-1) \\ (0.7*0.5)+(-1*0.5)+(0.6*0.3)+(0.4*-1) \end{bmatrix}$$

$$= \begin{bmatrix} -0.28 \\ -0.37 \end{bmatrix}$$

So, applying the threshold activation function, $\mathbf{y}(t)$, the vector of activations of u_4 and u_5, is:

$$\mathbf{y}(t) = \begin{bmatrix} y_4 \\ y_5 \end{bmatrix} = \begin{bmatrix} 0 \\ 0 \end{bmatrix}$$

Now we can calculate the weight change matrix $\Delta\mathbf{W}(t)$ as follows: the first row vector $\Delta\mathbf{w}_1(t)$ of the matrix is given by:

$$e_4 = (d_4 - y_4) = (1-0) = 1$$

$$\Delta\mathbf{w}_1(t)^T = \eta e_4 \mathbf{x}(t) = 0.1(1) \begin{bmatrix} 0.5 \\ 0.5 \\ 0.3 \\ -1 \end{bmatrix} = 0.1 \begin{bmatrix} 0.5 \\ 0.5 \\ 0.3 \\ -1 \end{bmatrix} = \begin{bmatrix} 0.05 \\ 0.05 \\ 0.03 \\ -0.1 \end{bmatrix}$$

$$\Delta\mathbf{w}_1(t) = \begin{bmatrix} 0.05 & 0.05 & 0.03 & -0.1 \end{bmatrix}$$

The second row vector $\Delta\mathbf{w}_2(t)$ of the matrix is given by:

$$e_5 = (d_5 - y_5) = (1-0) = 1$$

$$\Delta\mathbf{w}_2(t)^T = \eta e_5 \mathbf{x}(t) = 0.1(1) \begin{bmatrix} 0.5 \\ 0.5 \\ 0.3 \\ -1 \end{bmatrix} = 0.1 \begin{bmatrix} 0.5 \\ 0.5 \\ 0.3 \\ -1 \end{bmatrix} = \begin{bmatrix} 0.05 \\ 0.05 \\ 0.03 \\ -0.1 \end{bmatrix}$$

$$\Delta\mathbf{w}_2(t) = \begin{bmatrix} 0.05 & 0.05 & 0.03 & -0.1 \end{bmatrix}$$

So the weight change matrix $\Delta\mathbf{W}(t)$ and the new weight matrix $\mathbf{W}(t)$ after step t of training follow straightforwardly:

$$\Delta\mathbf{W}(t) = \begin{bmatrix} 0.05 & 0.05 & 0.03 & -0.1 \\ 0.05 & 0.05 & 0.03 & -0.1 \end{bmatrix}$$

$$\mathbf{W}(t) = \mathbf{W}(t-1) + \Delta\mathbf{W}(t) = \begin{bmatrix} 0.2 & 0.3 & -0.1 & 0.5 \\ 0.7 & -1 & 0.6 & 0.4 \end{bmatrix} + \begin{bmatrix} 0.05 & 0.05 & 0.03 & -0.1 \\ 0.05 & 0.05 & 0.03 & -0.1 \end{bmatrix}$$

$$= \begin{bmatrix} 0.25 & 0.35 & -0.07 & 0.4 \\ 0.75 & -0.95 & 0.63 & 0.3 \end{bmatrix}$$

The calculations for the next step of the training, step $t + 1$, follow exactly the same pattern, except that this time we are working with the new weight matrix $\mathbf{W}(t)$. So the activation vector $\mathbf{x}(t + 1)$ for the next pattern $\mathbf{x}(t + 1)$ is:

$$\begin{bmatrix} netinput_{u4} \\ netinput_{u5} \end{bmatrix} = \mathbf{W}(t)\mathbf{x}(t+1) = \begin{bmatrix} 0.25 & 0.35 & -0.07 & 0.4 \\ 0.75 & -0.95 & 0.63 & 0.3 \end{bmatrix} \begin{bmatrix} -0.4 \\ -0.2 \\ 0.1 \\ -1 \end{bmatrix}$$

$$= \begin{bmatrix} (0.25*-0.4)+(0.35*-0.2)+(-0.07*0.1)+(0.4*-1) \\ (0.75*-0.4)+(-0.95*-0.2)+(0.63*0.1)+(0.3*-1) \end{bmatrix}$$

$$= \begin{bmatrix} -0.58 \\ -0.35 \end{bmatrix}$$

The activation vector $\mathbf{y}(t + 1)$ will be:

$$\mathbf{y}(t+1) = \begin{bmatrix} y_4 \\ y_5 \end{bmatrix} = \begin{bmatrix} 0 \\ 0 \end{bmatrix}$$

The calculation of the weight change matrix and the new matrix is as follows:

$$e_4 = (d_4 - y_4) = 1 - 0 = 1$$

$$\Delta\mathbf{w}_1(t+1)^T = \eta e_4 \mathbf{x}(t+1) = 0.1(1) \begin{bmatrix} -0.4 \\ -0.2 \\ 0.1 \\ -1 \end{bmatrix} = 0.1 \begin{bmatrix} -0.4 \\ -0.2 \\ 0.1 \\ -1 \end{bmatrix} = \begin{bmatrix} -0.04 \\ -0.02 \\ 0.01 \\ -0.1 \end{bmatrix}$$

$$\Delta\mathbf{w}_1(t+1) = \begin{bmatrix} -0.04 & -0.02 & 0.01 & -0.1 \end{bmatrix}$$

$$e_5 = (d_5 - y_5) = 0 - 0 = 0$$

$$\Delta\mathbf{w}_2(t+1)^T = \eta e_5 \mathbf{x}(t+1) = 0.1(0) \begin{bmatrix} -0.4 \\ -0.2 \\ 0.1 \\ -1 \end{bmatrix} = 0 \begin{bmatrix} -0.4 \\ -0.2 \\ 0.1 \\ -1 \end{bmatrix} = \begin{bmatrix} 0 \\ 0 \\ 0 \\ 0 \end{bmatrix}$$

$$\Delta\mathbf{w}_2(t+1) = \begin{bmatrix} 0 & 0 & 0 & 0 \end{bmatrix}$$

$$\Delta\mathbf{W}(t+1) = \begin{bmatrix} -0.04 & -0.02 & 0.01 & -0.1 \\ 0 & 0 & 0 & 0 \end{bmatrix}$$

$$\mathbf{W}(t+1) = \mathbf{W}(t) + \Delta\mathbf{W}(t+1) = \begin{bmatrix} 0.25 & 0.35 & -0.07 & 0.4 \\ 0.75 & -0.95 & 0.63 & 0.3 \end{bmatrix} + \begin{bmatrix} -0.04 & -0.02 & 0.01 & -0.1 \\ 0 & 0 & 0 & 0 \end{bmatrix}$$

$$= \begin{bmatrix} 0.21 & 0.33 & -0.06 & 0.3 \\ 0.75 & -0.95 & 0.63 & 0.3 \end{bmatrix}$$

Solution to Exercise 2.3

This is just an application of the arithmetic of the delta rule. First of all, the net input to the single response unit u_4 is:

$$\mathbf{w}(t-1)^T \cdot \mathbf{x}(t) = \begin{bmatrix} 0.32 \\ -1.61 \\ 0.77 \end{bmatrix} \cdot \begin{bmatrix} 0.5 \\ 0.5 \\ 0.3 \end{bmatrix} = (0.32*0.5)+(-1.61*0.5)+(0.77*0.3)$$

$$= -0.414$$

And the activation y_4 of u_4 is:

$$y_4 = \frac{1}{1+e^{0.414}} = 0.398$$

Now we can calculate the error correction straightforwardly, using Equation 2.16:

$$\Delta\mathbf{w} = \eta(d_i - y_i)y_i(1-y_i)\mathbf{x} = 0.1(1-0.398)*0.398(1-0.398)\begin{bmatrix} 0.5 \\ 0.5 \\ 0.3 \end{bmatrix}$$

$$= 0.1*0.602*0.398*0.602\begin{bmatrix} 0.5 \\ 0.5 \\ 0.3 \end{bmatrix} = 0.014\begin{bmatrix} 0.5 \\ 0.5 \\ 0.3 \end{bmatrix} = \begin{bmatrix} 0.007 \\ 0.007 \\ 0.004 \end{bmatrix}$$

Finally, we just add this vector to the original weight vector $\mathbf{w}(t-1)^T$ to give the new weight vector $\mathbf{w}(t)$:

$$\mathbf{w}(t)^T = \begin{bmatrix} 0.32 \\ -1.61 \\ 0.77 \end{bmatrix} + \begin{bmatrix} 0.007 \\ 0.007 \\ 0.004 \end{bmatrix} = \begin{bmatrix} 0.327 \\ -1.603 \\ 0.774 \end{bmatrix}$$

Solution to Exercise 2.5

This is again a matter of arithmetical calculation. First, calculate the activation of u_6, as follows:

$$y_6 = \frac{1}{1+e^{-netinput}} = \frac{1}{1+e^{-3.22}} = 0.96$$

The error signal e_6 on u_6 is:

$$e_6 = y_6(1-y_6)\sum_{i=9}^{3} e_i w_{i6}$$

$$= 0.96(1-0.96)*((0.1*-0.77)+(0.32*0.21)+(0.46*1.6))$$

$$= 0.038*(-0.077+0.067+0.736)$$

$$= 0.038*0.726$$

$$= 0.028$$

From this we easily get $\Delta \mathbf{w}_i$, which is given by Equation 2.18:

$$\Delta \mathbf{w}_{6in} = \eta e_6 \mathbf{x}$$

$$= 0.5 * 0.028 \begin{bmatrix} 0.5 \\ 0.1 \\ 0 \\ -1.4 \end{bmatrix}$$

$$= 0.014 \begin{bmatrix} 0.5 \\ 0.1 \\ 0 \\ -1.4 \end{bmatrix}$$

$$= \begin{bmatrix} 0.007 \\ 0.0014 \\ 0 \\ -0.0196 \end{bmatrix}$$

Unit 3: Unsupervised learning in layers and lattices

CONTENTS

1	Introduction to Unit 3	118
	What you need to study this unit	119
	Learning outcomes for Unit 3	120
2	Unsupervised learning	121
3	Self-organisation and Hebbian learning	124
	3.1 Self-organisation	124
	3.2 Hebbian learning	125
	3.3 Experimental investigations with the Hebb Rule	126
	3.4 Practical applications of the Hebb Rule	129
4	Self-organising maps	130
	4.1 Background	130
	4.2 Artificial neural network maps	132
	4.3 Encoding the documents	150
	4.4 Training the map	152
	4.5 The WEBSOM browser	154
	4.6 Other applications	156
5	Summary of Unit 3	158
	References and further reading	213
	Acknowledgements	215
	Index for Block 4	216

Introduction to Unit 3

The previous unit offered an extensive discussion of feedforward networks: units arranged in layers, through which activity feeds in one direction from an input layer towards an output layer, and which are trained by some form of supervised learning, such as backpropagation. So popular and powerful have such systems proved to be that you might be excused for thinking that they are the only kind of neural network around, and that supervised learning is the only game in town. However, this is far from true.

Once again, I'd like you to think back – this time to Unit 1 of this block. There I discussed two general kinds of neural network architecture, or *topology*, other than the feedforward systems with which you are now familiar.

SAQ 3.1

Jot down a few notes describing each of these two alternative architectures. Look back at Unit 1 if you need to.

ANSWER..

I outlined two distinct types of architecture that are alternatives to feedforward: *lattices* and *recurrent networks*. Briefly, the details of each were as follows:

▶ **Lattices**: units are arranged in a one or more dimensional grid, often with *lateral* interconnections among them. Input is supplied from a separate set of dummy input units.

▶ **Recurrent networks**:these have at least one feedback connection (contrast this with feedforward networks). Units do not generally feed directly back to themselves.

In this unit, we will look in some detail at lattice architectures: variations on their basic topology, behaviour, learning and the uses to which they have been put. The behaviour of recurrent systems is the theme of Unit 4.

You've already seen that learning is perhaps *the* key question for any neural network system; and in the previous unit you worked intensively on supervised learning strategies, such as backpropagation. In this unit things will be different. Lattice systems in particular have been closely associated with *unsupervised learning* techniques, so throughout the unit, we will be taking a close look at unsupervised learning.

A rough plan of the way ahead, then, looks like this: in Section 2, I'll offer a short overview of unsupervised learning techniques and then, in Section 3, move on to look, again briefly, at one form of unsupervised learning you've encountered already: Hebbian learning. Although systems based on Hebbian learning have been used in some practical neural network applications, they have been much less successful than the networks that are the subject of Section 4: *self-organising maps*. These are a version of the lattice architecture closely associated with the theorist Teuvo Kohonen, whom you may remember I introduced you to briefly in Unit 1. In particular, we'll examine a form of unsupervised learning known as *competitive learning* that is frequently used with such lattice systems. At the end of the section I also want to present quite a lengthy case study on the use of self-organising maps in the exploration of very large document collections. Section 5 offers a summary and some conclusions.

What you need to study this unit

You will need the following course components, and will need to use your computer and internet connection for some of the exercises.

▶ this Block 4 text

▶ the course DVD.

LEARNING OUTCOMES FOR UNIT 3

After studying this unit, you will be able to:

3.1 write a few sentences explaining the general nature and purposes of unsupervised learning;

3.2 draw up a set of bullet points outlining the main principles of self-organisation;

3.3 draw diagrams and bullets sketching out how a system can self-organise under Hebbian learning;

3.4 briefly explain the process of vector quantisation and explain how this can be related to the concepts of Voronoi tessellation and a neural map;

3.5 write a very brief outline of an algorithm for competitive learning;

3.6 write a few sentences explaining the workings of lateral inhibition and excitation;

3.7 write a paragraph setting out the main processes involved in training a self-organising feature map (SOFM);

3.8 write a brief explanation of modern variations on this basic SOFM training process;

3.9 describe some applications of SOFMs.

2 Unsupervised learning

After the rigours of the previous unit, you should have a pretty firm grip on the main ideas of supervised learning, especially as they apply to multi-layer neural networks. However, you may feel a good deal less sure about unsupervised learning. So, again as a little exercise in recall, and to set the scene, think about this question for a moment.

SAQ 3.2

Write a couple of lines contrasting supervised with unsupervised learning. What examples of unsupervised learning have you already met?

ANSWER...

In supervised learning, there is a set of patterns or exemplars, each one accompanied by a teaching input that indicates the correct, or desired, answer. Learning takes place by adjusting the system according to some measure of the difference between the expected, correct answer and the actual answer, for each exemplar. In unsupervised learning a set of exemplars is also provided, but no desired response.

The only example of unsupervised learning you have met so far is Hebbian learning.

At first sight, one might ask how can unsupervised learning possibly work? If there is no indication of what the right or wrong response to an input pattern is, how can a system improve its performance by making changes in the 'right' direction? For example, in a classification task, how can we correctly assign an input pattern to the right category without teaching feedback? Yet at the same time, if we look back at our inspiration – the natural world – and at the performance of real nervous systems, it seems that unsupervised learning must work somehow. As you saw in Block 3, most creatures do possess some sort of elementary system for categorising the world and making sensible responses to it. Of course, the environment does provide some kinds of feedback, but by and large animals must have learned without teachers, books, maps, plans and outside guidance. How?

One clue comes from considering any large set of data. In normal circumstances, this will always contain *regularities* of some sort. Let's take a very simple example: the height and weight data for a large set of people. Set out in a table, this would look something like this:

Name	Height (m)	Weight (kg/100)
Tomkins	1.85	0.84
Butterworth	1.55	0.77
Hefty	1.80	0.99
Wisp	1.40	0.62

(I've scaled the weights in kilograms by one hundredth to make the numbers we are dealing with more tractable for a neural network.) In other words, we can think of each data item as a two-element vector $\mathbf{x}_n$ = [height, weight]. We would certainly expect to detect regularities within a large data set like this. But what kinds of regularities? This is worth thinking about for a moment.

Exercise 3.1

What general types of regularity might one find inside our height and weight data set?

Discussion ....

Actually there are a number of possible answers. I came up with the following general kinds:

▶ *Clusters of closely related patterns.* For example, men are generally heavier and taller than women, so one might expect to find a cluster corresponding to each of these two groups.

▶ *Frequency.* One might discover that tall people occurred much more frequently in the set than short people, or vice versa.

▶ *Relative variance.* There might be a much greater range of weights in the set than heights.

▶ *Ordering.* The patterns may be ordered in various ways.

There are other more complex possibilities.

The task of unsupervised learning is to detect these regularities without any input or prior knowledge of the set. To illustrate this, let's stick with our set of height and weight data and just concentrate on the idea of *clustering*, which I think is the most obvious and easy to picture. We can illustrate the idea graphically by going back to our tried and tested picture of an *input* or *pattern space* (see Section 2.2 of the previous unit). Our height and weight vectors x_1, x_2, x_3 ... x_n will obviously lie dotted around a two-dimensional space, illustrated in Figure 3.1, and if clusters exist they should be clearly visible.

Note that we have no way of telling what these clusters actually *are*: men v. women; one town v. another town? All we can see is a statistical regularity. The process of naming the cluster is known as **calibration**, and lies outside the scope of unsupervised learning.

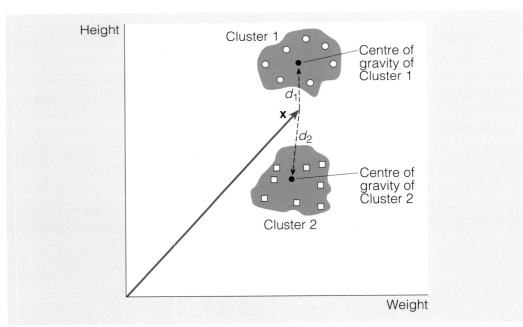

Figure 3.1   Clusters in data space

Now consider the new data pattern **x**, illustrated in Figure 3.1 as a vector. Which cluster should it be assigned to? This is not a trick question. We would naturally want to put **x** in the cluster it was closest to – or, to put it another way, it is the shortest *distance* from. From the figure, **x** obviously belongs in Cluster 1: this is absolutely straightforward, surely. Yes, it is, but we do need to be a bit careful. To us, distance seems an easily grasped concept: I'm relatively near to one thing and far away from another – simple. But in mathematics there are many different ways of measuring distance, some of them far from simple. The kind of distance we instinctively think of when the word is mentioned is known to mathematicians as **Euclidean distance**, and I've illustrated it in Figure 3.2. By contrast, another way of measuring the distance between two points is known as the **angular distance**, and is given by the cosine of the angle between the two vectors. I've also illustrated this in Figure 3.2.

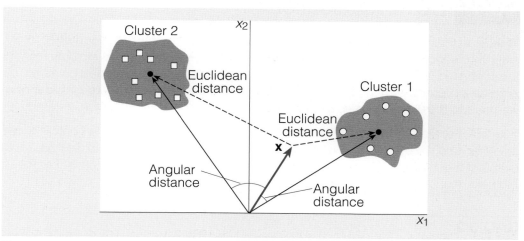

Figure 3.2   Distances between clusters in data space

To put it more formally, the Euclidean distance d between two vectors $\mathbf{x}_1$ and $\mathbf{x}_2$ is given by:

$$d = \sqrt{(\mathbf{x}_1 - \mathbf{x}_2) \cdot (\mathbf{x}_1 - \mathbf{x}_2)} \tag{3.1}$$

and the angular distance by:

$$d = \cos\theta = \frac{\mathbf{x}_1 \, \mathbf{x}_2}{\|\mathbf{x}_1\| \|\mathbf{x}_2\|} \tag{3.2}$$

Remember that the vertical lines represent the length or norm of a vector. See the Maths Guide for details.

where θ is the angle between the two vectors. There is no need to worry too much about these technicalities. Statistical techniques for discovering clusters and other patterns within data sets have been known for a long time. But our real concern here is with how we can make this process of discovery work in a neural network.

Once again – and as with so many of the complex phenomena found in nature – the answer lies in using the principle I introduced in Block 3: *self-organisation*. Unsupervised learning of artificial neural systems can be made to be an *emergent property* of *interactions* between the units that make them up, when coupled with the principle of *adaptation*.

Unsupervised learning in neural networks can be divided into two general kinds:

▶ Hebbian learning and variations on it;

▶ competitive learning.

Hebbian learning you have already met; I'm going to make some brief remarks on it and the principle of self-organisation in the next section. However, in this unit we will be mostly concerned with *competitive learning*, which I'll discuss in Section 4.

3 Self-organisation and Hebbian learning

3.1 Self-organisation

Without any external corrective input, unsupervised learning must depend on self-organisation in some way. How else could the system learn? And all forms of unsupervised learning are, in fact, designed to bring about self-organisation as an *emergent* property arising from *interaction* and *adaptation*. But before we consider how, we need to recall briefly some of the main principles of this phenomenon.

You first met the concept of self-organisation in Unit 2 of Block 3, in the context of ant colonies; and we discussed the principles underlying it in more detail in Section 2.3 of Unit 3 of that block. You might at some stage want to revisit these sections. For the moment, though, think about this question.

SAQ 3.3

What processes did we identify as leading to self-organisation?

ANSWER..

There were four:

▶ *multiple interactions*: as ever, in nature's systems we see order arising from interactions between simple units;

▶ *amplification of fluctuations*: some small initial variation, possibly a random one, becomes magnified, as a result of

▶ *positive feedback*, which reinforces some fluctuations, while others are diminished by

▶ *negative feedback*, by means of which certain other activity is suppressed.

We saw all these at work in the seemingly organised behaviour of insect foraging and construction.

Although he was expressing them in more Darwinian terms, the neurologist Christoph von der Malsburg expressed much the same ideas in these three principles of self-organisation:

▶ Fluctuations self-amplify. This self-amplification is analogous to reproduction in Darwinian evolution.

▶ Limitation of resources means that fluctuations compete and that some are selected at the expense of the others.

▶ Fluctuations cooperate. The presence of a fluctuation can enhance the fitness of some of the others.

You can see that the same ideas of amplification by positive and negative feedback are embodied here. Now let's try to apply these ideas to neural systems, and specifically to Hebbian learning.

3.2 Hebbian learning

You should recall that the basic Hebb Rule of synaptic modification can be stated in English as something like:

▶ If two units at either end of a weighted link are activated *simultaneously*, then the value of the weight is *increased* by some amount.

▶ If two units at either end of a weighted link are activated *at different times*, then the value of the weight is *decreased* by a certain amount.

And mathematically in a much more compact form as:

$$\Delta w_{kj}(t+1) = \eta x_k(t) x_j(t) \tag{3.3}$$

So how might the principles of self-organisation fit in with Hebbian learning and neural systems in general?

Exercise 3.2

What relationships can you see between the principles of self-organisation and the structure and behaviour of neural systems, particularly under Hebbian learning?

Discussion ....

Clearly there are multiple interactions: neurons are densely linked and signal to one another – this is an obvious enough point, and one I've made before. And when artificial neural systems are trained using *supervised* learning, some form of positive feedback is being supplied from outside the system by the learning algorithm. But what about unsupervised Hebbian learning? The point here seems to be that the positive and negative feedback come from *inside* the system. Some initial fluctuation causes two linked neurons to fire together and this co-incidence is amplified by the Hebb Rule, making it more likely that they will fire together in the future, by strengthening the connection between them. At the same time, connections between neurons that are not firing together are weakened, making it even less likely they will fire together in future.

All four processes – amplification of fluctuations, positive and negative feedback and multiple interactions seem to be at work in Hebbian learning.

But there is a problem with the simple formulation of the Hebb Rule that I gave above. This is related to von der Malsburg's second principle – the limitation of resources. What are the limits on Hebbian growth and diminution of synaptic weights? Presumably a weight can shrink to zero and no further. But can a weight go on growing indefinitely? There is nothing in Equation 3.3 to stop it from doing so.

In reality, some sort of restraint on the growth of weights has to be imposed. This can just mean setting limits beyond which weights cannot grow: *w+* as the upper positive limit and *w–* as the lower negative limit. This approach is often accompanied by a modification to the Hebb Rule involving adding a term which slows the growth in a weight that is being reinforced. Consider the simple network illustrated in Figure 3.3 and the neuron *k* within it.

In the modified form of the rule, the change in w_{kj} is given by:

$$\Delta w_{kj}(t+1) = \eta x_k(t) \left[x_j(t) - x_j(t) w_{kj}(t) \right] \tag{3.4}$$

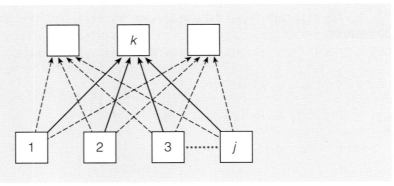

Figure 3.3 Simple network

Removing the terms indicating the time steps makes this clearer:

$$\Delta w_{kj} = \eta x_k \left[x_j - x_j w_{kj} \right]$$ (3.5)

You can easily see that the term $-x_j w_{kj}$ acts as a brake on the growth of w_{kj}. This renders the rule into a form which makes it easier to use in practical experiments. It is also possible to show mathematically that after many applications of the rule, all the weights of a neuron will reach their saturation values, either at $w+$ or at $w-$, after which they no longer change and the system is stable.

Exercise 3.3

Intuitively, why do you think all the weights of a neuron will stabilise in this way? Don't attempt a proof; just try to think about this in terms of the principles of self-organisation.

Discussion ....

This seems to be a case of the amplification of fluctuations. Consider a single neuron k, one weight of which, w_{kj}, is being reinforced positively, in accordance with Equation 3.5. This will cause the activation of k to be slightly higher on the next application of the rule, which will in turn cause the weight to grow further towards its maximum. The same consideration applies to all weights that are being positively reinforced. Using the same reasoning, you can see that all of k's weights that are being negatively reinforced will fall towards their minima. As the rule is applied over and over, all the weights will either fall towards their minima or grow to their maxima.

Armed with this formulation of the Hebb Rule, we can now look briefly at a well-known experiment in which its self-organising properties were demonstrated.

3.3 Experimental investigations with the Hebb Rule

Neural network research has always drawn its inspiration from scientific findings about the actual functioning of the brains and nervous systems of humans and other animals. Perhaps the best understood aspect of information handling in the nervous system is the issue of how *visual* data is processed in mammals.

The chain of processing that leads to the interpretation of visual signals in the brain starts in the eye, at the retina. There, specialised neurons – chiefly **rods** and **cones** (about 100 million of them in each human eye) – fire in response to light falling on them from the volume of space in front of the eye, known as the **visual field**. Their signals are passed via a number of intermediate cells to another kind of neuron, the **retinal ganglia**.

There are about 1.5 million of these in each human retina. The area of the retina that projects onto each ganglion is known as its **receptive field**. Without going into too much detail, ganglia have become specialised into two types: *on-centre* and *off-centre*. On-centre ganglia only fire if light is falling onto the centre of the receptive field; off-centre ganglia only fire if light is falling on the parts of the receptive field lying around the centre. I've illustrated this in Figure 3.4. Both kinds of cell will fire at low frequency if light falls on their entire receptive field.

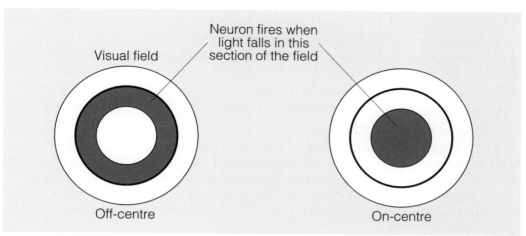

Figure 3.4   Off-centre and on-centre retinal ganglia

Further along the chain, neural signals finally reach the brain in an area at the back known as the **visual cortex**, at a receiving station known as **V1**. There, Nobel-prize winning neuroscientists David Hubel and Torsten Wiesel observed other specialised

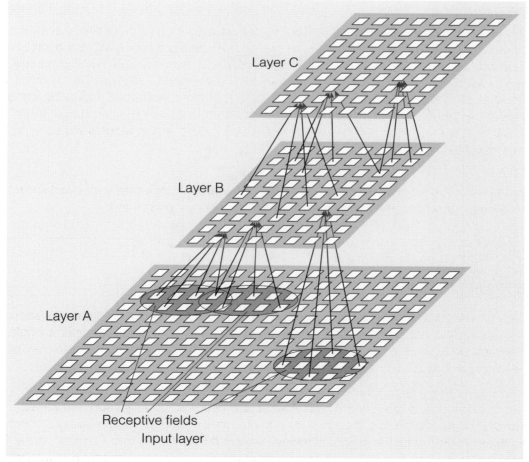

Figure 3.5   Experimental set-up for Hebbian learning

neurons and neuron groups that respond to the *orientation of lines* in the visual field. A vertical line might cause one group of cells to fire: a line at 45° or 90° (or some other angle) will stimulate others. Signals are passed up from V1 through a hierarchy of areas, V2–V4, each building a more complex and detailed analysis of the contents of the visual field.

The obvious question is: how did these specialisations come about? As with all neurons, the sensitivities of these various cells are governed by their synaptic strengths. So how are these set?

One possible answer lies in self-organisation under Hebbian learning. In a series of experiments begun by Linsker and continued by von der Malsburg, these researchers were able to show how on-/off-centre and orientation specialisation might arise in layers of artificial neurons, learning under a Hebbian regime. Here is a brief and somewhat simplified account of these experiments. The general experimental set-up is depicted in Figure 3.5 on the previous page.

A layer A of dummy input neurons is connected to a two-dimensional layer B of neurons in a set of overlapping fields, mimicking the receptive fields of the retinal ganglia. Layer B is fully connected to another two-dimensional layer C. There are no connections between units within a layer. Every unit's activation is given by:

$$x_j = b + \sum_{i=1}^{N} w_{ji} x_i \qquad (3.6)$$

where N is the number of units feeding into unit j, and b is a constant. All weights are updated according to the Hebb Rule. A series of randomly distributed patterns is presented over and over at layer A, until the weights of the units in B stabilise at their saturation values. The weights of the units in layer C are then trained until they stabilise.

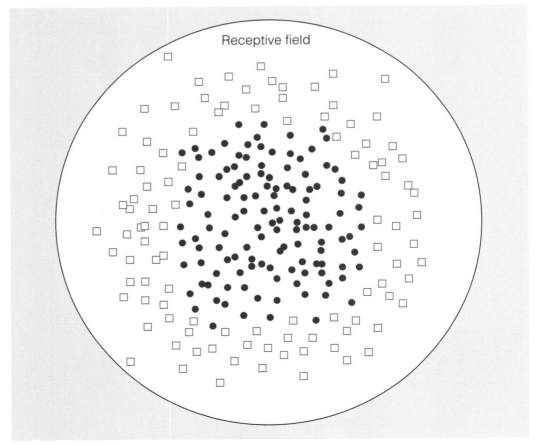

Figure 3.6   Receptive field of a single neuron in layer C

If we now depict the final state of a single unit j in layer C, we get a picture resembling Figure 3.6. The positions of the units feeding into j from its receptive field in layer A are all marked either by a square or by a dot: a square represents a weight that has grown to its maximum (in this experiment, +0.5); a dot represents a weight at its minimum. You can clearly see the off-centre pattern that has emerged. Stimulation of units in the circular band surrounding the central area of the field will mean strong positive input to j, as the weights there are strongly positive, causing j to fire. Stimulation of units in the central area will inhibit j, since the weights there are negative.

3.4 | Practical applications of the Hebb Rule

Hebbian learning has not been widely used in practical applications. Where it has been applied, its self-organising properties have been exploited to implement a statistical technique known as *principal components analysis*, to do the kind of feature detection I talked about in Section 2. As you'll see in the next section, the detection of statistical regularities can also be used in data compression and coding.

There has been some recent interest in using Hebbian techniques in internet searches. I've given some details of this on the course website.

ACTIVITY 3.1 (optional)

On the course DVD you will find a few links and resources to help you investigate some of the applications of Hebbian learning. If you have time, browse through some of these.

4 | Self-organising maps

4.1 | Background

The most intensively researched aspect of brain function is the working of the **cerebral cortex**. In the human brain, this very large structure is a deeply crumpled and fissured sheet of tissue, about 2–4 millimetres thick, forming a dome over the entire set of the brain's inner structures (see Figure 3.7).

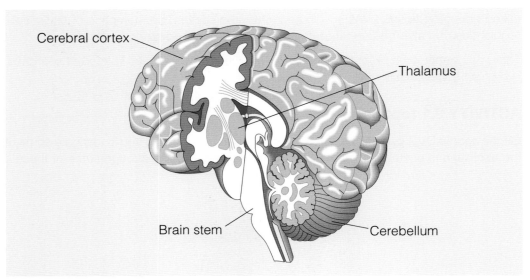

Figure 3.7   The cerebral cortex

Seen in cross-section, under magnification, this sheet comprises six distinct layers. Within the sheet, the axons of neurons tend to be directed up and down, across the layers, although there are also dense lateral connections between neurons in the same layer (see Figure 3.8), some of them over quite long distances. Although the cortex does receive axons from other areas of the brain – for example, you've seen that V1 receives signals originating at the eyes – over 75% of the connections come from within the cortex itself. Essentially, the cortex is a massive lattice of billions of neurons, connected by an impenetrable jungle of axons.

In 1957, the neuroscientist Vernon Mountcastle, exploring the properties of the somatic sensory areas of the cortex, observed that the neurons there appear to be organised in **cortical columns**, each made up of between 1000 and 10 000 neurons (see Figure 3.9).

Connections up and down within the column are much denser than lateral connections between columns, he noted, so that when cells inside the column become active, the whole structure reverberates with complex patterns of neural firings. Moreover, Mountcastle observed that cortical columns tended to be *specialised*: a column would become active in the presence of a certain stimulus (a touch on a finger, say), while others close by would remain inactive. Columns close by would become active in the presence of a different stimulus. Mountcastle's findings were confirmed when David Hubel and Torsten Wiesel (mentioned above) observed exactly the same columnar organisation and specialisation in the visual cortex. Columns, or small groups of

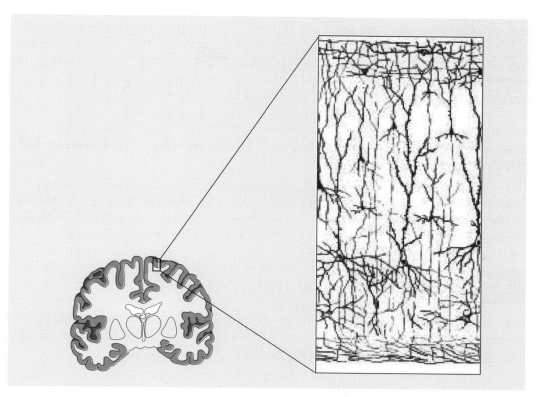

Figure 3.8   Cross-section of cerebral cortex

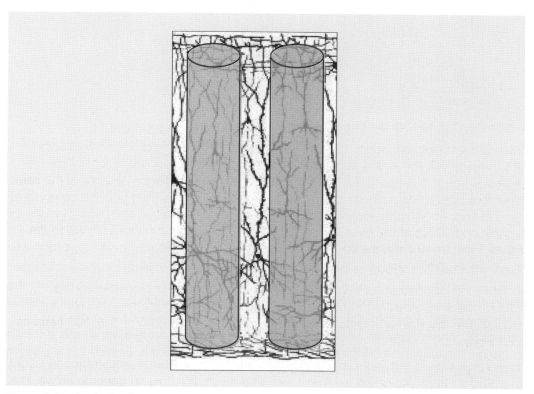

Figure 3.9   Cortical columns

columns, would tend to fire together in response to some particular component of a visual perception, such as a vertical line or a certain colour.

Now think back to the idea of a brain *map*, which I introduced in Unit 1 of this block. Look back at this section, if you need to. In discussing the somatosensory map I pointed out how assemblies of neurons in a certain area of the cortex respond by firing when a certain area of the skin – the left index fingertip, say – is stimulated, while groups of neurons in another area fire together in response to stimulation from another – the lips, maybe. In other words, a part of the cortical sheet forms a *map* of the body surface, in just the same way that areas of paper in a conventional map correspond to geographical areas of a real country. As you've seen, the same thing happens in the visual cortex: groups of neurons map the visual field, responding to various areas of it and to colours, shapes and orientations within it. This kind of ordering, where areas in a map correspond to certain groups of features, is known as **topographical ordering**.

Once again, how does this work? Assuming that such brain maps are not fixed from birth (and there is evidence they are not), how are they formed? Computer simulations based on the principles of artificial neural networks can offer us some insights into these questions.

4.2   Artificial neural network maps

The general structure of a neural network map will already look fairly familiar to you. It comprises a one-, two- or three-dimensional lattice of units, connected by weighted links to a layer of dummy input units (see Figure 3.10).

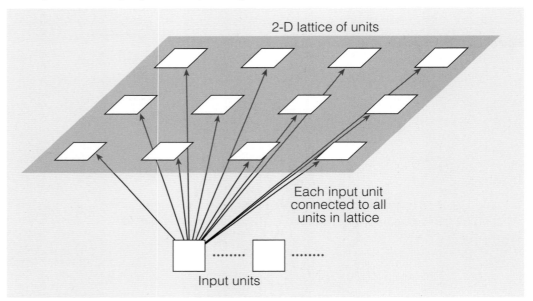

Figure 3.10   Neural network map

You might say that this looks pretty much like the single-layer perceptrons you learned about in the previous unit. So it does; but the strategy for training maps and interpreting their response is quite different. The idea is that the lattice should become *partitioned* in such a way that a certain unit, or cluster of units, will fire when one kind of input is presented, and a separate unit (or cluster of units) will fire in some other area of the map in the presence of a different input. To take the example I used in Section 2 – the height and weight data – we might find that a unit in the top left corner of the map responds when the input embodies data that is typically female, and a unit in a different part of the map fires when an input is presented that is typically male. To put it another way, we want the layer of units to form a map of the clusters or other statistical regularities within the input data set.

You can see that the cortical map, which I described in the previous section, is a specific version of the idea: certain clusters of neurons in one part of the map activate when certain areas of the body or the visual field are stimulated; when another area is stimulated, these clusters are dormant while other clusters fire. But how can we ensure that the layer of units becomes organised in such a way that it has these mapping properties? How can it discover these statistical properties of the input? The most common way is to use variations on an unsupervised learning procedure known to mathematicians as **vector quantisation**.

Vector quantisation

Using the notation with which you are now familiar, and sticking with the example I presented in my general discussion of unsupervised learning in Section 2, assume that we have a set of input vectors x_1, x_2, x_3 ... x_n (our set of height and weight data, maybe), with each x being a vector $[x_1, x_2, x_3 ... x_n]$ ($n = 2$ in the case of our height and weight set). And again using the concept of an input space, we can visualise the input vectors lying within an input space of the same dimension as the vectors. In Figure 3.11, I've represented this as two-dimensional. The idea of vector quantisation is to divide the entire space up into regions, known as **Voronoi tessellations**, **Voronoi regions** or **Voronoi cells**, and to represent each region with a single vector, termed a **Voronoi vector**, representing that entire region. Figure 3.11 depicts the two-dimensional space divided into nine Voronoi 'tiles', with the Voronoi vectors v_1–v_9 marked with black circles. Any input vector lying within that region is simply tagged with the index number of the region's Voronoi vector.

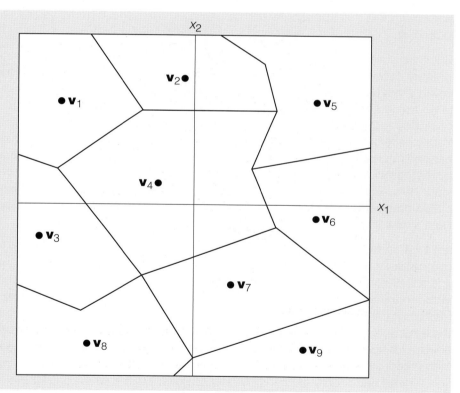

Figure 3.11   Two-dimensional vector space with Voronoi tessellation

As you can see, this is a kind of *coding*. A complex input is simply reduced to, and represented by, a single **code vector**, which we can tag with a specific index number or code word. This kind of reduction is immensely useful in any kind of *compression* technology, where the idea is to cut down a very large amount of data into something more manageable. In image compression (JPEG, PNG), for example, patches of adjacent pixels that are very similar to one another can be represented by a single code; in moving picture compression (MPEG) close correlations between frames can be similarly reduced. Vector quantisation is used today in a whole range of compression and coding applications.

Let's now consider how vector quantisation can be made to work in an artificial neural network map.

Vector quantisation in artificial maps

The relationship between the idea of a neural map and the Voronoi tessellations I depicted in Figure 3.11 must be a fairly obvious one, I think. But just to make it completely clear, think about this question for a moment.

SAQ 3.4

How exactly do you think the concept of a neural map and the Voronoi tessellations can be related?

ANSWER..

Figure 3.11 should give you an insight here, since the picture of the abstract input space, divided into regions, looks very like a map anyway. Each Voronoi region can be represented by a unit in the map and that unit (and no others) can become active when the input is a vector in that region of the input space. In this way, the neural layer forms a map of the clusters and regularities within the input data set.

Something like this appears to be happening in the cortical maps you've already looked at.

But if we start with the kind of system I illustrated in Figure 3.10 above, with all the weights between the input layer and the map randomised, it is of course incredibly unlikely that we will get the kind of mapping behaviour we want. Clearly, the network has to be trained in some way: but how? Some sort of supervised learning like backpropagation might be possible, certainly. However, neural maps have traditionally been trained using *unsupervised* techniques. Not only is this closer to what happens in nature, in our own brains, but it also has the immense interest and advantage of the network's being able to discover *for itself* the regularities within the input data. And this can be achieved by using an approach to unsupervised learning called **competitive learning**, sometimes also known as **winner-takes-all learning**. Here's how it works.

Let's return to the network depicted in Figure 3.10. As before, assume we have a set of input vectors $\mathbf{x}_1$, $\mathbf{x}_2$, $\mathbf{x}_3$ ... $\mathbf{x}_n$, with each $\mathbf{x}$ being a vector $[x_1, x_2, x_3 ... x_n]$, where each x is a real number. Every unit in the dummy input layer is fully connected to every unit in the map, so every map unit i will have its own incoming weight vector $\mathbf{w}_i$. For mathematical reasons which I'm going to gloss over, it is often common practice for all the input and weight vectors to be *normalised*, that is they are all made to be of length 1. Finally, for every input $\mathbf{x}$, the activation y_i of each unit i in this network is given by:

Refer to the Maths Guide for an explanation of normalisation.

$$y_i = \mathbf{w}_i^T \cdot \mathbf{x} \tag{3.7}$$

In other words, the activation will simply be the net input to the unit.

The idea of competitive learning can be summed up in the most basic way as follows:

1   When a pattern represented by the input vector $\mathbf{x}$ is applied to the dummy input units, one of the response units (call it m) 'wins' the competition by virtue of its weight vector $\mathbf{w}_m$ being the one with the smallest Euclidean distance from the input vector $\mathbf{x}$. Formally, the winning unit's weight vector $\mathbf{w}_m$ satisfies the property:

$$\|\mathbf{w}_m - \mathbf{x}\| = \min_i \|\mathbf{w}_i - \mathbf{x}\| \tag{3.8}$$

But we can identify the winning unit more simply than this. If all the weight and input vectors are normalised, then the winning unit is simply the one with the highest activation, expressed formally as:

$$\mathbf{w}_m^T \cdot \mathbf{x} = \max_i \mathbf{w}_i^T \cdot \mathbf{x} \tag{3.9}$$

From now on, in future discussions of unsupervised learning I'm going to assume that the network preconditions for Equation 3.8 being true are all fulfilled and that the winning unit is simply the one with the highest activation according to Equations 3.7 and 3.9.

2 m's weight vector $\mathbf{w}_m$ is altered by moving it closer to the input vector $\mathbf{x}$.

3 None of the other units or their weight vectors are altered.

4 This is repeated for all n patterns in the set.

Let's consider this in a little more detail by means of an example. Once again, I'll use our height and weight data set, giving us a very simple network, illustrated in Figure 3.12.

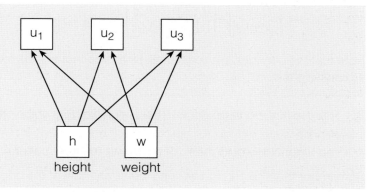

Figure 3.12 Simple network for height and weight data

Suppose the weight matrix of the network at time t is:

$$\hat{\mathbf{W}}(t) = \begin{bmatrix} 0.77 & 0.63 \\ 0.80 & -0.59 \\ -0.68 & -0.73 \end{bmatrix}$$

The cap over the vector and matrix symbols indicates that they have both been normalised.

We now apply the first height and weight vector:

$$\hat{\mathbf{X}}_1 = \begin{bmatrix} 0.91 \\ 0.41 \end{bmatrix}$$

at the input.

Returning to the four-step process outlined above, at time t we proceed as follows:

1 Calculate the activations of the three units and find the winner:

$y_1 = (0.91 * 0.77) + (0.41 * 0.63) = 0.96$

$y_2 = (0.91 * 0.80) + (0.41 * -0.59) = 0.49$

$y_3 = (0.91 * -0.68) + (0.41 * -0.73) = -0.92$

The winning unit m is therefore u_1.

2 Alter m's weight vector $\mathbf{w}_m$ to move it closer to the input vector. Obviously there are several ways in which we could do that, but we'll just adopt the simplest and apply the rule:

$$\Delta \mathbf{w}_m(t+1) = \eta \left(\mathbf{x}(t) - \mathbf{w}_m(t) \right) \tag{3.10}$$

where η is a learning constant. η is generally kept small, in the range 0.1–0.5. With η as 0.1, the new weight vector for m can be worked out easily.

Exercise 3.4

Calculate the new weight vector $\mathbf{w}_1(t + 1)$ for u_1.

Discussion ....

The calculation is just a matter of arithmetic. First we calculate the change vector $\Delta\mathbf{w}_1(t)$ and then add it to the original weight vector, giving $\mathbf{w}_1(t + 1)$, as follows:

$$\Delta\mathbf{w}_1(t+1) = \eta\left(\mathbf{x}(t) - \mathbf{w}_1(t)\right)$$

$$= 0.1\left(\begin{bmatrix} 0.91 \\ 0.41 \end{bmatrix} - \begin{bmatrix} 0.77 \\ 0.63 \end{bmatrix}\right) = 0.1\left(\begin{bmatrix} 0.14 \\ -0.22 \end{bmatrix}\right) = \begin{bmatrix} 0.014 \\ -0.022 \end{bmatrix}$$

$$\mathbf{w}_1(t+1) = \Delta\mathbf{w}_1(t+1) + \mathbf{w}_1(t)$$

$$= \begin{bmatrix} 0.014 \\ -0.022 \end{bmatrix} + \begin{bmatrix} 0.77 \\ 0.63 \end{bmatrix} = \begin{bmatrix} 0.78 \\ 0.61 \end{bmatrix}$$

Note that the changes are very small. Note also that $\mathbf{w}_1$ has moved slightly closer to $\mathbf{x}$ as a result of them.

---

3 There is nothing to be done to the weight vectors of the other units, as they were not winners.

4 The algorithm would then continue with the next pattern.

Remember that the change will only be to one row of the original weight matrix, Row 1, as these are the weights of u_1. So the new matrix becomes:

$$\hat{\mathbf{W}}(t+1) = \begin{bmatrix} 0.78 & 0.61 \\ 0.80 & -0.59 \\ -0.68 & -0.73 \end{bmatrix}$$

I think it's helpful to try and depict graphically what we are doing in this sort of operation. Assume for a moment that all the input and weight vectors are normalised at length 1. If they are then plotted in the input space, they will all lie around the circumference of a circle, and any clusters will show up as sets of points close together. I've depicted this in Figure 3.13.

On presentation of a new input $\mathbf{x}$, the weight vector of the winning unit $\mathbf{w}_m$ (which is the minimum Euclidean distance from the input vector) moves closer to $\mathbf{x}$, making a new weight vector $\mathbf{w}'_m$. You can see that, after many presentations of many inputs, the weight vectors of the units in the map will each have moved near to the centre of a cluster. They have become the Voronoi vectors for regions in the input space.

Vector quantisation can be made to work in artificial neural networks, but no one would claim that anything of that kind is actually going on in the brain. However, the general idea has been taken up by neural network theorists and used as a basis for rather more realistic models of cortical mapping. One of the best known and successful of these is the self-organising feature map.

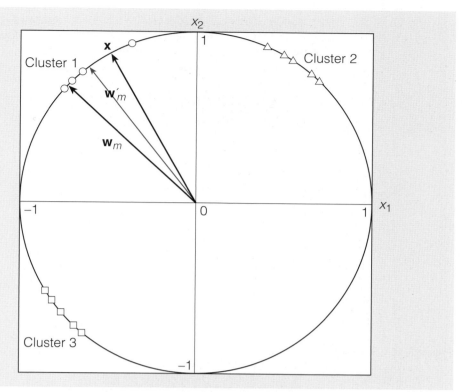

Figure 3.13   Normalised vectors moving through space under training

Self-organising feature maps

The Finnish scientist Teuvo Kohonen, whom I introduced you to briefly in Unit 1 of this block, set out to model this mapping process in an artificial neural network. The result was a neural architecture known as the **self-organising feature map** (**SOFM**) – sometimes just known as a **self-organising map** (**SOM**) – and a training process based on vector quantisation.

Kohonen has had a lifelong interest in the processes that go on in the cortex, and in the practical applications that could come out of an understanding of these. He found that the formation of cortical maps is another example of *self-organisation*. Once again, we can see them as an *emergent property* of *interactions* between neurons, and the *adaptation* of the links between them. In the model of the specialisation of neurons in the visual cortex arising from Hebbian learning, which I discussed in the previous section, the links were generally of the feedforward kind. In the formation of maps the interactive processes at work are believed to be rather different: specifically, they are termed **lateral excitation** and **inhibition**.

Figure 3.14   Teuvo Kohonen

Now consider the lattice of units illustrated in Figure 3.15 overleaf. As in every model you've met so far, each unit receives forward input from a layer of dummy input units. However, in contrast to the feedforward systems you studied in the previous unit, the units within the lattice are connected by a set of *lateral* links (only a very few of these are illustrated in the figure – you can assume that every unit in the lattice is connected to every other unit). So, not only does each unit receive stimulation from the input, its response is also affected by the units around it. And its response affects those units, in turn – a classic example of interaction.

What about the weights of these lateral connections? If they are simply set to random values, it is unlikely that any useful patterns would emerge – at least not in the short term. But if the connection strengths follow a certain general pattern, more interesting results are likely. Focus on a single unit *j*, illustrated in Figure 3.16.

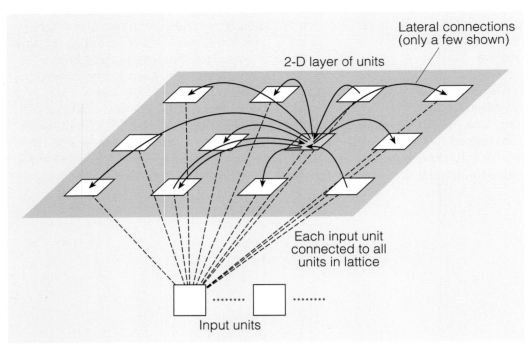

Figure 3.15 Self-organising feature map

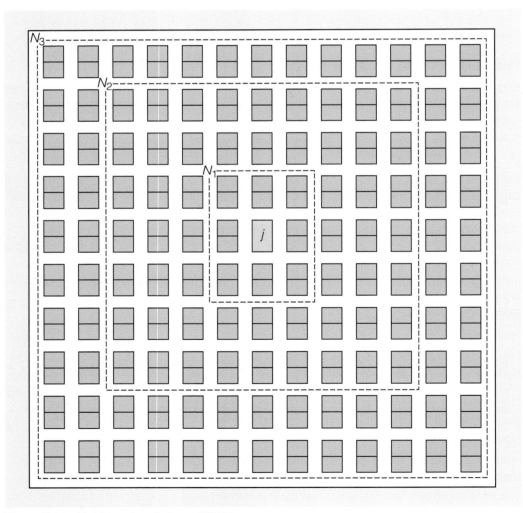

Figure 3.16 Neighbourhoods in an SOFM

Now, let's mark out a certain area, or *neighbourhood*, N_1 around j, and assume that the lateral connections between j and the units in this neighbourhood are all strongly positive, causing j to *excite* these units (and be excited by them, in turn). Further, we can mark out a wider neighbourhood N_2 around j's immediate excitatory area, to and from which all the lateral connections are negative: the units in this neighbourhood will *inhibit* (and be inhibited by) j. Beyond this, we can mark out a third area N_3 with very weak positive connections to the units in it. This set-up is summarised by the well-known 'Mexican hat' function, illustrated in Figure 3.17. The connections between j and the units in N_1 are an example of *lateral excitation*; those between j and N_2, *lateral inhibition*.

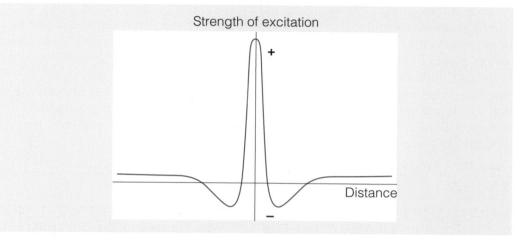

Figure 3.17   The Mexican hat function

Now, suppose we have set up similar neighbourhoods for every unit in the lattice, and we then apply a vector of some kind to the input layer, making j become active – or rather, slightly more active than other units in the map. Think about this question for a moment.

Exercise 3.5

What would you expect to happen as a result of j's becoming active?

Discussion ....

j will excite the units in its immediate neighbourhood, which will then feed back their excitation to j and j's activity will tend to grow. At the same time, j will be inhibiting units further away, preventing them from exciting the units in their neighbourhoods. After a short period of time, a bubble of activity will form around j, while other areas of the layer are forced into quiescence.

Dissimilar though the two processes may seem at first glance, I think this once again demonstrates the principle of self-organisation. An initial fluctuation gets amplified by positive feedback, suppressing other activity though negative feedback, until it comes to dominate the entire scene. In our neural example here, when we apply the input vector, it is likely that a number of units in the layer will start to become active. Then a battle will start between positive and negative feedback until one unit and its neighbourhood becomes dominant and smothers all the others. Simulations indicate that this is exactly what happens.

Computer Exercise 3.1

Load up and complete Computer Exercise 3.1 on the course DVD.

Exactly the same principles apply in lattices of one, two and three dimensions. However, two-dimensional systems are the most common. I'll concentrate on these from now on. As usual, the main question is how such systems can be trained to a state in which they produce the desired kind of clustering behaviour. We can now look at this in some detail.

Training self-organising feature maps

Actually implementing systems with lateral inhibition can be difficult and costly in computer power for systems of any size, although with modern computers it can be done. However, Kohonen devised an elegant shortcut. He envisaged an SOFM as a simple sheet of units, without lateral connections, fed by a layer of dummy units – the topology I illustrated earlier in Figure 3.10. Then, by combining the idea of a neighbourhood with the competitive learning process for achieving vector quantisation that you've just studied, he was able to simulate the kind of clustering behaviour observed in the cortex in a lattice of artificial units. It's best to start, therefore, by reflecting briefly on competitive learning.

SAQ 3.5

Think back to the process for competitive learning you looked at in the section on vector quantisation in artificial maps a few pages back. What are the three basic phases of this learning procedure?

ANSWER..

After the weights are initialised, a vector is applied and then:

▶ a pattern is presented at the input;

▶ a winning unit is identified;

▶ the weight vector of this winning unit is then modified.

This pattern is repeated for every vector in the training set.

We can call these three steps the *presentation*, *competition* and *adaptation* steps, respectively. To these, Kohonen added a *clustering* step, between competition and adaptation. Taken together with initialisation of the weights, then, SOFM learning is a five-step process, as follows:

1   *Initialisation.* Here, the weights of the connections between the input layer and the map are set to random values. In practice, SOFMs are very sensitive to the initial weight settings, so a certain amount of research has been done on what the ideal distribution of these initial weights should be. I'll return to this point a little later. One restriction, however, is that none of the weight vectors should be identical.

2   *Presentation.* In the supervised learning strategies you looked at in the last unit, the procedure was generally to start with the first pattern in the training set, then select the second, then the third, and so on sequentially through the set. However, remember we are dealing here with an unsupervised learning process, where the statistical distributions of data within the set are crucial – in fact, they are precisely what we want the network to discover. Consequently, the usual process with SOFMs is to select input vectors from the training set at random, or according to a certain pre-determined probability. From now on, we'll assume that inputs are selected randomly.

3   *Competition.* The learning procedure involves selecting a winning unit. As before, the winner is selected by using Equation 3.8, which is equivalent to Equation 3.9 if all vectors are normalised.

4   *Clustering.* Now, denoting the winning unit as m, we draw a symmetrical neighbourhood N_m around m containing the units that will participate in the adaptation that takes place in the next step. The neighbourhood will have a certain width d, and can be one of many different shapes, depending on the nature of the problem and the number of dimensions of the map. In a one-dimensional map, of course, the neighbourhood can only be a set of one or more units on either side of m; in a two-dimensional map, an area around it, as illustrated in Figure 3.15; and so on.

The main point, however, is that d *varies with time.* At the start of training, it may be wide enough to take in most of the units in the map. As the training process proceeds, after each cycle, or some multiple of cycles, through the entire training set, d is shrunk until, after many thousands of iterations, N may just contain the winning unit.

5   *Adaptation.* Here, the procedure is just a slight modification of the one you met in the discussion of competitive learning above. The weight vector of m and those of all the units i in the neighbourhood N_m of m are adjusted according to the rule:

$$\Delta \mathbf{w}_i = \eta(\mathbf{x} - \mathbf{w}_i) \qquad \text{for } i \in N_m \tag{3.11}$$

where η is a learning constant. Another important point: η also decreases with the number of iterations through the set and may also be made to depend on the size of the neighbourhood. In fact, Equation 3.11 might be rewritten as:

$$\Delta \mathbf{w}_i = \alpha(d,t)(\mathbf{x} - \mathbf{w}_i) \qquad \text{for } i \in N_m \tag{3.12}$$

where $\alpha(d,t)$ is some decreasing function of the width of the neighbourhood at that time and the time step the algorithm has reached. This is usually referred to as a *neighbourhood function.* All sorts of functions have been proposed, but for simplicity I'm going to assume that η decays linearly with the time step and is independent of the width of the neighbourhood.

Summing up, then, let's consider for a moment the differences between the SOFM process and the supervised learning techniques you considered in the previous unit.

Exercise 3.6

Draw up a list of some of the major differences between the Kohonen learning process and a feedforward, supervised algorithm, such as backpropagation.

Discussion ....

There are lot of differing features one could single out. I identified four:

▶   no teaching input, and thus no error signals;

▶   weight adjustments only applied to a subset of the units;

▶   competition, together with the concept of a winning unit and its neighbourhood;

▶   parameters that change through time, such as the learning constant and the size of a neighbourhood.

You may have come up with alternatives.

We are now in a position to state the SOFM learning algorithm in full. Given a large training set of vectors x_1, x_2, x_3 ... x_n, the algorithm can be set out as follows.

SOFM training algorithm

1   Set the elements of the weight vectors w_j of all units j in the map to small random values.

2   Set an initial neighbourhood width of d ; set the learning constant η to some small initial value.

3   Extract a vector x_i, where i is a randomly generated number, from the training set and clamp the activations of the input units to the values of its elements.

4   Identify the winning unit in the map, using the criterion that the winner is the unit whose weight vector is the minimum Euclidean distance from x_i:

$$\|w_m - x_i\| = \min_j \|w_j - x_i\|$$

5   For all units j in the neighbourhood N_m, width d, of m, adjust the weight vectors according to the rule:

$$\Delta w_j = \eta(x_i - w_j) \qquad \text{for } j \in N_m$$

6   If a certain pre-decided number of time steps have passed then decrement η and d.

7   If the weights have shown no significant change in the last cycle through the training set then terminate   // map is fully formed

else go to step 3   // map is still forming

The number of steps that pass before decrementing η and d are generally settled on by trial and error. I'll discuss these questions shortly, but in the meantime it would also be useful to attempt another visualisation of what is happening during the learning process. Kohonen himself offered a very striking and suggestive way of doing this in his 1982 paper in which he first introduced the concepts of the lateral inhibition and of the SOFM. Adapting his picture slightly, we can go back to an idea I discussed briefly in Section 2.3 of the previous unit, that of a *weight space*. Suppose we have a very simple SOFM system, comprising an input layer of just two units and a two-dimensional lattice of 6 × 8 = 48 units making up the map. The weight vector of every unit will then just be a two-dimensional vector with elements w_1 and w_2. This gives us an easily visualised weight space of two dimensions. Now let's plot the initial weight vectors of each of the 48 units in this space: since the weights have been set to random values we would expect them to be dotted randomly around the space, as indeed they are (see Figure 3.18(a)). The vectors are clustered near the centre of the space as their elements were all started off as small random values. In the figure, I've also drawn a line between each unit and its immediate neighbours on either side, and above and below it, in the grid. Again, since the weight vectors are completely random, you can see there is no obvious relation between the vector's position in the space and its unit's position in the lattice, resulting in a confused mass of lines.

Now let's consider what happens as training proceeds. Figures 3.18 (b) through to (d) show the map gradually 'unfolding' as the weights grow and move around the space, towards the positions of points, or clusters of points, indicated by the training set. By the end of training, each weight vector has come to occupy a position in the space that preserves the neighbourhood ordering of the grid.

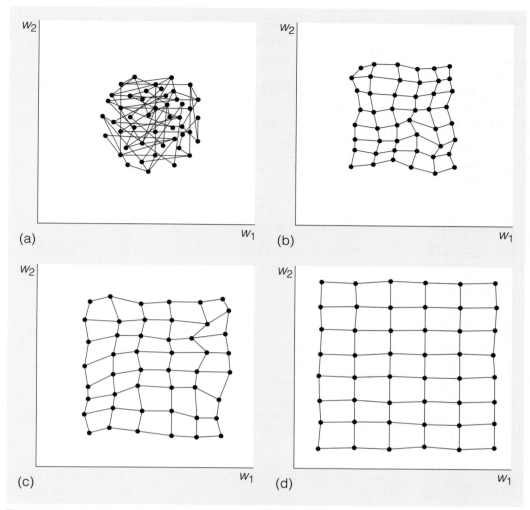

Figure 3.18　Evolution of weight vectors under SOFM training

Computer Exercise 3.2

Load up and complete Computer Exercise 3.2 on the course DVD.

You may well have concluded from the computer exercise that the success or failure of SOFM training is much more sensitively dependent on the selection of the values of key parameters than the algorithms you encountered in the previous unit. I think this is true. It is worth spending a brief while considering these factors.

SOFM learning – factors affecting performance

In my experience, working with real SOFMs can be a lot trickier than the theory suggests. Now that you have concluded an exercise involving such a system, this is a good time to reflect on some of the factors that seem most to affect the performance of SOFM learning.

Exercise 3.7

List some of the factors that you felt most affect the performance of SOFM learning, based on your understanding of the theory covered above, and your experiences with such a network.

Discussion ....

I thought the most important parameters were possibly:

1   the initialisation values of the weights;

but definitely:

2   the neighbourhood width and its rate of diminution;

3   the learning constant and its rate of diminution;

4   the number of iterations of the algorithm.

These seem to me to cover most of the key factors governing the success or failure of clustering behaviour in an SOFM.

There is a whole range of options for these. Let's now discuss what theory and the experience of other researchers has to tell us about these options.

1   *Initialisation values of the weights.* There doesn't seem to be a great deal of agreement here, except for the general consensus that weights should be set initially to small random values and that the weight vectors must all be different. However, with such a starting point it is always possible that the map may stagnate, or weight vectors get stranded in isolated regions, and thus fail to form clusters. Robert Hecht-Nielsen has suggested an alternative approach, with all vectors starting at the value:

$$\mathbf{w}_i = \frac{1}{\sqrt{n}}[1,1,\ldots 1]^T \tag{3.13}$$

and training with an initially very small learning constant.

Before considering the other three key parameters in the list in Exercise 3.7, we need to look a little more closely at the exact way in which the map adapts under training. Kohonen has pointed to two semi-distinct phases:

▶   the **self-organising phase**, in which the unfolding and ordering of the map depicted in Figure 3.17 above takes place; this is followed by

▶   the **convergence phase**, in which the map is fine-tuned and an accurate representation of the statistical regularities in the data set is formed.

The choice of values for the key parameters depends on which phase of the adaptation process they are being applied in. Armed with this knowledge, we can now look at these.

2   *Neighbourhood width, d.* As I stated earlier, this should start large and gradually shrink as time passes. Theorists seem to agree that the width at the start of the ordering phase may encompass every unit in the map, but by the end of the self-organising phase it may simply enclose the winning unit alone, or perhaps the winning unit and one or two units around it. During the convergence phase, the neighbourhood should remain at this final size.

The rate at which *d* should diminish is a matter of rather more controversy. A simple linear rate of reduction may suffice, but some theorists suggest an exponential fall-off in value, so that the value of d_t of *d* at time step *t* is given by an equation such as:

$$d_t = d_0 e^{-t/\tau} \tag{3.14}$$

where τ is a constant and d_0 is the width of the neighbourhood at initialisation.

3   *Learning constant, η.* During the self-organising phase, this should start small – many theorists suggest 0.1 as a good initial value – but should fall to about 0.01. Once again, there is a choice between a linear or exponential rate of decrease, with some theorists favouring the same form as equation 3.14, namely:

$$\eta_t = \eta_0 e^{-t/\tau}$$

(3.15)

with τ a constant as before. During the convergence phase η should remain at about 0.01 and not be allowed to fall to 0.

4   *Number of iterations.* Remember that vector quantisation is a process of statistical discovery, which is likely to be a much slower process than supervised learning. Consequently, one must expect the training of a self-organising map to require many iterations. In many of the practical supervised learning examples you worked through in the previous unit, 500 iterations of the backpropagation algorithm may have been sufficient to provide good results. For an SOFM, a minimum of 1000 iterations has been suggested for the self-organisation phase and many, many more for convergence: Haykin recommends 500 times the number of units in the map as a minimum. Zurada suggests 100 000 iterations as probably necessary for the most effective regularity discovery.

The issue is clearly a complex one and can only be settled by experiment. You may have formed your own ideas about this in the course of Computer Exercise 3.2. So round off this theoretical section with a few conclusions of your own.

Exercise 3.8

Write a few sentences summarising your own experiences of SOFM training, in the light of what you've just read above.

Discussion ....

There are no right or wrong answers in neural networks. Neural systems are tricky to work with and, unlike conventional computer systems, don't always give the results theory tells us they should. It's important you should have drawn your own conclusions here.

Now I want to conclude the theoretical discussion with a few words about two variations on the theme of training an SOFM.

SOFM learning – batch map

Given the large number of iterations that are needed for full convergence of an SOFM, some way of speeding up the algorithm is very desirable, especially when dealing with the kind of huge map you will meet in the next case study. To this end, Kohonen's group has developed a variation on the algorithm, in which groups of input vectors are gathered together and dealt with in a batch.

First of all, consider a single unit *i* in the map with weight vector $\mathbf{w}_i$. Now let V_i be the set of all the input vectors $\mathbf{x}$ that are close to $\mathbf{w}_i$ – that is within the Voronoi cell that $\mathbf{w}$ represents. Now the algorithm has three principal stages: initialisation, quantisation and smoothing, as follows.

Batch map

1   *Initialisation:* set up the weight vectors of the map units; this can be done randomly or with some very rough initial ordering.

2   For each unit *i* in the map, create a list *L* of the input vectors that lie within its Voronoi cell V_i.

3   *Quantisation*: for each unit i in the map, calculate the average vector of all the vectors in the list in L.

4   *Smoothing*: for each unit i in the map, calculate a new weight vector $\mathbf{w}'_i$ for it, by taking the average of the averages (calculated in step 3) of all the units within a certain neighbourhood of i.

5   If the weights have shown no further significant change then terminate, else go to step 2.

In step 4, the kind of decreasing neighbourhood function illustrated in Equation 3.14 may be used. I've kept it simple here, to illustrate the main point.

SOFM learning – learning vector quantisation

You've already seen that the learning of an SOFM falls naturally into two phases: *self-organisation* and *convergence*.

SAQ 3.6

Note down very briefly what happens in each of these phases.

ANSWER...

In the self-organising phase, the network makes its discovery of the basic regularities in the data set, forming itself into clusters. In the convergence phase, the map fine-tunes itself, building accurate Voronoi regions and vectors.

Learning vector quantisation (LVQ) is a supervised learning technique for fine-tuning the map during (or after) the convergence phase. Here is how it works.

Assume that we have, as before, a very large set of input vectors $\mathbf{x}_1, \mathbf{x}_2, \mathbf{x}_3 \dots \mathbf{x}_n$, and a map that has formed a set of Voronoi vectors $\mathbf{w}_1, \mathbf{w}_2, \mathbf{w}_3 \dots \mathbf{w}_k$, with n being very much larger than k, and each $\mathbf{w}$ acting as a code for a certain class of input C. Since LVQ is a supervised learning technique, we require a teaching input, so each input vector $\mathbf{x}_i$ is accompanied by a label C_i giving the class that the vector actually belongs to. Now the LVQ algorithm becomes a classic case of supervised learning.

LVQ training algorithm

1   Choose a vector $\mathbf{x}_i$, where i is a randomly generated number, from the training set and clamp the activations of the input units to the values of its elements.

2   Identify the winning unit in the map using the criterion that the winner is the unit whose weight vector is the minimum Euclidean distance from $\mathbf{x}_i$:

$$\|\mathbf{w}_m - \mathbf{x}_i\| = \min_i \|\mathbf{w}_i - \mathbf{x}_i\|$$

3   If the class C_m indicated by the vector w_m is the same as the teaching input C_i given for $\mathbf{x}_i$ then alter $\mathbf{w}_m$ to move it closer to $\mathbf{x}_i$ using the formula:

$$\mathbf{w}'_m = \mathbf{w}_m + \eta(\mathbf{x}_i - \mathbf{w}_m)$$

4   If the class C_m indicated by the vector $\mathbf{w}_m$ is not the same as the teaching input C_i given for $\mathbf{x}_i$ then alter $\mathbf{w}_m$ to move it away from $\mathbf{x}_i$ using the formula:

$$\mathbf{w}'_m = \mathbf{w}_m - \eta(\mathbf{x}_i - \mathbf{w}_m)$$

5   If the weights have shown no significant change in the last cycle through the training set then terminate   *// map is fully tuned*

     else go to step 1   *// map is still tuning*

Once again, various ways of decreasing the value of η as training proceeds have been suggested. However, I will not look at these here.

Applications of SOFMs

Kohonen's model is a huge simplification of the natural reality, as all neural models are. However, he and others have been able to show that numerous practical systems can be based on it. In this section I'm going to look briefly at one area in which SOFMs have been successfully applied to a serious practical problem: *data mining*.

As you read through Section 2 at the start of this unit, I hope that you sensed a faint echo of familiarity. Remember that in that section I looked at the basic question of discovering statistically significant relationships within a large data set. Does this seem at all familiar? If it doesn't, let me remind you of Case Study 3.4 of Unit 3 of Block 3, where exactly the same issue came up. This is the question of *data mining*. Most large institutions, such as banks, universities, manufacturing companies, publishers, and so on, maintain colossal databases of information. But perhaps 'information' is the wrong term here: these databases contain mountains of *facts*, but the *information* is hidden among these facts, in statistical properties of the entire collection. To use the slightly misleading analogy, the useful information has to be *mined out*, meaning that the information has to be discovered inside the mountain.

Data mining has been usefully defined as:

> Nontrivial extraction of implicit, previously unknown and potentially useful information from data, or the search for relationships and global patterns that exist in databases.

> Source: Klevecz (1999)

Data mining is most often carried out using statistical techniques, such as stepwise regression. However, it should be clear from the discussion of SOFMs that you've just worked through that these systems are a plausible alternative.

Before looking at the case study, here is a rather general question, but one worth considering.

Exercise 3.9

Can you see any possible pitfalls in the whole process of data mining, no matter what techniques are used to carry it out?

Discussion ....

I think the most striking potential pitfall is this: that one might discover regularities within the data that simply do not correspond to reality – in other words, the discovery process might *impose* a view on the data that is not justified. A related concern is that relationships are discovered that are simply a matter of pure chance, rather than arising from any real relationships existing in the data.

Data mining is big business at the time I'm writing this; but – for the reasons given in the discussion above – it has plenty of detractors, too. Here's one pithy comment I found on the Web, commenting on data mining as a means of analysing sporting results:

> Data mining is the sports-betting equivalent of sitting a huge number of monkeys down at keyboards, and then reporting on the monkeys who happened to type actual words.

Source: http://sports.betfirms.com/glossary.shtml

For this reason, data mining is sometimes contemptuously referred to as **data dredging**. There is clearly an important debate to be had here, but unfortunately no space to enter into it in M366.

Case study 3.1: WEBSOM

A colossal amount of printed material now exists in electronic form. Not only has much of the world's literature been recorded electronically, but there are also innumerable vast databases of other kinds of documents: encyclopedias, patents, scientific publications, and so on. Although it is usually possible to search these databases by means of keywords and catalogues, the results are often unsatisfactory. Long lists of hits may appear in no particular order, and with no clear means of telling to what extent any item in such a list relates to the searcher's actual needs.

What is really required is that textual databases, and thus the results of searches on them, should be *organised* in some way that is significant to those who use them. And since users of such databases are almost exclusively interested in the *content* of the documents contained in them, then ideally this organisation should in some way be based on content. Moreover, users are likely to want to know about significant relationships between the subject-matter of documents, and to be able to retrieve texts by relevance and similarity. For instance, if I enquire in an encyclopedia database about 'whales', I may also be interested in other documents about 'marine life' or 'mammals'; but I'm unlikely to care about texts on 'flying saucers' or 'cholesterol'. And finally, the average user will probably be perplexed when a search engine simply supplies a long list of hits, even if they are sorted according to some broad measure of relevance. In general, searchers want query results to be visualisable in some useful way, browsable and easily readable; so an excellent user interface to the query system is needed, one which displays results in a way in which the underlying organisation is clear.

Imposing an order based on the content of documents in a textual database is a task that can, in principle, be done manually, but may require superhuman amounts of effort. The kinds of databases I'm talking about here are typically enormous, perhaps running to many millions of documents. So, as always, some way of automating the process of bringing order to a collection is an urgent need. And document collections may have some immunity to the main potential pitfall of data mining – the problem of data dredging for spurious relationships you looked at earlier.

SAQ 3.7

Why do you think mining document collections might be less likely to throw up spurious relationships?

ANSWER..

Because documents are made of words, and words have inbuilt semantic relations to one another. Granted, these are often fuzzy and ambiguous, but it is much harder to imagine completely arbitrary relationships between them. This is not true of numerical data.

SOFMs seem on the face of it to be excellent candidates for automated pre-ordering of a document collection. As you've seen, they are capable of discovering relationships between items in large data sets and of mapping these topographically on a (typically) two-dimensional lattice. The application of SOFM models and strategies to the pre-ordering and search of massive document databases is the goal of WEBSOM.

Work on WEBSOM (see the M366 website and course DVD for access details) is based at the Neural Networks Research Centre at Helsinki University of Technology and is led by Teuvo Kohonen. Their research into mapping large data collections has, at the time of writing, been going on for about eleven years. In the group's own words:

> WEBSOM is a full-text information retrieval and exploration method for large document collections. Self-Organizing Map (SOM) is used to statistically analyse relations between the words, and then, based on this analysis, to create a document map. Similar documents become positioned close to each other on the document map. Therefore, this document landscape provides a good basis for search and exploration.
>
> Source: Lagus et al. (1996)

In pursuing this goal, the group has had to tackle three main problems:

1 finding an economical means of encoding the documents in a suitable form for neural network processing;

2 developing very efficient algorithms for building and fine-tuning the map;

3 constructing a user interface that will enable users to browse search results effectively.

It is on the first two of these problems that the group has had to concentrate their main efforts. Why? For the simple reason that the raw numbers involved are *huge*. For a start, the sheer numbers of documents in the collections that have been given the WEBSOM treatment are enormous, varying from 115 000 long articles from the *Encyclopaedia Britannica*, through 1 124 134 texts from 85 Usenet newsgroups (a total of 245 592 634 words), up to the current (2006) staggering record of 6 840 568 documents, a database of abstracts of patent applications (about 850 million words). To add to this, the range of vocabulary to be found in such collections is also vast: the *Encyclopaedia Britannica* articles embodied a vocabulary of nearly 326 000 different words, while the patent abstracts altogether used 733 129! To map such a huge number of documents and range of vocabulary was found to require an enormous lattice of neurons: 1 002 240 were required for the largest database.

Dealing with numbers like this is very difficult computationally, even on the most up-to-date computers. Supercomputers and grid computation could probably handle data volumes of this size, but the WEBSOM group took the line from the start that the formation of the document map and its subsequent browsing should all be possible on general-purpose machines. This meant that at every stage they had to concentrate on the most efficient and economical strategies for carrying out steps 1 and 2 above. Let's now look at some of the approaches they took.

4.3   Encoding the documents

Case study 3.1 – WEBSOM (continued)

There is general agreement that an excellent way to compare the content of one document with that of another is through an analysis of the actual words used in them. One way to do this is to build a **word histogram** of each document. Assuming the two texts both draw on a common vocabulary of, say, 100 000 words, then the word histogram of each will be a vector with 100 000 elements, one for each possible word, with a 0 if the word represented by that element is not present in the document, and a 1 if it is. More sophisticated variations on this basic scheme are possible: elements can be weighted to reflect the number of times the word appears. The similarity between the word histograms of the two documents can then be measured, using one of a number of distance measures, as described in Section 2 above.

A word histogram would be a suitable *form* to serve as an input vector to an SOFM, but working with vectors of this *size* is quite out of the question, especially in view of the number of such vectors involved, and the amount of fine-tuning an SOFM requires. Some way of cutting down the vector size without too much loss of information was urgently necessary.

One obvious starting point was to decrease the size of the *vocabulary*, since this determines the dimensionality of the histogram vector. The WEBSOM group found that by pre-processing all of the documents, to remove:

▶ words of no semantic interest ('a', 'the', 'and', etc.);

▶ grammatical variations ('dog'/'dogs', etc.);

▶ numerical expressions;

▶ common words, with little discriminatory power ('important', 'main', 'thing', etc.);

▶ words which appeared in fewer than five documents;

they were able to make substantial reductions. For example, the vocabulary of the Usenet document database, was cut from 1 127 184 to about 63 000 words.

But vectors of this size are still far too large for an SOFM running on a standard computer. The WEBSOM group tried several methods of reducing the size still further, two of which deserve mention here:

▶ *Word-cluster coding*. The initial approach, used in the early days of WEBSOM, was to map each original document vector onto a relatively small set of *word clusters*. These clusters were created by using an SOFM. Here is how it was done: each word in the vocabulary was encoded as a vector consisting of three sections, basically:

Average context before	The word	Average context after

with each section represented as a string of numbers. In one experiment, these vectors were then used as input to an SOFM with 315 units and the network trained using the SOFM training algorithm you studied above. 315 clusters of related words formed. Figure 3.19 shows a portion of the map, with some of the word clusters illustrated.

This map was then used to encode each document into a much more compact form. Each word in the document was input to the map and the index of the word-cluster unit that activated most strongly was recorded for every word. A 315-element *word-cluster histogram* was then built, each element of which represented the number of times one particular word-cluster had activated. This much more tractable vector could then be used as an input to the main document map.

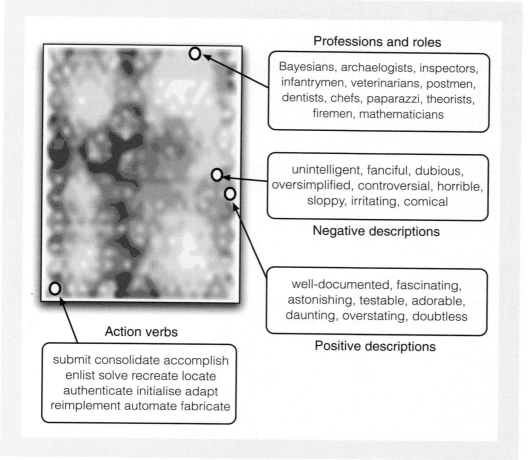

Figure 3.19   Illustration of the word-cluster map

▶ *Random projection.* Although it proved quite successful, word-cluster encoding was later abandoned in favour of a much simpler and more computationally tractable technique: *random projection*. Without going into too much detail here, each huge document vector n_i was multiplied by a matrix R to give a much smaller *projection vector* x_i, R being a sparse matrix, consisting mostly of 0s, with a few 1s scattered through each column. It was discovered that the similarity measure of any pair of the projection vectors (x_1, x_2) was very much the same as that between the original word histogram vectors (n_1, n_2) – little if any discrimination information had been lost. Using this technique, the group were able to reduce word histogram vectors of dimension 43 222 to projection vectors of dimension 500. Still large, but quite usable for training the SOFM.

But as I stated above, even though input vectors could be much reduced, the sheer numbers of these, and the huge size of the lattices required to map the entire document set, were also enormous. Techniques to speed up the formation of the map under training were needed too.

4.4 Training the map

Case study 3.1: WEBSOM (continued)

It was into the training algorithms used for the map that the WEBSOM group poured most ingenuity over the years. It's only possible for me to give a brief summary of some of the shortcuts they found. The researchers used a combination of the following strategies:

▶ *Batch training.* Standard SOFM training was much too slow for the datasets and lattices involved in WEBSOM work. The batch map training strategy I outlined earlier was used in all experiments.

Now, recall from our discussions of SOFM learning above that the training of an SOFM falls into two phases: self-organisation and convergence. For the self-organisation phase, the group developed the following strategies:

▶ *Growing the map.* Rather than starting with a full-size, dense map of many hundreds of thousands of units, the process started with a much smaller and sparser map, which was self-organised and fine-tuned. This small map was then increased in size by adding new units between existing ones. The weight vectors of these new units were estimated using distance measurements from the weight vectors of units around it, as illustrated in Figure 3.20. In the diagram, a new unit has been added and its weight vector estimated on the basis of the weights of the units around it. The diagram also shows where the vectors of other additional units might lie in the denser map, given certain assumptions about the homogeneity of the training set.

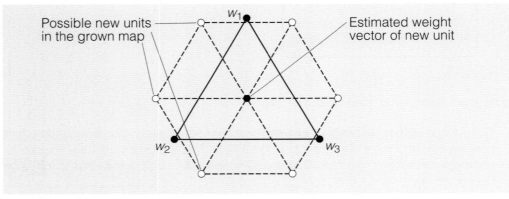

Figure 3.20   Adding new units according to estimated weight

In most experiments, this process of growing the map and then fine-tuning it was repeated many times, until the map had reached its final size. For example, in the development of the map of patent applications, the initial map contained only 435 units and grew by three increments to its final size of over one million units.

▶ *Exploiting 0s.* Since the input vectors contain a very large number of 0s (many of the words in the vocabulary will simply not appear at all in a typical document), and these naturally contribute nothing to the calculation of the winning units, the WEBSOM researchers found ways of excluding all 0s from the computations, greatly speeding up the process.

And as you learned, the convergence phase is likely to be very lengthy, even for small networks, so the group took some of the following steps to speed this up:

▶ *Fast searching for winners.* Finding the winning unit in a one million unit map can itself be a computationally expensive operation. The team devised two shortcuts:

▶ To find the winning unit the first time an input vector was presented, the algorithm simply estimated the area of the map in which it is likely to be found, using a similar technique to the one illustrated in Figure 3.21, and then doing a local search in that area. As soon as the winning unit is found, a pointer to it is stored with the input vector.

▶ On future presentations of each input vector, this stored pointer is used to locate the winning unit. The algorithm then searches locally in the area around this unit for a new winner, if any.

▶ *Parallel computation.* The algorithm proved suitable for parallelisation and in some experiments was carried out on a six-processor Silicon Graphics machine. This obviously speeded up performance markedly.

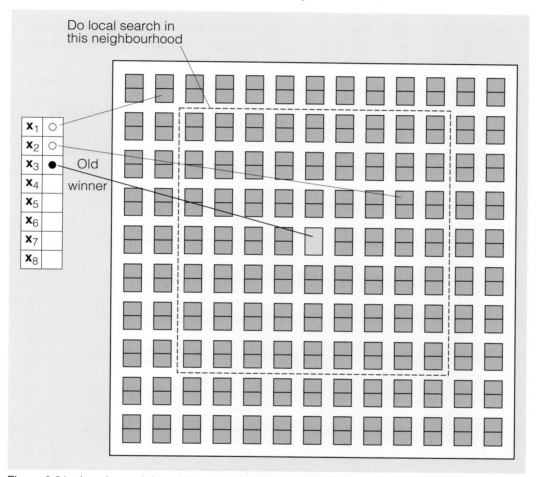

Figure 3.21   Local search in neighbourhood of previous winner

The group also used a number of other statistical techniques to improve the efficiency of encoding and to speed up computation. By combining all the shortcuts I've outlined above, the group were able to cut the processing time required to a tenth of what straightforward, non-batch SOFM computation would require. Nevertheless, the preparation of the document map of the patent application database required six weeks (!) of processing time on a six-processor parallel machine.

Once the document map is finally prepared, though, recall that it is very swift, so querying and browsing can easily be done in real time. But as I remarked above, the effectiveness of the query and browsing will depend very much on the user interface that is devised for it. So finally, let's look at the WEBSOM browser.

4.5 The WEBSOM browser

Case study 3.1: WEBSOM (continued)

WEBSOM seeks to exploit the topographical nature of the map in the browser. Our familiarity with maps and the often visual nature of the way we understand the world works very much in favour of such an approach. When two concepts, or documents, or pieces of information are *similar* to one another, a natural way to represent them is *close together* in space. This is the whole idea of a map.

The WEBSOM browser is a set of HTML pages through which users can query and browse the final map. On first accessing the root page, the user is presented with a visualisation of the map, as in Figure 3.22.

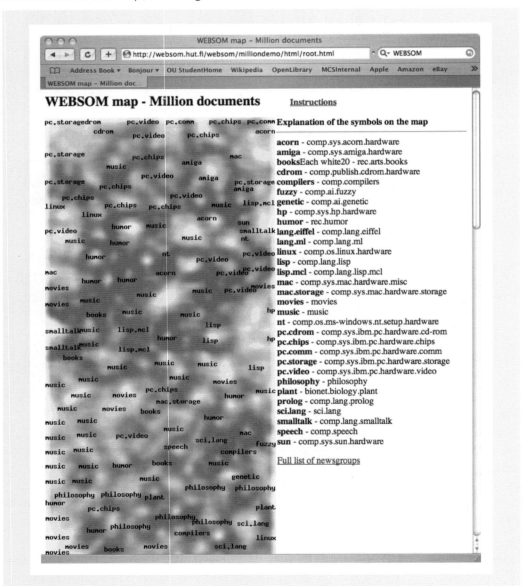

Figure 3.22   Map of the Usenet collection

Obviously, with many hundreds of thousands of units, very little detail is visible, although, as you can see from the figure some landmark keywords are provided. Users can search or explore in three ways:

▶ direct exploration through clicking and zooming;

▶ keyword search;

▶ content addressable search.

On clicking on any portion of the map, a new window appears, presenting a zoomed-in view of the area of the map around the point selected. Alternatively, users may enter keywords, or a fuller length query, such as 'Tell me about the philosophy of AI' (content addressable search). In either case, the underlying software transforms the query into a word histogram vector of exactly the same form as the ones used to train the system, which is then presented to the input of the map. The best activated units in the map are then marked by circles (see Figure 3.23). The width of each circle is an indication of how strong the activation at that point is. Clicking on one of the circles causes a zoom window to appear (see inset to Figure 3.23).

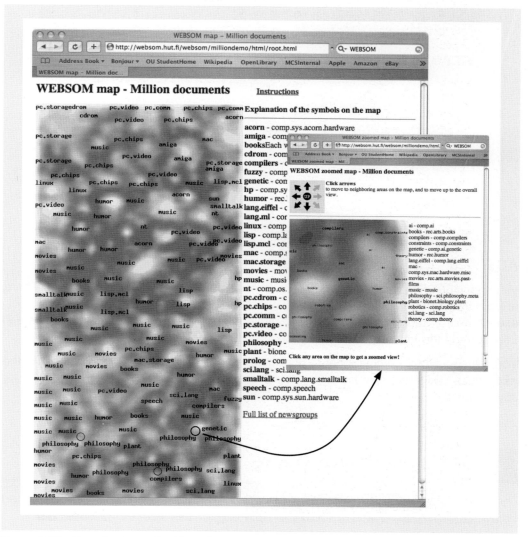

Figure 3.23   Zooming in on the Usenet map

Clicking on any point in the zoom window will cause another zoom in: up to three levels of zoom are provided, depending on the size of the map. When the lowest level is reached, individual units are visible, but not labelled. Clicking on one of these brings up a window displaying the documents available that are clustered at that unit, as illustrated in Figure 3.24. These can then be accessed and downloaded directly.

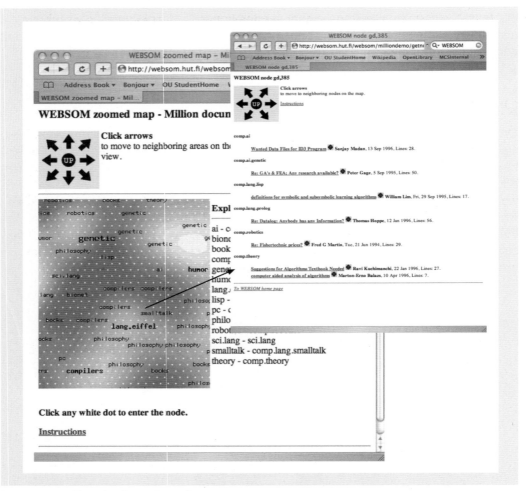

Figure 3.24   Zooming in on the sub-map

ACTIVITY 3.2

Visit the WEBSOM website (see the M366 website and course DVD for details). There are a number of demonstrations available there. Spend twenty minutes or so experimenting with these. At the time of writing, some of these are in Finnish, others in English, and the actual documents are not available from the demonstrations.

You will also find a complete set of publications giving greater detail about some of the techniques and strategies that I've outlined in this case study. These are all downloadable.

4.6   Other applications

There have been numerous other applications of SOFMs, some of which are described below.

Financial analysis and forecasting

SOFMs have been used for a huge range of financial and economic tasks, including:

▶   financial applications (analysis of financial statements, financial forecasting, selection of investment managers);

- ► economic applications (analysis of economic trends, mapping socio-economic development);
- ► marketing applications (customer profiling and scoring, analysis of customer preferences).

Optimisation

In theoretical work, self-organising maps have been used to tackle our old friend the TSP. *Cities* are represented as vectors on a two-dimensional plane, and a *tour* as a ring of units. Plotting the weight vectors of these units in weight space and initialising them with random values, we get the situation depicted in Figure 3.25(a). Then, applying a modified version of the SOFM training algorithm, the nodes move through weight space, converging on the points representing cities and eventually coming to represent a tour (see Figures 3.25 (b) to (d)).

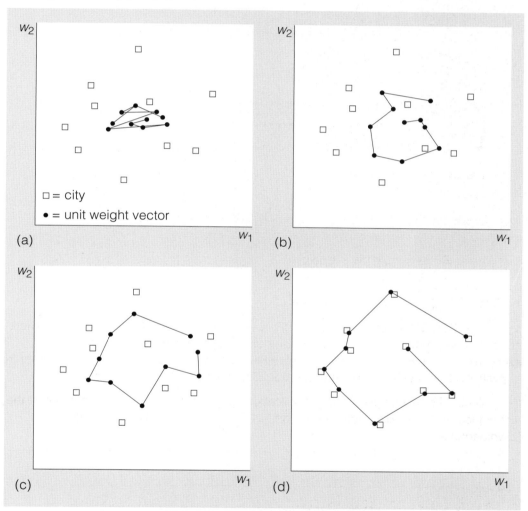

Figure 3.25   An SOFM evolving towards a solution tour for the TSP

In actual experiments based on a 1000-city set, results were very encouraging, with tour lengths being less than 3% greater than optimum.

Bioinformatics

As you probably know, one of the greatest research efforts currently underway in modern biology is to understand how genes function. One of the main techniques in the armoury of the modern genetic researcher is **gene clustering**, in which related genes are grouped in clusters. However, new analysis technologies have resulted in a mass of genomic data, so vast that it is difficult to extract meaningful clusters. SOFM techniques have been used in the clustering process, yielding good results.

In some work, SOFMs have been combined with strategies from particle swarm optimisation (see Block 3, Unit 3).

If you have time, you can follow up some of these in the following activity.

ACTIVITY 3.3 (optional)

On the course DVD you will find a number of links and resources to help you investigate further some of the applications of SOFMs. If you have time, browse through some of these.

5 Summary of Unit 3

In this unit, we've mainly been concerned with unsupervised learning. We started with an analysis of this idea, arriving at the conclusion that it was a process that looks for statistical regularities in large volumes of data, and that this can be brought about in artificial neural networks by relying on the phenomenon of self-organisation.

Unsupervised learning systems fall mostly into one of two categories: Hebbian learning and competitive, or winner-takes-all, learning. After a fairly short, and mostly theoretical, section on Hebbian learning, I then moved on to consider competitive learning in the rest of the unit. Starting with the idea of vector quantisation, we moved on to learn about a simple way of doing vector quantisation in a neural lattice. This led to a discussion of self-organising feature maps (SOFMs) and the related concept of lateral inhibition and excitation. You learned about methods of training SOFMs based on vector quantisation.

The unit ended with quite a lengthy discussion of the WEBSOM project, in which SOFMs have been applied to the mapping and browsing of massive document collections.

Look back at the learning outcomes for this unit and check these against what you think you can now do. Return to any section of the unit if you need to. We will then move on to our final challenge in this block: the whole question of *recurrence* and *time*.

Unit 4: It's about time: recurrence, dynamics and chaos

CONTENTS

1	Introduction to Unit 4	162
	What you need to study this unit	163
	Learning outcomes for Unit 4	164
2	Layered recurrent networks	165
2.1	Temporal inputs	165
2.2	General structure	167
2.3	Elman networks	169
2.4	Backpropagation through time	176
2.5	Making music with recurrent networks	178
3	Fully recurrent networks	188
3.1	Content addressable memory	188
3.2	Structure of fully recurrent networks	189
3.3	Brain-State-in-a-Box	194
3.4	The Hopfield model	196
3.5	Other examples of recurrent networks	202
4	Dynamic and chaotic neural networks	204
5	Summary of Unit 4	209
	References and further reading	213
	Acknowledgements	215
	Index for Block 4	216

1 Introduction to Unit 4

The previous three units have presented you with a wide variety of neural topologies and training methods. You've scanned a panorama of diverse ideas. However, there is one feature that all the systems you've studied so far have had in common; they are *static*. What do I mean by this? Well, consider a simple feedforward system: an input is clamped to the first layer, activation flows through the system to the output and stops there. There is a clearly determined pattern to the way the system behaves: the system takes an input, operates on it, produces an output and then stops, having reached its goal. Broadly speaking, this input–operation–output process is reminiscent of the sort of conventional computing we are all familiar with. Even when the weights of static systems are being developed under training, there are clear patterns of convergence, and proofs that the weights will eventually reach a stable final state. There is a clear goal and finishing point, with no unpredictability, no instability and no real evolution over time.

Natural systems of the kind you studied in Block 3 are not really like this at all. They exist *in time*. Animals move about, act, respond to a world that is continually changing. There is no final stable state, no ultimate goal that an animal is seeking, and no stopping either, as the world never stops changing around it. Interesting and novel though they are, there is something unrealistic – in terms of natural intelligence – about static neural networks.

The issue here, therefore, seems to be how neural networks can be made to handle considerations of *time*. In this unit, we'll take up the theme of time, as I introduce and discuss one or two varieties of *recurrent network*. I introduced you to the concept of a recurrent network in Unit 1 of this block. First of all, let's try to recap some of the points I made there.

SAQ 4.1

What is a recurrent network?

ANSWER...

A recurrent network is one that has at least one *feedback* connection (contrast this with feedforward networks). Units do not generally feed directly back to themselves.

And, as you also learned in Unit 1, the behaviour of recurrent networks is in sharp contrast to the stable behaviour of, say, a feedforward system or a lattice.

SAQ 4.2

What is peculiar about the behaviour of a recurrent network that contrasts with that of a conventional, feedforward system?

ANSWER...

Recurrent systems generally behave quite differently from feedforward systems and lattices, the behaviour of which is relatively stable and predictable. As you learned in Unit 1, recurrent networks are generally *dynamic*, their state *evolving* over time, and often in unpredictable ways. This makes them difficult to work with and to reason about.

In this unit, I'll try to scratch the surface of some of these difficulties and to show how neural networks can be developed that are capable of handling time. But the phrase 'handling time' needs quite a bit of clarification before we can move on. What can it mean to claim that a neural system is capable of 'handling time'? Briefly, I think it can mean two things:

1   that the system is able to deal with inputs whose main significance is their pattern of *change over time*; and/or

2   that the state of the system itself *evolves as time passes*.

If this still seems a bit obscure, I hope things will become clearer when we get down to considering actual cases. Here is a rough plan of the path ahead for this unit. In the next section, I want to consider types of networks in which the basic multi-layer, feedforward topology has been adapted to cope with inputs that evolve in time, as in point 1 above. I've called these systems collectively **layered recurrent networks**. I'll principally be focusing on one such a system, known as an **Elman network** – its topology, (supervised) training and capabilities. I'll also discuss some of the problems that arise in layered recurrent networks, and a potential solution to them in the **long short-term memory** (**LSTM**). Along the way, to illustrate the theoretical points, we will look at one particular application of recurrent networks – the composition of music.

Then, in Section 3, I will move on to talk about a different kind of recurrent topology, one without layers, and with much denser recurrent connections than are generally found in simple recurrent networks. I've called these **fully recurrent networks**. In order to talk sensibly about them it will be necessary to start by introducing a bit of terminology. This will open the way to discuss two powerful theoretical models: the **Brain-State-in-a-Box** system of John Anderson and the model introduced by John Hopfield (look back at Unit 1 of this block for an introduction to Hopfield and his work), now known – naturally enough – as a **Hopfield network**. Among other properties, the state of systems such as these evolves over time. We'll look in some detail at how this works, at the training of Hopfield networks and at their computational power and limitations.

Hopfield networks belong to a much broader category of systems (not limited to neural networks) known as **dynamic systems**. One property of certain kinds of dynamic system is **chaos**, a word that has been much on people's lips in the last ten years (and often hopelessly misused). This is a difficult subject, but in the final section I am going to discuss, very briefly, the concept of chaos: how it arises in recurrent neural networks and how computer scientists are currently trying to harness it in practical systems. This will take us to the very frontiers of research.

What you need to study this unit

You will need the following course components, and will need to use your computer and internet connection for some of the exercises.

▶   this Block 4 text

▶   the course DVD.

LEARNING OUTCOMES FOR UNIT 4

After studying this unit, you will be able to:

4.1 draw up a set of bullet points detailing the problems for neural network training caused by inputs that are sequences ordered in time;

4.2 draw diagrams illustrating the topology of an Elman network and other layered recurrent topologies;

4.3 give examples of the applications of layered recurrent networks to practical problems;

4.4 draw up a set of bullet points explaining possible features of network evolution of a recurrent system: attractors, periodic attractors, transients and dynamic behaviour;

4.5 describe in a paragraph, with illustrative diagrams, the structure and function of the Brain-State-in-a-Box model;

4.6 describe in a paragraph, with illustrative diagrams, the structure and function of the Hopfield models;

4.7 summarise how a fully recurrent network can be used as a simple content addressable memory system and to solve optimisation problems;

4.8 describe in one or two paragraphs the possible role of chaos in recurrent neural systems.

2 Layered recurrent networks

2.1 Temporal inputs

Let's start with an idea I raised in the Introduction above: that of an input which *evolves over time*. You've seen from Units 2 and 3 of this block that various kinds of neural network are very good at handling static inputs – a fixed pattern say – taking it and then classifying it, or recognising it, or completing it. Similarly, other kinds of network are excellent at discovering relationships within large *collections* of fixed patterns. But all the patterns that are used as inputs are predetermined; they have been prepared and finalised before they are used as input to the network. What about patterns which are *sequences over time*?

Exercise 4.1

Try to think of some sequences in everyday life in which the ordering of the parts in time is the most important feature.

Discussion ....

This might have seemed a difficult exercise at first, but in fact life abounds with such sequences. Here are two examples I thought of:

► *Sentences*. When I utter a sentence, I pronounce a string of words that come out one after another as time passes. The temporal ordering of the words in the sequence is crucially important in English: 'John loves Mary' may be true, but 'Mary loves John' may conceivably get you into trouble. And 'I live near the gasworks' makes perfect sense, whereas 'gasworks the near live I' makes none.

► *Stock market data*. On a much more practical note, financial analysts are always looking for trends. They will examine the performance of certain stocks over long periods of time in an attempt to predict which way they will move in the future. These kinds of data are usually known as **time series** information.

You probably thought of many others.

The conventional way to handle a sequence in a neural network is to pre-prepare it and present the entire sequence to the network as a whole. Essentially, what we are doing here is translating the *time* aspect of the sequence into a representation in *space*. The first event is the first element in the input vector, the second event is the second element, and so on (see Figure 4.1).

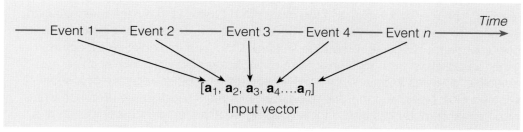

Figure 4.1   Sequence evolving in time

SAQ 4.3

Why would it be impossible to represent a temporal sequence as a series of input vectors, $\mathbf{x}_1$, $\mathbf{x}_2$, $\mathbf{x}_3$ ... $\mathbf{x}_n$, applied one after the other to a conventional static network?

ANSWER...

The problem is that the network *has no memory*. With each new input, it starts afresh, retaining no trace of any previous inputs.

However, there are considerable drawbacks to coding of time information spatially. The computer scientist Jeffrey L. Elman has suggested three:

▶ It means that there has to be an upper limit on how long the pattern sequences can be and (worse) that all sequences have to be the same length.

▶ It is impossible to distinguish between patterns that represent the same sequence shifted in time, and patterns representing quite different sequences. For example, consider these two vectors:

[1 1 1 0 0 0 1 1 1 0 0 0]

[0 0 0 1 1 1 0 0 0 1 1 1]

These certainly look as if they might represent the same sequence, but with the pattern shifted three time steps. But do they? We could certainly train a network to recognise them as being the same sequence. But then this would make it very difficult to accommodate new patterns that were quite similar to either of the above, and close to them in Euclidean space, but which represent different sequences.

▶ It's unrealistic. All the psychological evidence is that humans do not process sequences in this way.

Since our concern here is with natural intelligence, it's worth expanding that last point briefly. Returning to my example of sentences in natural language as sequences of words ordered in time, quickly read through the following little sentences:

The old man the boats.

When Fred eats food gets thrown.

Mary gave the child the dog bit a bandage.

That Jill is never here hurts.

Now think about this question for a moment.

Exercise 4.2

How did you feel as you read these sentences? Why are they difficult to make sense of at first? Jot down a few thoughts about this.

Discussion ....

If you're like me you probably felt a slight feeling of discomfort as you read each sentence for the first time. They are certainly not that easy to understand at first reading. The reason for this, and the discomfort, I think, is that each one raises an *expectation* and then lets you down. Take the first one, for example, and consider how you read it over time. I read the first word 'the' and immediately expected either an adjective or a noun next. Sure enough, the next word 'old' is an adjective, so I was happy. What next? Again, either another adjective or a noun seemed most likely, and the due appearance of 'man' satisfied me. But then what was I expecting? By this time, I think you'll agree, there is strong anticipation of a verb. But all I got was another determiner, 'the', and suddenly I was lost. What had happened?

The process I've described above was almost certainly unconscious. But again, if you are at all like me, what you probably did next was to quite consciously retrace your steps back along the sentence to find the place where things might have gone wrong. Eventually, I got back to 'old'. It wasn't an adjective, after all: it was a noun, meaning that 'man' had to be a verb. From that point, I was then able to read forward again and make sense of the sentence.

You'll see that the other sentences have much the same structure and play exactly the same trick: they gradually increase your expectation and then let you down. For this reason, they are often called **garden path sentences**, as they lead you up the garden path and abandon you there. They are quite fun; but I hope you appreciate the serious point I'm trying to make. They work the way they do because our understanding of a sentence evolves over *time*, as it is being uttered or read. We don't see the sentence all as one whole after it has been completed. We build up as we go along, we are all the time making predictions and guesses. It's all about time.

A moment's reflection suggests that much human cognition, and probably animal cognition, is structured in this way. In Block 2, for example, there was considerable discussion of the way Symbolic AI tackles *planning* – which was basically to work out a plan in full and then execute it. But this seems extraordinarily unrealistic in terms of how we actually operate. Plans, like most of our actions, develop in real time as they are being executed and change continuously as the world changes about us. The temporal ordering of our experience is all important. But I don't want to labour the point any further here. We can now move on to consider neural networks that are structured to take account of this temporal ordering.

2.2 General structure

A simple recurrent network is, of course, a recurrent network, so we would expect it to have at least one feedback connection. One class of recurrent topologies exploits the power of multi-layer feedforward networks by combining their layered structure with feedback connections. I'll refer to these kinds of systems as **layered recurrent networks**. There are three basic types of layered recurrent network.

1   **Input–output networks**. These are made up of a multi-layer perceptron with a single output. This output is fed directly back to become part of the input. The output may be fed into a delay line so that many past inputs are included at once (see Figure 4.2). This is similar to one of the adaptive filter models you met in Case Study 2.1 in Unit 2 of this block.

2   **State space models**. I've illustrated a generic state space model in Figure 4.3. Here, the feedback connection is from one of the hidden units. The number of hidden units that feed back is known as the *order* of the network. The network in Figure 4.3 is therefore order 1.

3   **Recurrent multi-layer perceptrons**. These are a generalisation of the state space model, comprising a multi-layer perceptron with more than one hidden layer, the activation vector of each hidden layer being fed back into that layer (see Figure 4.4).

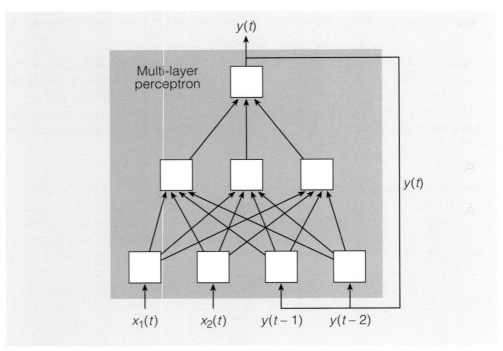

Figure 4.2   An input–output network

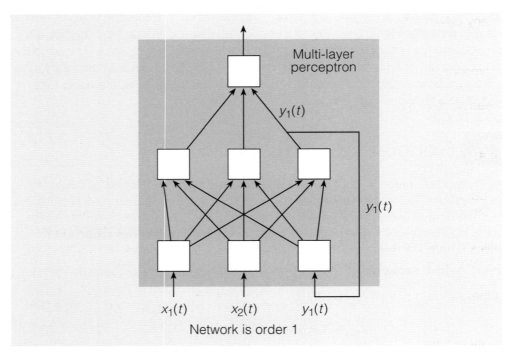

Figure 4.3   A state space model

Fairly clearly, things can get complicated here, so to give you some idea of the power of such systems I want to concentrate on one particular kind of state space model: the simple recurrent network, sometimes known, after its originator, as the *Elman network*.

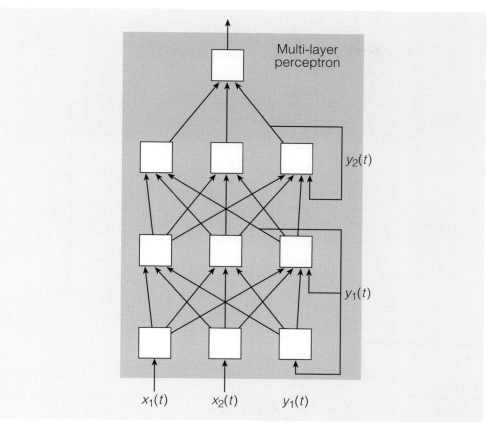

Figure 4.4   A recurrent multi-layer perceptron

2.3 | Elman networks

Elman was interested in *language* and in the temporal problems its processing by neural networks posed. And he was especially concerned with finding new ways of coding the kind of temporal information buried in language, in ways other than spatially pre-prepared input vectors. In his own words:

> The spatial representation of time ... treats time as an explicit part of the input. There is another, very different, possibility: Allow time to be represented by the effect it has on processing. This means giving the processing system dynamic properties that are responsive to temporal sequences. In short the network must be given memory.

> Source: Elman (1990)

An *Elman network* is a proposed solution to this problem. It is a state space model of order n, where n is the number of hidden units: in other words, all the hidden units feed back to become part of the input. This part of the input is known as the **context units**. The **local field** of a unit in the network is simply the net input from context units, internal units and external inputs. Figure 4.5 depicts a typical simple recurrent network: you'll note that *all* of the hidden units feed back into context units, making the network order 3.

Most of Elman's examples are based on issues of language. I'll look at two of these in a moment. However, perhaps his simplest demonstration involved a classic problem with which you are already familiar: XOR.

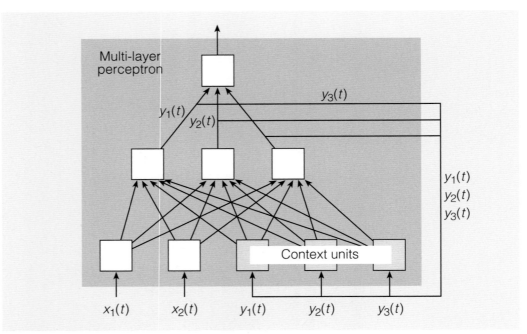

Figure 4.5   Elman network

SAQ 4.4

Quickly note down a definition of the XOR problem.

ANSWER..

The problem is to compute the following truth table.

x_1	x_2	x_3
1	1	0
1	0	1
0	1	1
0	0	0
XOR		

You'll recall that this cannot be computed by a single-layer perceptron.

Of course, you now know that XOR can be perfectly satisfactorily computed by a multi-layer perceptron trained under backpropagation. Therefore, it is generally treated by supplying two inputs at the perceptron's input layer and then waiting for a single output unit to activate (or not). On the face of it, there doesn't seem to be any time involved.

Elman, however, added a temporal perspective to this simple problem in this way. He devised a very long sequence of XORs, as in the following example:

[1 1 0 1 0 1 0 0 0 0 1 1 0 1 1 0 0 0 1 0 1 1 1 0 ...]

I've inserted spaces into the series so you can get a clearer view of what is going on. The vector consists of a sequence of three element groups, repeated over and over. The first two elements of each group are the input to XOR and the third the expected answer. A vector encoding a sequence of 3000 elements was put together in this way and used to train the network shown in Figure 4.6.

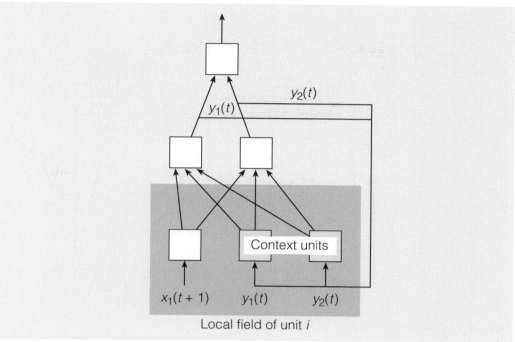

Figure 4.6   Elman network for XOR

The idea was to apply the input vector, one element at a time, to the input unit x_1 in this network, and that the activation of the output unit would represent the network's *guess* as to what the next element in the sequence was going to be – 0 or 1. After training (I'll discuss training of simple recurrent networks in the next section), the results were interesting.

Put yourself in the position of the network, if you can. Your situation is really quite similar to the one you were in as you read through the garden path sentences above. Let's work it through in this new context.

1   The first element comes in: let's say it is a 1. What expectation do you have for the next element? None really, as there's a 50% chance that it may be another 1 and a 50% chance it will be a zero. Your guess will be just that – a pure guess.

2   But assume that you now receive the second element – it's a 1. What do you anticipate next? If you know the XOR table then you should have an overwhelming anticipation that it will be a 0. You guess 0.

3   You read the third element and find you got this right.

4   Now the fourth element is presented, a 1. You are in exactly the same position you were in at step 1, but the network now has a context – a memory of the previous inputs.

Obviously this sequence will repeat itself 1000 times. But note what is happening within the network as you proceed. On presentation of each element, the context units will be supplying information about the state of the network on the *previous* step. The network is preserving a short-term memory as it goes along.

Elman discovered that the trained network followed exactly this pattern. Plotting the squared network error, averaged over 1200 cycles, over 12 time steps, he got the graph in Figure 4.7.

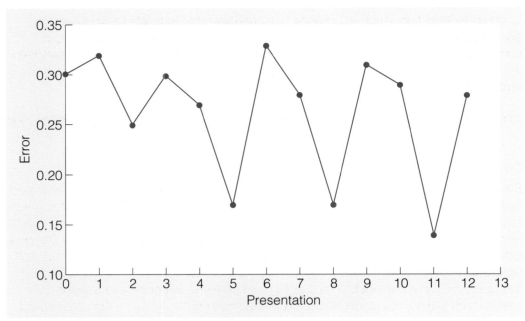

Figure 4.7　Error graph of Elman XOR network

SAQ 4.5

What basic trend can you discern here? Can you account for the degrees of error on each cycle?

ANSWER...

The basic trend is quite clear: on every third cycle, the error is much lower. Since this is the point at which the network would be expected to provide the right answer on the basis of the XOR rule, this is to be expected. On other cycles, there is 50:50 chance of guessing the correct response, so the error might be expected to be relatively high in these cases.

In fact, certain information is rather concealed by the averaging process. Elman remarks that direct observation of the network at each third cycle showed that it was, indeed, getting the correct response in most cases, showing that it had mastered this sequential form of the XOR rule. Moreover, he also noted the behaviour of the two hidden units: one became active when the inputs comprised a series of identical elements, either 1s or 0s; the other became active when inputs tended to alternate between 1 and 0. Elman interpreted this as the hidden units having developed into feature detectors, distinguishing between high- and low-frequency input, and indicating that the network had learned temporal features of the sequence.

In a series of more ambitious experiments, Elman attempted to probe some of the problems of *language processing*. In each experiment he used a layered recurrent network with the same general structure as the one you've just met: a set of input units and context units; hidden units feeding back to the context units; and output units, the task of which is to predict the next input. These experiments are described in detail, with a lucid discussion, in Elman's 1990 seminal paper. What follows is a brief account of two of them.

Words and word boundaries

We naturally think of language as being composed of *words*, so you might be surprised to learn that among linguists the very notion of a 'word' is controversial, with no agreed definition or understanding of what such a thing might actually be. (In fact, even the briefest study of linguistics will quickly convince you that linguists rarely agree on anything.) Elman set out to investigate whether a recurrent neural network could somehow detect words when they are expressed as individual characters embedded in a stream of characters that together make up a sentence. See Figure 4.8 for an ambitious example.

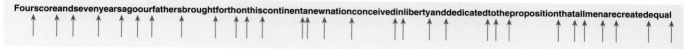

Figure 4.8   Word boundaries

Starting with a basic vocabulary of fifteen words, 200 valid sentences were generated, their lengths varying from four to nine words. These were then combined into a single stream of 1270 words – 4963 letters in total. Finally, representing each letter as a five-bit vector yielded a complete input sequence of 24 815 bits. This was applied five bits (one letter) at a time to a simple recurrent network with five input units, twenty hidden units (and thus twenty context units) and five outputs. The network was trained to predict the next letter on each input. After training, the network demonstrated a significant pattern over time, once again illustrated in the graph of the error on the output units (see Figure 4.9).

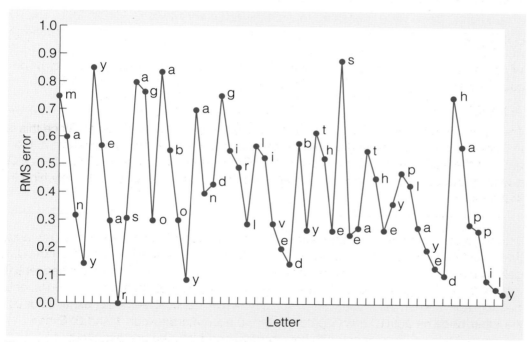

Figure 4.9   Error graph of Elman word boundary network

The highest error occurs at the first letter of each word, at the point when – obviously – there is most uncertainty as to what can be expected next, and gradually falls as each new letter is presented, reaching a minimum at the end of the word. On the onset of the first character of the next word, it rises sharply again. This consistent rising and falling pattern suggests that the network has gathered information from the unfolding of the sequence in time.

Simple sentences and lexical classes

As we all know, words do not exist in isolation: they form sentences; and much of our information about them – especially in languages like English – comes from their position in the sentence. Another important property of words is that they all fall into one or more **lexical classes**. Persons of my generation had these drummed into them at school, despite the fact that – naturally – there is no agreement among linguists about what the lexical classes are. However, you've already had a taste of them in the garden path sentences we looked at above. As each new word is read, the expectation of a certain *kind* of word coming next gradually rises. These 'kinds' are the *lexical classes* of the word: nouns, verbs, adjectives, and so on.

In this second experiment, Elman explored the possibility of a recurrent network not only being able to predict the next word in a sentence, but also deducing information about the lexical classes of words along the way. This time he worked with a vocabulary of 29 words, a mixture of simple nouns and verbs such as 'man', 'dragon', 'glass', 'move', 'smell', 'see', etc. However, the lexical categories were constructed to include a certain amount of semantic information also, with classes such as

NOUN-HUM (man, woman),

NOUN-ANIM (cat, mouse),

VERB-DESTROY (break, smash)

and so on. Each word was encoded as a 31-bit vector, all 0s except for a single bit switched to 1, the position of this 1 signifying which word the vector represented (the extra two bits were reserved for future words). A simple sentence generator program then produced a list of 10 000 tiny sentences, each one or two words long. This gave an input sequence of 27 534 31-bit vectors. Following the same pattern as earlier experiments, these were presented to a simple recurrent network, with 31 input and 31 output units and 150 context and 150 hidden units. Once again, the task of the network was to predict the next word in the sequence.

Several interesting results came out of the experiment:

1   Elman found that a simple measure of error at the output was insufficient for measuring the system's performance on this particular set of inputs. Since every training vector has only one bit set to 1, then the network quickly and unerringly discovered that a good way to reduce the overall error was just to respond with an output vector consisting of thirty-one 0s! This was clever of it, but nothing to do with the kind of linguistic information it was hoped the system would acquire. A considerable number of training epochs were therefore needed to force the system to distinguish properly between inputs. The best way to quantify performance after training was to compare the system's output against a vector in which the active bit was a measure of the statistical *likelihood* of that word occurring in that context. So, for example, if the word 'dog' was represented by the vector:

    [0 **1** 0 0 0 0 0 0 0 0 0 0 0 0 0 0 0 0 ... 0 0 0 0 0 0 0]

    then the vector:

    [0 **0.13** 0 0 0 0 0 0 0 0 0 0 0 0 0 0 0 0 ... 0 0 0 0 0 0 0]

    might represent the fact that 'dog' will occur next in that context with a probability of 0.13. These vectors were calculated from an analysis of the training set. When performance was calculated according to this measure, the final error was less than 0.06. The network had learned to predict the next word in the sequence.

2   In a follow-up analysis, Elman attempted to discover what it was the network had actually learned. Here the technique was to ignore the output units and concentrate on what the *hidden units* are doing. You should recall from Unit 2 of this block that, after training, hidden units often take on the role of *feature detectors*, responding to significant patterns within the input. Elman collected the vector of the hidden unit activations for every word in the vocabulary and averaged these, coming up with twenty-nine 150-element vectors, each reflecting the average hidden unit response for that word across all presentations of it. He then did a *hierarchical cluster analysis* on these.

SAQ 4.6

You met the idea of cluster discovery in the previous unit. What is it? What do you think hierarchical cluster discovery might be?

ANSWER..

Cluster discovery, as its name suggests, attempts to find regularities in a large set of data – specifically groups of data items that are clumped closely together, and are thus very similar to one another. In vector terms, it involves finding groups of vectors that are only short distances from one another in the vector space.

Hierarchical cluster discovery just means turning a magnifying glass on these clusters, looking inside them to see if they contain clusters, looking inside sub-clusters for further clusters, and so on.

The results of the analysis displayed a beautiful ordering, part of which I've tried to display in Figure 4.10. There were two main clusters, neatly corresponding to nouns and to verbs. Within these, verbs clustered into groups of intransitive verbs (these do not require an object: e.g. 'sleep', 'exist') and verbs that may require an object (e.g. 'like', 'chase'). Nouns clustered into various classes, which I've marked in the figure. It appears that the network had grasped certain important linguistic facts without ever having been told these explicitly. It had deduced them from word sequences extended over time.

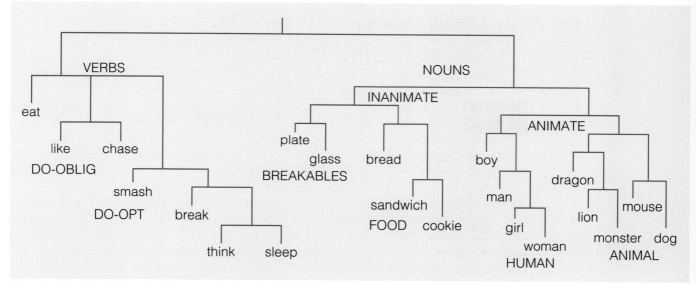

Figure 4.10   Word clustering in semantic experiment

But in fact Elman was quite wary about the significance of these results and added several notes of caution.

Exercise 4.3

Do you think Elman was right to be cautious about any claim that the network had learned important linguistic facts?

Discussion ....

Definitely. First of all, there is the ever-present danger of discovering statistical artefacts, patterns which are thrown up by the analysis but may have no real significance. Secondly, we should remember that all the network is doing is finding regularities in very large numbers of sequences of symbols. It would be foolhardy to deduce from this that the network had really acquired any grasp of *language*.

Of course, Elman understood this. He wrote:

> The *content* [my italics] of categories is not known to the network. The network has no real information which would 'ground' the structural information in the real world. In this respect, the network has much less information to work with than real language learners.
>
> Source: Elman (1990)

But remember, this was never Elman's claim. His interest was how a neural network could be constructed that would be able to handle inputs that evolve in time. In that respect, he was surely successful.

Computer Exercise 4.1

Load up and complete Computer Exercise 4.1 on the course DVD.

2.4 | Backpropagation through time

Elman generally used simple backpropagation to train the networks in these experiments. The weights of the recurrent connections were fixed to 1 (ensuring that the hidden units fed back their full activation to the context units) and they were not altered at all during training. But clearly, this approach is not altogether satisfactory. The XOR sequence requires two inputs before it is possible to say what the desired response is. After the first input there is no obvious way of specifying any desired response at the output, and so of computing the error signals on the output and hidden units. And the XOR sequence is relatively short; for longer sequences the problem becomes greater, and the training process is likely to be prolonged by fluctuations in the network weights.

To compensate for some of these drawbacks, a modified version of backpropagation called **epochwise backpropagation through time** (EBPTT) is often used. This is a general-purpose algorithm for training any kind of layered recurrent network, not just Elman systems. Here is a brief summary of how it works.

The idea of EBPTT is that the network should not be treated as a fixed entity, with a certain number of layers, but as a network that *grows* layer by layer at each computational step. Each new time step adds a new layer to the network, so the passage of time is represented as the spatial growth of the network, each new layer representing the state of the network at a new time step. I've tried to illustrate this in Figure 4.11, with Elman's simple XOR network, which I described above.

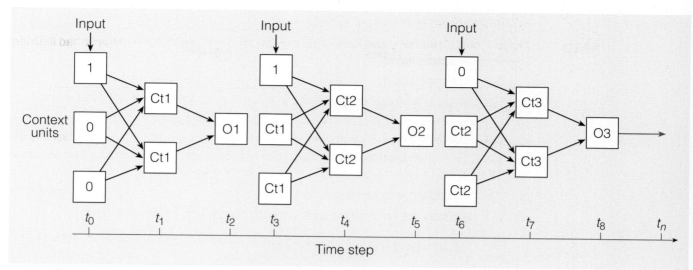

Figure 4.11   Error backpropagation through time

As each layer activates and as each new pattern is presented, the network grows, until the end of the sequence. Given this basic idea, EBPTT comprises the following basic steps.

1   Divide the input sequence into epochs, each of which represents a complete sequential pattern. For example, in the case of XOR, an epoch might be a single row of the XOR table, e.g. 1 1 0, or a sequence including the entire table, e.g. 1 1 0 1 0 1 0 1 1 0 0 0.

2   Apply the input patterns to the network, one after the other, to the end of the sequence, at each stage growing the network and saving its state at each time step. Here we are running the network *forward* in time through the sequence, from the initial time step t_0 through t_1, t_2 ... etc. to the final step t_n.

3   Now run *backward* in time, from t_n to t_1 calculating the error signal e on every unit, using the standard backpropagation equations (see Unit 2, Section 3.2, Equations 2.17 and 2.20 – I've also given them below in the EBPTT algorithm). We don't need to go all the way back to t_0, as that is an input and will consequently have no errors.

4   For each unit in the network, sum up the error signals on it over all epochs and use this combined value to calculate the changes to its incoming weight vector.

The process can be repeated for many epochs, if necessary.

This might seem familiar to you if you have a clear memory of some of the technicalities of Unit 2 of this block. The whole idea is based on the technique of batch backpropagation that I discussed there, where weight changes are summed across all training examples before being applied to the network. One advantage of EBPTT is that it is designed to cope with situations where no real desired output can be specified, such as the first step of the XOR.

A formal summary of the EBPTT algorithm is given below, with the equations included. I'm assuming the activation functions of all the units in the network are unipolar sigmoids, such as Equation 2.10 in Unit 2.

EBPTT algorithm

1   Set all weights to small random values.

2   Set n to the number of steps in the epoch; set x to the number of epochs.

3   Set a counter t to 0; set a counter i to 1.

4   Extract the next input pattern $\mathbf{x}_i$ from the training set and clamp the activations of the input units of the perceptron to the values of its elements.

5   Feedforward in time from t_0 to t_n:

5.1 calculate the activations of all the hidden units; save these activations and weights as layer t;

5.2 increment t by 1;

5.3 calculate the activations of all the output units; save these activations and weights as layer t;

5.4 increment t by 1; increment i by 1;

5.5 if $i \neq n$ then feed back activations of hidden units to context units and return to step 4.

6   Feed backward in time from t_n to t_1:

6.1 calculate the error signal $e_j(t)$ on each output unit j in layer t, using:

$$e_j(t) = \left(d_j(t) - a_j(t)\right) a_j(t)\left(1 - a_j(t)\right)$$

where $d_j(t)$ is the desired activation of j at step t and $a_j(t)$ is the actual activation. If no d_j is specified then $e_j = 0$;

6.2 decrement t by 1;

6.3 calculate the error signal $e_k(t)$ on each hidden unit k in the network in layer t, using:

$$e_k(t) = a_k(t)\left(1 - a_k(t)\right) \sum_k e_j(t+1) w_{jk}$$

6.4 decrement t by 1;

6.5 if $t \neq 1$ then return to step 6.1.

7   Adjust weights:

7.1 for the all weights w_{jk} in the network calculate the weight adjustment Δw_{jk} using:

$$\Delta w_{jk} = \eta \sum_{t=t_1}^{t_n} e_j(t) a_{jk}(t-1)$$

where η is the learning constant;

7.2 adjust all weights w_{jk} in the network by adding the weight adjustment Δw_{jk};

8   If $j = x$ then end   // final epoch

else $j = j + 1$ and go to step 3   // more epochs

This is almost identical to the batch update procedure discussed in Unit 2, Section 3.5.

It's evident that for large networks and for very long sequences, EBPTT places heavy demands on computer resources, as each new layer of the network has to be saved – all the weights and activations – as the sequence of inputs unfolds. So a revised version, **truncated error backpropagation through time**, is sometimes used, in which an arbitrary cut-off point is imposed.

2.5 | Making music with recurrent networks

One good candidate for an application of layered recurrent neural network looks like the composition of *music*. A musical piece is, after all, a sequence of notes or chords unfolding over time. And music is never random: it is bound by strong conventions, such as the fixed intervals of the musical scale, chord progressions, the conventional structures of pieces such as fugues and sonatas, and so on. And contrast the relative simplicity of music as compared to language. You probably noted, in our earlier discussion of Elman's work with simple recurrent networks, that many difficulties stand in the way of modelling language.

SAQ 4.7

Try to sum up some of these difficulties, as you understand them from Elman's work and your own general knowledge.

ANSWER...

Human languages have huge vocabularies and incredibly intricate grammatical rules; words can be ambiguous or have many shades of meaning; words are embedded in complex sentence contexts, and sentences embedded in larger discourse structures. Finally, there is the constant question of semantics: words *mean* things – they are grounded in the real world.

All researchers in artificial intelligence know that the problems natural language presents are endless. At first glance, music looks a great deal less difficult: musical notes are unambiguous; the number of them is relatively small; and there are many conventions and regularities. And notes and chords don't mean anything: music doesn't have any definite semantics; it's just music – a 'concord of sweet sounds', as Shakespeare described it. So musical composition appears to be just the sort of thing a recurrent network could do.

CONCERT

A notable attempt to use a simple recurrent network as a composer was made by Mike Mozer (1994) of the University of Colorado in his CONCERT system. The idea was one now familiar to you: a melody is presented to the system one note at a time, and the output is the next note. As in Elman's experiments, the network is trained on a large set of examples. After training, the system can be seeded with a starting note and then feed back its own output on the next step, thus composing a melody as time unfolds.

I've illustrated the architecture of CONCERT in Figure 4.12 overleaf. As you can see, it fits the familiar pattern of a simple recurrent network, the only difference being an additional layer, NNL. (I've not explicitly shown the set of context units the hidden units feed back into, but you can see that what I've depicted is equivalent.) Mozer put an immense amount of ingenuity into constructing CONCERT.

Here is a very brief review of the steps he took:

▶ *Representation of musical notes.* In music, a note is characterised by its pitch and duration. Additionally, a note may be part of a chord, a group of notes played simultaneously. In CONCERT, notes were represented by a vector made up of three component vectors, representing, respectively, pitch, duration and chord:

   ▶ *Representation of pitch.* Mozer based this representation on one derived from psychological studies of music appreciation: the *chromatic circle* and the *circle of fifths*, enabling him to represent a note's pitch as a 13-element vector.

   ▶ *Representation of duration.* A compact form of expressing the duration of a note over time was needed here. Splitting the input over many time steps was not a good option, for reasons we'll see later; so Mozer again used a scheme based on psychological research and boiled the representation down to a 10-element vector.

   ▶ *Representation of chords.* Mozer used a method based on the harmonics of a base note and was able to represent any chord as a 13-element vector.

Some twentieth-century composers, notably the American John Cage, have written pieces based on random processes. You will have to judge for yourself whether these can actually be called 'music'.

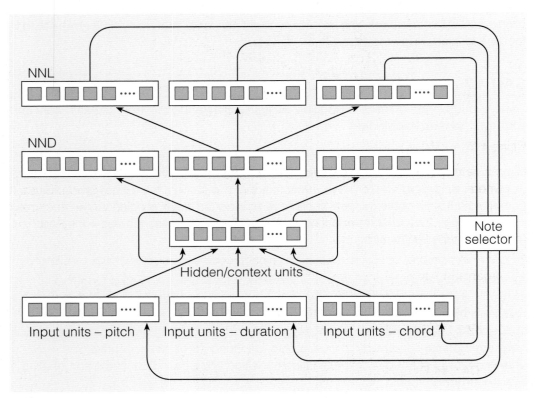

Figure 4.12   CONCERT

▶ *Output.* The first output layer, NND, expresses the network's prediction of the next note in the sequence. However, the idea was that CONCERT should be a composer, so had to have the facility to vary the melodies it had been taught with. Therefore the NND layer could represent up to three alternative possibilities simultaneously, by superimposing three different note vectors. These activations are then passed to the NNL layer.

Without going into great detail, the NNL layer transforms the input it receives from NND, which is the network's prediction of the next note, into a vector expressing the *probability* that the next note will be a certain pitch.

▶ *Unit activation functions.* These are all bipolar sigmoids, as described in Unit 2.

▶ *Training.* Training was carried out using EBPTT, as outlined in the algorithm in the previous section. Each epoch was a separate melody.

Mozer conducted a number of experiments with CONCERT, varying the number of hidden and context units, and the size of the training set, as required. Here is a summary of the initial investigations into the system's learning capacities.

▶ *Learning C major.* Every aspiring concert pianist starts with this scale. You probably recognise it yourself from Figure 4.13. CONCERT, with fifteen context units, easily learned to predict the next note from any input over three octaves.

▶ *Learning other scales.* With twenty context units, CONCERT was trained on 37 scales in various keys over the range of one octave. It predicted the next note with 98.4% accuracy.

▶ *Learning random walks.* One hundred ten-note sequences were generated by selecting a starting note at random and then choosing the next from either the note immediately above, or immediately below this in the scale of C major. With fifteen context units, CONCERT was trained on these. On testing, the correct next note in the sequence was among the networks top two predictions 99.5% of the time.

▶ *Learning interspersed random walks.* This time, 200 random, ten-note sequences were generated by intermingling two five-note sequences, each built according to

Figure 4.13   C Major

the same rule as in the experiment above. The pattern was $a_1, b_1, a_2, b_2 \ldots a_5, b_5$, where a_n is a note from the first sequence and b_n a note from the second. Since it would be impossible to predict the note b_n from a_n, these predictions were ignored in judging CONCERT's performance. With 25 context units, the system was able to predict with 99.9% accuracy.

▶ *Learning phrase structures.* Most classical pieces consist of musical *phrases*, organised into structures in which phrases are repeated and varied. Mozer generated 200 training examples, each consisting of twenty notes, in which two five-note phrases, A and B, are organised on the pattern AABA. For example:

F#2 G2 G#2 A2 A#2 –	(A)
F#2 G2 G#2 A2 A#2 –	(A)
C4 C#4 D4 D#4 E4 –	(B)
F#2 G2 G#2 A2 A#2	(A)

> The 2 and 4 represent the octave the note occurs in.

is such a sequence. Note that there are two kinds of structure here:

▶ local structure arising from relationships between notes within the phrases;

▶ global structure in the relationships between the phrases.

CONCERT was set up with 35 context units and trained on these patterns. This time, the analysis demonstrated rather more disappointing results. The succeeding notes at some positions in the sequence were predicted with up to 97% accuracy. But on many other sequence positions, CONCERT's performance was much less encouraging: about 58%.

This last experiment raises such an important point that it's worth dwelling on it for a moment. Think carefully about this question.

Exercise 4.4

Why do you think it was so difficult for CONCERT to infer certain notes?

Discussion ....

Again, it's all about *time*. In his analysis, Mozer points out that some notes can be confidently predicted from local information alone, from their position within the phrase; others require a global view of the pattern. For example, after F#2 G2 and G#2, A2 is a very safe prediction: it's integral to the pattern of phrase A. But consider the difficulty of predicting, from position 15 in the sequence, the first note of the third appearance of phrase A, at position 16. What knowledge must this prediction be based on? Mozer suggests the network needs to know:

▶ the first note of the A phrase;

▶ the fact that the previous phrase has ended;

▶ the fact that current input is part of the third phrase.

All this implies a *memory* that stretches back at least eleven time steps.

This problem with recurrent networks has been known for a long time. It is often known as the problem of **vanishing gradients**. Simply stated, it is this: in a long sequence, certain very early elements may have a strong influence on items that occur much later on. However, with the passing of time, this influence may gradually be diluted within the network as it unfolds, and may be forgotten altogether by the time the later item appears. Therefore, during training, error signals flowing back in time tend to vanish (or in certain cases they may explode). You can see that this must be a universal problem in recurrent networks. I'll return to it shortly.

But what about CONCERT's performance as a *composer*? Quite rightly, Mozer insisted that the results should be judged aesthetically, as pieces of music, in contrast to some researchers' assessment of their own work, where the ability to produce any kind of tune is enough. In further experiments, the system was trained firstly on ten short pieces by J. S. Bach and secondly on twenty-five waltzes by various composers. The resulting 'compositions' were certainly tunes of a kind. But, with engaging candour, Mozer quotes the view of one of his critics that they were '... compositions only their mother could love'. He goes on:

> To summarise more delicately, few listeners would be fooled into believing that the pieces had been composed by a human. While the local contours made sense, the pieces were not musically coherent, lacking thematic structure and having minimal phrase structure and rhythmic organisation.

Source: Mozer (1994)

The sad truth is that music is a great deal more complicated than one might have first supposed. Composers and listeners tend to think in terms of phrases and larger structures, of rhythmic and melodic motifs perhaps spanning many bars. All of this takes us back to where we started, to the problem of time and the matter of vanishing gradients.

Give me excess of it! More music with LSTMs

More recent research into neurally generated music has attempted to tackle the problem of vanishing gradients in several ways. Many approaches have concentrated on trying to refine the input representation so as to encapsulate more global information. Mozer himself experimented with abandoning the note-by-note approach in favour of more general input structures that reflected the upward and downward flow of pitch across the whole piece. This approach has had a certain amount of success, but has the obvious drawback that important local information can get lost in the process of making the input more general.

Another strategy is to abandon the simple Elman topology for something a bit more sophisticated. One such alternative is the **long short-term memory** (LSTM). LSTM is a fairly recent innovation in neural network design, aimed at tackling the vanishing gradient problem. The analysis of LSTMs can become rather complex, so my aim here is just to present a fairly broad picture of how they work.

I've illustrated a typical LSTM in Figure 4.14. Superficially, it looks rather like a simple recurrent network; the difference is in the bank of **memory cells** that replace the context units.

However, a memory cell is a much more complex affair than a simple unit. I've shown the architecture of a typical memory cell in Figure 4.15. At the heart of it is a single unit known as the **constant error carousel** (CEC). The activation of the CEC is calculated using a linear function, usually just the sum of the inputs it receives. Notice, however, that the CEC has a recurrent *self-connection*, with a fixed weight of 1, so some of the input it receives is its own output. You can see already that this alone would keep the unit in a steady state of activation, which would only be altered by outside events.

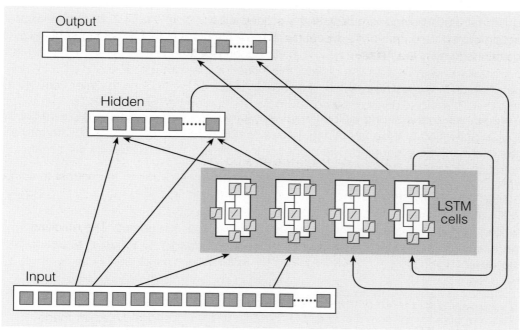

Figure 4.14   LSTM network

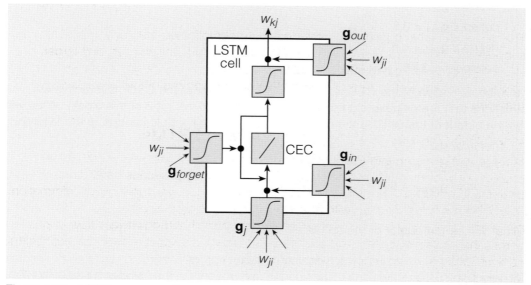

Figure 4.15   LSTM memory cell

These outside events enter the memory cell through four paths:

1   the normal input flowing into the cell net, the conventional weighted sum which you are now perfectly familiar with; this flows into a unit $\mathbf{g}_j$ with a non-linear activation function such as a unipolar sigmoid;

2   an *input gate*, marked $\mathbf{g}_{in}$ on the diagram. This is also a conventional unit, which sums its weighted inputs in the usual way and activates according to a non-linear function;

3   an *output gate*, marked $\mathbf{g}_{out}$ on the diagram, of exactly the same design as the input gate;

4   a *forget gate*, marked $\mathbf{g}_{forget}$ on the diagram, with the same design as the other gates.

The combined inputs of the input gate and the input to the cell are *multiplied* by the small unit depicted as a dark circle in Figure 4.15. Similarly, the output of the CEC is passed through another non-linear unit and then multiplied with the input from the output gate, the result being the output of the cell. Feedback from the CEC to itself is also multiplied by the output of the forget gate. The activation of the CEC at time t, $a_{CEC}(t)$, is calculated using the formula:

$$a_{CEC}(t) = a_{forget}(t)\,a_{CEC}(t-1) + a_{in}(t)\,a_j(t) \tag{4.1}$$

You can see that a strong inhibitory activation from the forget gate could cause the CEC's activation to drop to nothing, hence its name – it can cause the CEC to forget the information it is carrying. The output of the cell a_{cell} is calculated by the simple formula:

$$a_{cell} = a_{out}\,f(a_{CEC}) \tag{4.2}$$

where $f(a_{CEC})$ is also a non-linear function, again usually a sigmoid. You can gain an appreciation of the way the gates work by working through the following simple exercise.

Exercise 4.5

Consider an LSTM memory cell like the one depicted in Figure 4.15. At time t_1 the cell is receiving the following net inputs:

netinput $\mathbf{g}_{in}$ = –4.7

netinput $\mathbf{g}_{out}$ = 3.8

netinput $\mathbf{g}_{forget}$ = 6.1

netinput j = 3.78

and the activation of the CEC is 1.23. All the units except the CEC have activation functions that are unipolar sigmoids (see Equation 2.10 in Unit 2 of this block). What will be the output of the cell? At the next time step t_2, the net inputs change to the following:

netinput $\mathbf{g}_{in}$ = 3.1

netinput $\mathbf{g}_{out}$ = –3.8

netinput $\mathbf{g}_{forget}$ = 6.0

netinput j = 1.14

What will be the output of the cell at t_2?

Discussion ....

At time step t_1, the activations of the various components of the cell can be calculated as follows:

a_{in} = $1/(1 + e^{4.7})$ = 0.009

a_{out} = $1/(1 + e^{-3.8})$ = 0.978

a_{forget} = $1/(1 + e^{-6.1})$ = 0.998

a_j = $1/(1 + e^{-3.78})$ = 0.978

Now we can apply the formulae in Equations 4.1 and 4.2 to get the output of the CEC, as follows:

a_{CEC} = (0.998 * 1.23) + (0.009 * 0.978) = 1.236

and the output of the entire cell will be given by:

a_{cell} = $1/(1 + e^{-1.236})$ * 0.978 = 0.775 * 0.978 = 0.758

You can see that the activation of the CEC has been barely perturbed by the input. This is because of the effect of the input gate $\mathbf{g}_{in}$, which is weakly activated and thus – because of its multiplicative effect – cuts the additional input to the CEC almost to nothing.

At time step t_2, the activations of the various components of the cell are as follows:

$$a_{in} = 1/(1 + e^{-3.1}) = 0.957$$

$$a_{out} = 1/(1 + e^{3.8}) = 0.022$$

$$a_{forget} = 1/(1 + e^{-6.0}) = 0.998$$

$$a_j = 1/(1 + e^{-1.14}) = 0.758$$

Now we can apply the formulae in Equations 4.1 and 4.2 to get the output of the CEC, as follows:

$$a_{CEC} = (0.998 * 1.236) + (0.957 * 0.758) = 1.959$$

and the output of the entire cell is given by:

$$a_{cell} = 1/(1 + e^{-1.959}) * 0.022 = 0.876 * 0.022 = 0.019$$

Now the opposite effect is evident. The input gate has opened and allowed the external input to the cell to significantly increase the activation of the CEC. However, the output gate has now closed and is more or less completely choking off the output from the cell.

There is no need to repeat the exercise to show the effect of the forget gate. This has exactly the same multiplicative effect on the feedback of the CEC to itself. Potentially, it can shut down the activation of the CEC altogether.

LSTM memory cells can be connected into neural networks in various topologies and with many different patterns of connection. The exact arrangement is up to the researcher and to the application being worked on, although LSTMs are generally incorporated into some sort of feedforward, layered structure, as in Figure 4.14. The memory cells are arranged in banks, and there may be more than one bank in a typical network. Very dense connection patterns are common, in which memory cells feed back to themselves and to other memory cells, as well as accepting connections from units in the layers of the feedforward structure and feeding activation into these layers. I've tried to illustrate some of the possible connection patterns in Figure 4.14.

The idea of the LSTM is obviously that information can be retained indefinitely within a cell, but will only be updated, or influence the feedforward network, when its gates allow. Since these are controlled by units that receive weighted connections in the normal way, the network must learn the appropriate patterns of gate access to and from the cell, by adjustment of these weights, as in any other neural network. Training of a feedforward system incorporating LSTM memory cells is usually done by backpropagation, with the weights in the feedforward part of the system being trained using the standard algorithm, described in Unit 2 of this block, but with the weights passing in and out of the memory cells being subjected to EBPTT. Thus error signals can be preserved inside the cell indefinitely, rather than vanishing, as may happen with conventional EBPTT.

In 2002, Douglas Eck and Jürgen Schmidhuber conducted experiments using LSTM-based networks as music learners and composers. Their aim was to see if a neural network based on LSTMs could overcome some of the temporal problems Mozer had encountered. This aim was rather less ambitious than Mozer's: their network was to learn the chord sequences and melodies of the blues, and then improvise short blues compositions of its own. The experiment fell into two parts:

1   First of all, the researchers constructed a network that would be able to learn and reproduce the chord sequence in Figure 4.16. The network is depicted in Figure 4.17. In place of a separate hidden layer, it had four blocks of two LSTM cells, each cell of identical structure to the ones in Figure 4.15 above. The cells had a full set of recurrent connections, each being connected to itself and to all the other cells, as

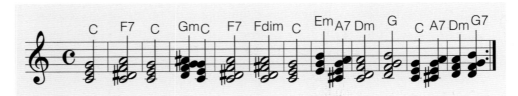

Figure 4.16   Blues chord sequence

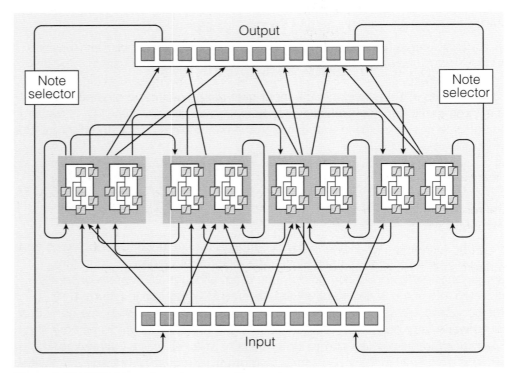

Figure 4.17   LSTM-based music composition system

well as to all the units in the input layer. All the units in the output layer had recurrent connections back to all the units in the input layer. Overall, you can see that this was a very rich and dense pattern of connectivity, and I've only been able to show some of the links in Figure 4.17.

The complex distributed input representation devised by Mozer was abandoned in favour of a much simpler local representation, where every possible note was represented by a unit and that unit activated if that note sounded. Twelve notes were possible. The durations of notes were handled by simply slicing time up into steps, each representing one eighth-note, with a separate input vector for each step. The output would be a vector expressing the probabilities that each of the allowable notes would be sounded at the next step.

The network was trained using a mixture of backpropagation and EBPTT, as described above. The network learned the chord sequence in Figure 4.16 very quickly. Eck and Schmidhuber note that this was unsurprising, as it is well known that LSTMs are excellent at counting and timing tasks.

2   In the second experiment, the network was expanded to cope with a melody line, in addition to the chord sequence. The input layer was divided into two, with thirteen inputs for chords, as before, and a further twelve input units for melody. Another four blocks of two memory cells each were added to handle the melody. Like the chord memory blocks, these had a full set of recurrent connections, as well as connections to the melody input. The chord LSTMs were fully connected to the melody cells, but there were no connections the other way.

Figure 4.18   Simple scale for improvisation

The researchers composed a training set of ten melodies on the scale illustrated in the Figure 4.18. After training, the network was able to improvise blues tunes on its own.

How good were these results? Clearly Eck and Schmidhuber had set themselves an easier task than Mozer. They themselves comment that blues improvisation over a fixed chord structure required fewer network resources and allowed them to take more shortcuts than, say, a classical piece. As for whether the results were aesthetically pleasing, you can judge for yourselves.

ACTIVITY 4.1

Visit the website Eck and Schmidhuber set up to demonstrate the results of their experiment. You can find details of this on the course DVD and website. There are several recordings of their network's output there, which you can sample. The researchers claim:

> It can be said that the network compositions are remarkably better than a random walk through the pentatonic scale ... [they] follow the structure of the musical form.

Source: Eck and Schmidhuber (2002)

See what you think.

In my discussion of the possible applications of layered recurrent networks, I've dwelt almost entirely on music composition. However, don't run away with the idea that this is the only area to which these systems have been applied. Layered recurrent networks have been used in robotics, control systems and language analysis. You'll find links and suggestions for further reading on the course DVD and website.

3 Fully recurrent networks

This unit is concerned with time. In the previous section, we explored various neural systems that were adapted to deal with inputs that were sequential, in which their most important feature was the changing pattern of the input over *time*. Most of the examples we looked at were variations on the layered systems you dealt with in Unit 2, the basic pattern of which is the familiar one:

▶   present an input;

▶   process;

▶   retrieve the output.

But remember from my introduction to this unit that inputs that evolve in time – what we learned to call *time series* information – was only the first of two issues with time. In this section, I want to move on to think about the second of my two concerns: networks whose state evolves in time.

3.1 Content addressable memory

But first, recall one important feature of human memory – and of natural intelligence generally – that I discussed near the start of Unit 1 of this block: *content addressability*.

SAQ 4.8

Do you recall what this term means? Look back if you need to, and jot down a brief definition.

ANSWER...

Content addressability is a feature of memory by means of which an entire complex memory can be retrieved from a small cue, which may be any part of the original.

It's worth pausing for a moment to contrast this with computer memory. Computer memories are **key addressable**. In a key addressable memory, a piece of information can only be retrieved by means of one special part of it, known as the key. So a typical database entry, say one of the rows in Table 4.1, can only be located if the Customer Number, its key, is known. None of the other pieces of information in the row will suffice. This is not just true of databases, but of computer memory generally. Information is retrieved from memory by knowing its *address*: if the address is lost, the memory is lost too.

Table 4.1   Sample database

Customer No.	Name	Phone	E-mail
S3428695	Milton, J.	01865 438294	jm@paradise.net
S5943933	Keats, J.	01817 562820	jk@nightingale.com

Contrast this with human memory. Picture a complex scene from your past: a birthday party, maybe; or the moment you recall that you were happiest. There are no special keys here. More or less any tiny part of that scene – an aroma, a snatch of birdsong, a familiar face – is usually enough to recall the scene in its entirety. The memory reconstructs itself from the tiniest of cues.

Now place this in the context of a system that is evolving over time. Consider Figure 4.19(a). Each numbered square represents the state of a neural network with one hundred units. Each unit is depicted within the square as either active (black) or inactive (white). Look along the row and you'll see the evolution of the network from the start, time step t_0, through to t_3. After t_3 there is no further change in the network state: we say it has *stabilised*. From a certain starting point, the system has evolved to retrieve a memory: the letter P. Figure 4.19(b) shows the same network starting at a different state and evolving to stabilise at a different memory: the letter C.

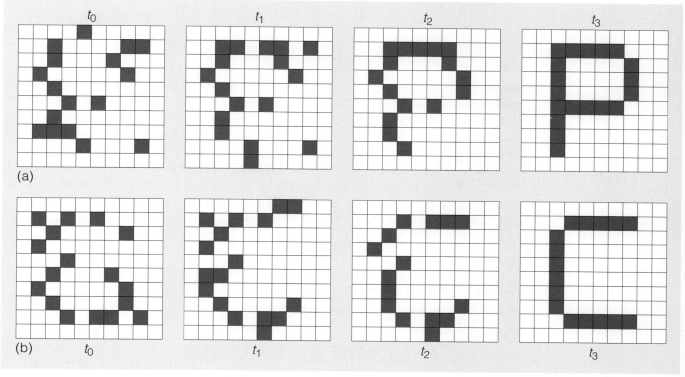

Figure 4.19   Pattern evolution

Can we persuade a neural system to behave in this way? Yes. Fully recurrent systems can be trained to do just this.

3.2   Structure of fully recurrent networks

Let's start with the very simple recurrent network I've portrayed in Figure 4.20.

You met this briefly in Unit 1 of this block. It has three units only. Each unit u_k is quite conventional: it sums up its inputs in the usual manner to find the net input:

$$netinput_k = \sum_{j=1}^{n} w_{kj} x_j \tag{4.3}$$

and activates according to a simple threshold activation function:

$$a_k = \begin{cases} 1 & \text{if } netinput \geq T_k \\ 0 & \text{if } netinput < T_k \end{cases} \tag{4.4}$$

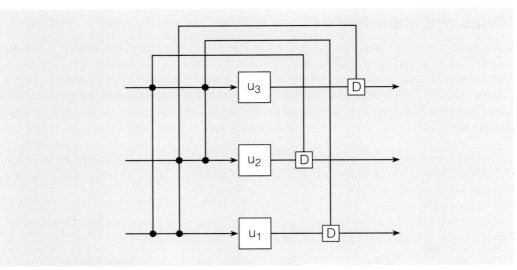

Figure 4.20   Simple fully recurrent network

where T_k is the threshold for unit k. Nothing new here. But now note the recurrent connections. In this case the connections flow backwards from each unit to the others, rather than just feeding forward. So u_1 influences both u_2 and u_3, but is itself influenced by them in turn. No unit feeds back to itself. We'll assume for simplicity from now on that the weight of the connections in both directions is the same: the weight on the link from u_i to u_j is always equal to the weight from u_j to u_i. So in this case $w_{12} = w_{21} = -0.8$; $w_{13} = w_{31} = 1.6$; and $w_{23} = w_{32} = -1.7$. The threshold T_1 of u_1 is 0.2, the thresholds for the other two units, T_2 and T_3, are both 0.

Let's set the time step to t_0 and start by clamping the activations of the three units into a set pattern. We'll set $a_1(t_0) = 0$, $a_2(t_0) = 0$ and $a_3(t_0) = 0$.

Exercise 4.6

Work out what will happen next, at time step t_1.

Discussion ....

All the units will recalculate their inputs and activate according to the rules given above. Specifically, the new activations will be as follows:

$netinput_{u1} = a_2 * w_{12} + a_3 * w_{13} = 0 + 0 = 0$; activation $a_1(t_1) = 0$

$netinput_{u2} = a_1 * w_{21} + a_3 * w_{23} = 0 + 0 = 0$; activation $a_2(t_1) = 1$

$netinput_{u3} = a_1 * w_{31} + a_2 * w_{32} = 0 + 0 = 0$; activation $a_3(t_1) = 1$

The network has moved into a new pattern of activations.

There are two points I want to make here before moving on to consider the implications of this result.

▶   Notice that we have chopped the passage of time up into slices, t_0, t_1, t_2 ... . Each time step is like the tick of a clock: nothing is deemed to happen between one tick of the clock and the next. But at each tick, a new era instantaneously begins and all the units in the network update simultaneously, using information from the previous time step.

▶   Also note the dense pattern of recurrence of the network. There are no layers – or, if you like, there is a single layer – and every unit is connected to every other unit (except itself). From now on, I'll refer to this sort of system as a **fully recurrent network**.

Now we can move on to consider the implications of the Exercise 4.6.

States and state spaces

In the previous exercise you worked out that from a starting set of activations $a_1(t_0) = 0$, $a_2(t_0) = 0$ and $a_3(t_0) = 0$, the network in Figure 4.20 clicked into a new set at t_1: $a_1(t_1) = 0$, $a_2(t_1) = 1$ and $a_3(t_1) = 1$. Let's call the set of activations $\{a_1, a_2, a_3\}$ at time step t_i the **state** of the network at that time. So the state of the little network we've been working with up to now is $\{0,0,0\}$ at t_0 and $\{0,1,1\}$ at t_1. Between t_0 and t_1 there has been a **state transition**.

This is a concept that will be quite familiar to you from Block 2. There we were dealing with states such as chessboard positions, or dispositions of blocks in a planning application. Here we are dealing with sets of unit activations. But the idea is just the same: the system can be in a certain state and then move to another. And if we are dealing with states then we can bring back the notion of a **state space**: the set of all possible states that the system can be in.

SAQ 4.9

How many possible states can the network be in, and what are they?

ANSWER..

With our present network, the three units can each only be in either state 1 or 0, so there are 2^3 states: the full set is $\{0,0,0\}$, $\{0,0,1\}$, $\{0,1,0\}$, $\{1,0,0\}$, $\{1,0,1\}$, $\{1,1,0\}$, $\{0,1,1\}$ and $\{1,1,1\}$.

As always, we can profitably represent this geometrically. We have a three-dimensional space, one dimension for the activation of each unit. Since the units can only have activations 1 or 0 then the possible system states lie at the vertices of a cube, as I've illustrated in Figure 4.21. The transition from $\{0,0,1\}$ to $\{0,1,1\}$ is marked by an arrow: all transitions will be between vertices of the cube.

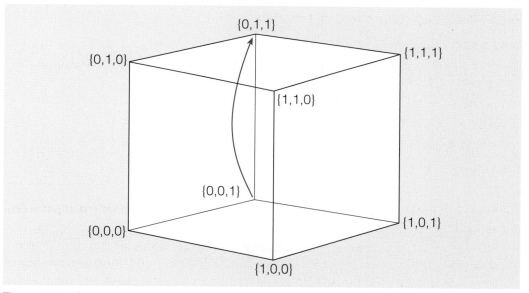

Figure 4.21   State transition in a recurrent network

Presumably, the network may switch state again at the next tick of the clock, and then again at each step. Now let's explore the time course of our network in a little more detail.

Computer Exercise 4.2

It would be tedious to go through any more arithmetical calculation, so load up and complete Computer Exercise 4.2 on the course DVD. This contains instructions for automating our network.

My system indicated that the time course of the network would be as follows:

$t_0 \rightarrow \quad \{0,0,0\}$

$t_1 \rightarrow \quad \{0,1,1\}$

$t_2 \rightarrow \quad \{1,0,0\}$

$t_3 \rightarrow \quad \{0,0,1\}$

$t_4 \rightarrow \quad \{1,0,1\}$

$t_5 \rightarrow \quad \{1,0,1\}$

$t_6 \rightarrow \quad \{1,0,1\}$ ......

The network visits a number of different states and then at t4 it seems to have entered a state after which no further change is possible.

Exercise 4.7

Mark these transitions out on the state space cube and then use your system to find the evolution of the network from a number of other starting states.

Discussion ....

You probably found that $\{1,1,0\}$ was the most interesting starting state. Most of the others very quickly converge on state $\{1,0,1\}$, with all activity ceasing after that point. For the sake of completeness, I did all the eight possible starting states and marked the transitions on Figure 4.21, giving Figure 4.22.

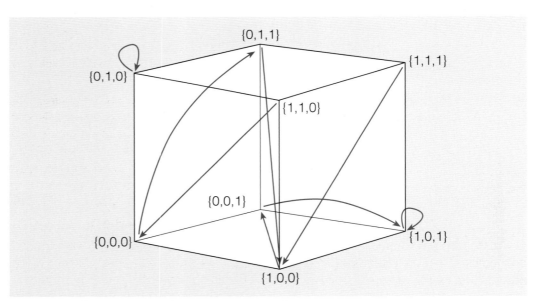

Figure 4.22 State transitions in a recurrent network

Note the rather peculiar state $\{0,1,0\}$. It is stable – no arrows lead away from it. But neither do any arrows lead into it. It is not reachable from any other state of the network.

You might care to try networks with the same topology but different weights and thresholds. For example, keeping the same thresholds but altering the weights such that $w_{12} = w_{21} = 1.0$; $w_{13} = w_{31} = 1.6$; and $w_{23} = w_{32} = -1.7$ leads to different results. Starting at {0,0,1}, we find the network immediately stabilises at {1,0,1}. A start at {0,1,0} leads immediately to {1,1,0}, which is also a stable state. Starting at {1,1,1}, however, leads to a more interesting result: the network immediately moves to {1,0,0} and then flips backwards and forwards between this state and {0,1,1} for ever. It appears this network has (at least) three stable states, one of which consists of an alternation between two other states.

Does this remind you of anything? It should. It's exactly the picture we encountered in Block 3, in our discussions of the Game of Life and other highly interactive systems. *Interaction* and *feedback* are the key, both of which – naturally – are present in a densely recurrent neural network. Think back for a moment to your experiments with the Game of Life.

SAQ 4.10

Note down some of the kinds of structures that emerged from the evolution of the Game of Life over time.

ANSWER..

You encountered:

▶ stable, unchanging structures, such as *blocks*;

▶ oscillating patterns, like *blinkers*;

▶ reconstituting patterns, for example *gliders*;

▶ very complex evolving patterns, like *puffer trains*.

There was also behaviour that is impossible to classify.

We can use these models to develop some terminology, taken from the theory of complex systems:

▶ Stable states such as blocks or patterns of activation – {1,0,1} in our first network – towards which the system tends to converge, are termed **attractors**.

▶ Stable states consisting of oscillations between two or more states, such as blinkers or the flipping of the network above between {1,0,0} and {0,1,1}, we will call **periodic attractors**.

▶ Patterns like gliders that reconstitute themselves after a certain number of steps, we will call **transients** or **quasi-periodic states**. Note that a glider is not the same kind of thing as a periodic attractor such as blinker: the glider rebuilds the same pattern, but in a different part of the grid. The recurrent network we've been examining is probably too small and simple to exhibit that sort of emergent structure.

▶ The network state evolves in time and moves around the state space (also sometimes known as the **phase space**), from state to state. I'll refer to the path of the system through the state space from now on as the system **trajectory**.

Given that the brains and nervous systems of animals contain millions of recurrent connections, we would expect this kind of emergent behaviour to be found there. And we would certainly expect it to play a part in the functioning of the nervous system, in memory, action and perception.

3.3　Brain-State-in-a-Box

One early investigation into this type of recurrent neural network was James Anderson's **Brain-State-in-a-Box** (BSB). In Anderson's model, we have a similar topology to the one in the little network above in Computer Exercise 4.2, except that there are no constraints on the feedback connections: a unit may feed back to itself and w_{ij} need not be equal to w_{ji}. There are further differences in the update rules for each unit. Units sum up their weighted inputs in a somewhat different way: rather than using Equation 4.3, the net input to a unit j is given by:

$$netinput_j = a_j + \alpha \sum_i^N w_{ji} a_i \qquad (4.5)$$

where a_j is the current activation of unit j and α is a constant. The activation is also calculated according to a rather different rule:

$$a_j(t+1) = \begin{cases} 1 & \text{if } netinput_j(t) > 1 \\ netinput_j(t) & \text{if } -1 \le netinput_j(t) \le 1 \\ -1 & \text{if } netinput_j(t) < -1 \end{cases} \qquad (4.6)$$

You can see that the activation grows linearly with *netinput* until it reaches +1 and then can increase no further. Similarly, under the influence of inhibitory input, the activation can fall no further than −1. The graph of the function is shown in Figure 4.23.

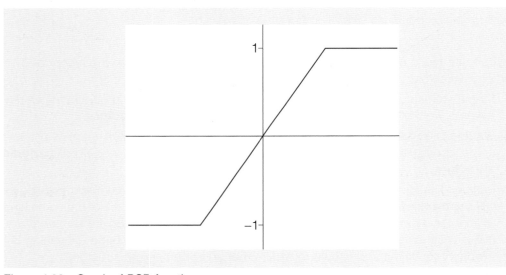

Figure 4.23　Graph of BSB function

Since the units in this model can take on any real number value between −1 and 1, the trajectory of the system through state space will be slightly different also. For a three-unit network the interior of the cube can now be visited, rather than just the vertices, as in our earlier example. So we would expect the trajectory to start somewhere within the cube and move through it. But how?

Computer Exercise 4.3

It will be useful to model the behaviour of a small BSB system. Load up and complete Computer Exercise 4.3 on the course DVD.

You might perhaps have guessed the typical behaviour of a BSB system by examining the equations. Figure 4.24 shows the results I got from two separate runs of the system, each from different starting points.

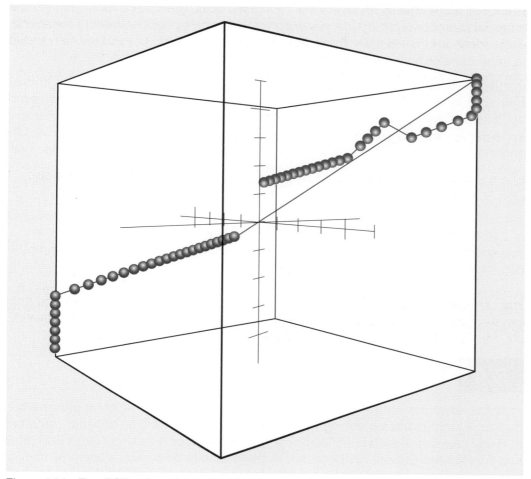

Figure 4.24 Two BSB trajectories

You'll see that the trajectories, although their starting points are fairly close together immediately move off in different directions. You'll also note that each finishes at one of the vertices of the cube, stabilising there because the activation can go no higher than 1 or lower than −1.

Exercise 4.8

Why do you think such a result is implicit in the connectivity of the system and in Equations 4.5 and 4.6?

Discussion ....

This is a simple example of self-organisation caused by the amplification of fluctuations by feedback. Equation 4.5 takes the current activation of a unit and boosts it by some increment of the current input it is receiving from other units, tending to push it further up the trajectory it is travelling along: if the activation is positive it is likely to become more positive; if negative, more negative. Eventually one unit will reach 1 or −1, thus hitting the wall of the box. As other units follow suit the trajectory then slides along the wall, finally reaching a corner. I've already made the point that Equation 4.6 prevents the trajectory ever leaving the box.

So quite a small initial difference in starting points may well push the system in radically different directions that will be progressively reinforced by feedback.

BSB models have been used for data clustering applications. The networks we've been looking at so far have been very small – just three units, giving us a nicely visualisable cuboidal state space. But of course many more units are possible, making the space into a *hypercube*. Since the corners of the hypercube are stable points, they can be said to correspond to memories, or data clusters.

In 1990 Anderson used a BSB to classify radar signals. A radar beam emitted from a particular source can be seen as a complex pattern of variables. Different emitters send out different characteristic patterns, and an obviously useful application would be a system that can recognise and categorise signals according to the source that is emitting them. As you can imagine, though, this is far from straightforward. In the real world, the radar data is extremely noisy, and an actual signal may look substantially different from the idealised one that supposedly characterises that emitter. Therefore, the kind of data clustering analysis that you learned about in the previous unit is necessary. Using a simple version of supervised learning, Anderson trained the weights of a BSB network to values that caused it to stabilise at one particular corner of the hypercube for each different input pattern. Each corner was associated with a particular data cluster.

A further important characteristic of BSB and many other fully recurrent networks is the *energy function* that is associated with them. I'll introduce you to the idea of an energy function in Section 3.4, in the context of the Hopfield model.

3.4   The Hopfield model

I introduced you to John Hopfield in the first unit of this block. A scientist of immense distinction, a physicist by training but now working in genomics, he became interested in neural networks in the early 1980s, shortly after Anderson's early work with BSB. BSB and the Hopfield network (as Hopfield's system came to be known) share a number of features, but have several significant differences.

Structure of the Hopfield model

Like BSB, a Hopfield network has a fully recurrent topology, with the difference that units are *not* connected to themselves. So topologically, a Hopfield network is more or less identical to the recurrent system with which we started this section, and which I depicted in Figure 4.20. It also shares with that network the property that the weights are symmetric: that is, $w_{12} = w_{21}$; $w_{13} = w_{31}$; $w_{23} = w_{32}$ and so on, and that units usually have threshold activation functions, for example:

$$a_k = \begin{cases} 1 & \text{if } \sum_{j}^{N} w_{kj} a_j \geq T_k \\ -1 & \text{otherwise} \end{cases} \tag{4.7}$$

or

$$a_k = \begin{cases} 1 & \text{if } \sum_{j}^{N} w_{kj} a_j \geq T_k \\ 0 & \text{otherwise} \end{cases} \tag{4.8}$$

where T_k is the threshold of unit k, and N is the number of units. Although there are continuous-valued versions of the Hopfield model, I'm not going to discuss them in this unit. So far, nothing new. What's so special about the Hopfield model?

Network dynamics and energy

Two things, really. Remember that the *state* of networks like these is their position in the state space, which is determined entirely by the activations of the network units at that time step. So, for a three-unit network, its state S at time t is given by $S = \{a_1(t), a_2(t), a_3(t)\}$. Hopfield derived a function of the network state, the value of which changes as the state changes, and which he called the **energy function**. This function has useful properties, but is quite complex, so I'm going to take it a step at a time.

The energy E_k of a single unit k in a Hopfield network with N units at time t is given by:

$$E_k = -a_k \left(\sum_{j}^{N} w_{kj} a_j - T_k \right) \tag{4.9}$$

where again T_k is the threshold of unit k. I've dropped the time step symbols to make this easier on the eye. Simplifying Equation 4.9 slightly, we get:

$$E_k = -\sum_{j}^{N} w_{kj} a_j a_k + a_k T_k \tag{4.10}$$

So it's reasonable to suppose that the energy of the whole network will be the sum of the energies of all the units in the network. Not quite. The overall energy is actually given by:

$$E = -\frac{1}{2} \sum_{k}^{N} \sum_{j}^{N} w_{kj} a_j a_k + \sum_{i}^{N} a_i T_i \tag{4.11}$$

This might look intimidating or impressive, but it's no more than a modified form of the sum of Equation 4.10 over all the units in the network: the sum of half the first term plus the sum of the second term. But why half? This is simply because the connections are symmetric, running in both directions.

Try this exercise.

Exercise 4.9

Consider a three-unit Hopfield network, with the following characteristics at time step t.

    Unit 1: $a_1 = 1$; $T_1 = 0.4$

    Unit 2: $a_2 = -1$; $T_2 = 0.5$

    Unit 3: $a_3 = -1$; $T_3 = 0.1$

and $w_{12} = w_{21} = -0.8$; $w_{13} = w_{31} = 1.6$; $w_{23} = w_{32} = -1.7$

What is the energy of the network at this time step?

Discussion ....

The energy is given by Equation 4.11. To make the calculations a little more straightforward, I took them a step at a time. Start by calculating the first two sigmas:

$$\sum_{k}^{N}\sum_{j}^{N} w_{kj}a_j a_k = \left((-0.8 * -1 * 1) + (1.6 * -1 * 1) + (-0.8 * 1 * -1) + (-1.7 * -1 * -1) \right)$$

$$+ \left((1.6 * 1 * -1) + (-1.7 * -1 * -1) \right)$$

$$= \left((0.8 - 1.6) + (0.8 - 1.7) \right) + \left(-1.6 - 1.7 \right)$$

$$= -0.8 - 0.9 - 3.3$$

$$= -5.0$$

Halve this and make it negative, giving 2.5. Then substitute this into Equation 4.11 giving:

$$E = 2.5 + \sum_{i}^{N} a_i T_i$$

$$= 2.5 + (0.4 - 0.5 - 0.1)$$

$$= 2.5 - 0.2$$

$$= 2.3$$

It would be a mistake to think of the energy as being in any way related to energy as defined in physics – the capacity to do work – still less to our everyday meanings of the term. Broadly, energy in this context is the amount of stimulation a neuron needs to make it fire: the smaller the unit's weights and the higher its threshold, the more stimulation it will require. And the energy of the network is just the sum of the energies of all its units.

I'll return to network energy in a moment and explain its significance. The second distinctive feature of the Hopfield network is the way it updates. Hopfield proposed a system known as **asynchronous stochastic update**. This weighty term disguises a very simple idea. In our experiments at the beginning of this section we updated all the units of our little three-unit network at each time step. In the Hopfield model, we only update *one*, chosen randomly at each step.

Hopfield was able to show that under this regime the network energy would always progressively diminish until it reaches a low energy state and then stabilise there. Any network will have one or more possible states at which the network energy is at a minimum. These *attractors*, as with BSB, correspond to network memories.

Training

Hopfield networks can be trained in both supervised and unsupervised mode. The simplest and most common approach is to use Hebbian learning. Given a Hopfield network of N units and a set of p memories, each an N-dimensional vector $\mathbf{m}_1, \mathbf{m}_2 ... \mathbf{m}_p$, then the weight w_{ji} from unit i to unit j are set according to the following rule:

$$w_{ji} = \begin{cases} \dfrac{1}{N}\sum_{k}^{p} m_{k,j} m_{k,i} & j \neq i \\ 0 & j = i \end{cases} \tag{4.12}$$

where $m_{k,i}$ is the ith component of the kth vector. This only works in networks with bipolar (i.e. 1 and -1) activations. Once the weights are set, they do not change thereafter.

ACTIVITY 4.2

On the course DVD you will find a few links and resources with which to investigate Hopfield systems. Browse through some of these.

Limitations of the Hopfield model

False attractors

In the Hopfield model, then, memories or solutions are simply the stable states, or *attractors* of the network. Once again, the best way to think about this is pictorially, by reviving the potent image of a landscape. We can picture the energy states of the network as just such a landscape, with *hills* representing high-energy states and *valleys* low-energy states. You're already familiar with this kind of picture from your study of particle swarm optimisation (PSO) in Block 3. You'll meet it again in Block 5, in the shape of a fitness landscape.

I've pictured an energy landscape in Figure 4.25. You appreciate, of course, that in a discrete-valued Hopfield network we don't actually get this kind of smooth surface: the landscape will be a set of points, with no ground between them. However, it's still useful to picture the landscape in the way I've shown. In it, the minimum energy states would be the deepest valleys. The areas around these are known as **basins of attraction**, because the system state, when it enters such a region, will be drawn inexorably down to the bottom, like water flowing down a hill, into the attractor – the lowest energy state. Figure 4.26(a) depicts this idea in terms of a contour map; Figure 4.26(b) depicts the landscape in two-dimensional cross-section.

Figure 4.25   System state traverses and energy landscape

But Figure 4.26(b) reveals that the problem that plagues every optimisation problem – and indeed every search problem – appears here as well. What about the states marked as **false attractors** in the figure? They are nowhere near an energy minimum, in fact they are very high energy states. However, all the other states it is possible to move to from them are higher energy still. A system entering such a state can never leave it, as energy can only diminish or stay the same. The system is trapped in a false attractor.

Several approaches have been taken to tackling this problem, many of which may seem familiar to you by now. One strategy is to inject some *uncertainty* into the state transitions. Instead of having a threshold activation function, the units are given a function that changes the activation of the unit with a certain *probability*. One kind of system based on this idea is the *Boltzmann machine*, which uses a complex system of training known as *simulated annealing*. However, to describe this would take us beyond

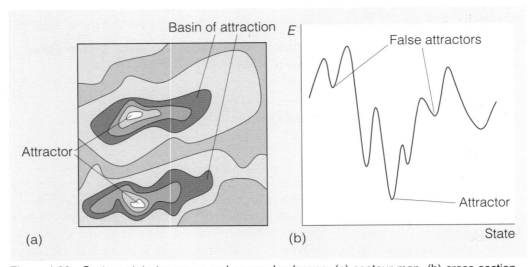

Figure 4.26 System state traverses and energy landscape: (a) contour map. (b) cross-section

the scope of this course, so I've given some more details and web links on the course DVD.

Memory constraints

If recurrent networks like Hopfield systems and BSB store memories as their lowest stable energy states, then a key question is this: *how many memories*? Given a network with, say, N units, how many memories can the system store?

A lot of theoretical work has been done on this question, the details of which need not concern us here. Consider a Hopfield network with N units. The aim is to store a series of memories, $\mathbf{m}_1$, $\mathbf{m}_2$ ... $\mathbf{m}_p$, each of which is a vector of dimension N. Fairly clearly, if p is too large the vectors will interfere with one another and there will be less than perfect recall. So what is the maximum value of p? This depends: do we want *perfect* recall of *some* of the memories, or perfect recall of *all* of them? Can we do without perfect recall and make do with something a bit less? Research has shown that the maximum value of p, p_{max}, is given by:

$$p_{\mathrm{max}} = \frac{N}{2 \ln N} \tag{4.13}$$

for perfect recall of some of the memory vectors, and:

$$p_{\mathrm{max}} = \frac{N}{4 \ln N} \tag{4.14}$$

for perfect recall of all memories. This is a very disappointing result. It means in practice that the storage capacity of a Hopfield system must always be kept small, limiting its usefulness as a recognition and classification system.

Applications of the Hopfield model

Despite these limitations, there is an important potential application of Hopfield networks – to *optimisation problems*. As you know by now, all optimisation problems consist in finding a best (or very good) solution, usually buried among myriads of alternatives. Hopfield networks can be trained to find states of minimum energy. So, if we can *associate* an optimum with a minimum energy state, then the network will naturally seek out the optimum. Think back to our old friend the Travelling Salesman Problem, specifically the little five-city example I introduced in Block 1, and consider the recurrent network I've depicted in Figure 4.27(a). Each *unit* represents a city and each *column* represents one stage in a tour, with the shaded box showing which city is visited

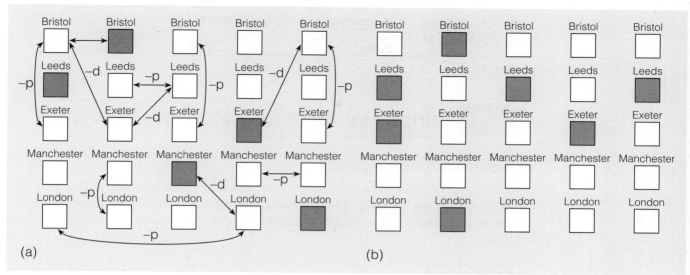

Figure 4.27   Hopfield network for the TSP

on that stage. The network is depicted as being in a state that represents the tour {Leeds, Bristol, Manchester, Exeter, London}.

The network is fully recurrent, including self links to every unit. I've represented only a few of these links in the diagram, but these are important. To understand how and why, first consider the constraints on the network state.

Exercise 4.10

What constraints do you think there must be on any final network state if it is to represent a legitimate tour? It might help to consider Figure 4.27(b), which represents a useless and contradictory tour.

Discussion ....

Remember that each column represents a single stage in the tour. So:

▶ only one unit must be active in each column (otherwise this would mean that the salesman was in two cities at the same time);

▶ there must be only one unit active in each row (otherwise it would mean that the salesman had visited the same city twice);

▶ there must be one unit active in every row (otherwise some cities would be missed out).

And, of course, the tour must represent a minimum distance overall.

This explains the significance of the weighted links I illustrated. Units in the same column are connected by strongly negative weights, to discourage more than one from becoming active. The same is true of the links between units in the same row. Units' self-connections are strongly positive, to reinforce their activation. The diagonal links represent distance: the greater the distance between two cities, the more strongly negative the weight. You can see that this will push the network state towards a minimum tour length.

Using a continuous-activation version of the model, Hopfield and Tank, working in 1985, were able to find a set of weights that associated energy minima with short tours. They were able to find good solutions for up to thirty-city problems. However, beyond this limit, performance was not so good. Since Hopfield and Tank's original work, much research has gone into improving it: new update schemes and activation functions, the addition of noise, modified energy function and other fixes have all led to better results.

Hopfield networks have been used in numerous practical optimisation applications, including routing in packet-switched communication networks (look back to Block 3 for information about this); medical image analysis; and scheduling of satellite broadcasts.

3.5   Other examples of recurrent networks

Bi-directional memories

To finish our discussion of fully recurrent networks, let's consider one further style of recurrent topology, in which a layered structure is combined with the fully recurrent network's property of state evolution over time: the **bi-directional associative memory** (BAM).

You may recall that you met associative memories in Section 2.6 of Unit 2 of this block. In these simple single-layered feedforward systems, the network learns to *associate* certain input vectors with specific output vectors. As with any associative network, the system can be trained on a sequence of pairs of vectors, $(\mathbf{x}_1, \mathbf{y}_1)$, $(\mathbf{x}_2, \mathbf{y}_2)$, $(\mathbf{x}_3, \mathbf{y}_3)$ ... $(\mathbf{x}_n, \mathbf{y}_n)$, with the **x** vectors being subject to the orthonormality constraints on stored patterns you learned about in Unit 2. In some cases, $\mathbf{x}_i$ and $\mathbf{y}_i$ may be identical vectors, in which case the network is an auto-associator. After training, the presence of $\mathbf{x}_i$ at the input means that the network should respond with $\mathbf{y}_i$ at the output, even if the input pattern is damaged or incomplete. All vector elements are generally either bipolar binary (i.e. all 1 or −1), or unipolar binary (1 or 0).

A simple associative memory can be made into a BAM simply by modifying the feedforward connections to run in *both* directions. To illustrate this, look at Figure 4.28. This depicts a network of familiar appearance, consisting of two layers fully connected, with no links within each layer.

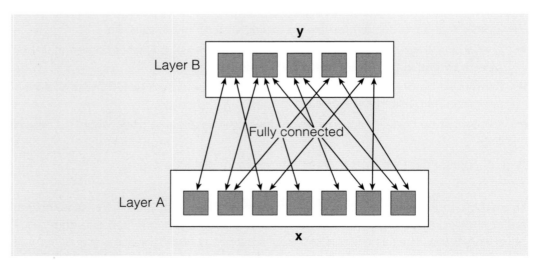

Figure 4.28   A BAM

Suppose for the moment that the network has been trained and we are testing it out on a number of incomplete or noisy versions of $\mathbf{x}_1$, $\mathbf{x}_2$, $\mathbf{x}_3$ ... $\mathbf{x}_n$, say $\mathbf{x}_a$, $\mathbf{x}_b$, $\mathbf{x}_c$ ... etc. Now the network state evolves in cycles, like this:

1   Present a pattern **x** at layer A.

2   Feedforward in the normal way to layer B.

3   Switch so that the response at layer B becomes the input and feed back to layer A.

4   Go back to step 2.

5   Continue until patterns **x** and **y** have stabilised and there is no further change.

The question is, will the network stabilise? And if so, how? Well, like other recurrent networks BAMs also have an associated energy function, diminishing (or remaining the same) as the network state evolves. The function is:

$$E = -\mathbf{x}^T\mathbf{Wy} \qquad (4.15)$$

for each associated pair of input vectors **x** and **y**. Then, when a mutilated version of one of the stored patterns is presented, the network energy should steadily diminish from cycle to cycle until the network stabilises at a reconstructed version of the closest stored input and output vectors.

4 Dynamic and chaotic neural networks

At this point, it might be a good idea to stand back and take a critical look at fully recurrent networks and their behaviour. You've learned about the structure of the BSB and Hopfield models, done experiments with them, and looked at their inner workings: activation rules, update algorithms, etc. Consider this question for a moment.

SAQ 4.11

Think about the activation functions of BSB and the update rules of Hopfield networks. Did any general features of their design strike you?

ANSWER...

You may have been rather unclear what I was getting at here. My main idea was that I was trying to suggest that they were very *constrained* by their designers. For example, in BSB the possible activations of the units were forced to plateau at 1 and −1 to limit the system to the inside of the box. In the Hopfield system, only one unit is allowed to update at each time step, the weights are symmetrical and there are no connections w_{jj}.

There is one reason for these limitations being deliberately built in to the networks, I think.

Exercise 4.11

Why do you think Hopfield and Anderson chose these limitations?

Discussion ....

I think their motivation was simply this: *stability* and *convergence*. Anderson wanted the system states of BSB to converge on the vertices of the box and stabilise there. Hopfield wanted a smooth decline in the energy function and eventual stabilisation in low-energy optima.

From time immemorial, engineers have striven to bring stability to the systems they construct. Their enemies have always been volatility, disruption and flux. Mechanical engineers worry about vibration; electronic engineers fret about feedback and noise; electrical engineers battle with voltage unsteadiness and external fields. For engineers, instability is a foe to be eliminated, minimised or filtered out. And you can see that the same considerations must surely apply to recurrent neural networks: their essence is feedback; and feedback, as we noted in Section 3.3 above, does not necessarily lead to stability: a feedback system *may* converge to a stable state, but other outcomes are just as likely – periodic attractors, transients, and so on.

SAQ 4.12

In the Game of Life simulation, we observed periodic attractors (e.g. blinkers) and quasi-periodic structures (e.g. gliders). Do you recall there being any other possible outcomes?

ANSWER..

You may remember the strange case of the r-pentomino. Starting from this state, there seemed to be an explosion of activity across the grid, with no clear order or pattern to it.

It was once thought that only complex systems can produce complex behaviour; and if a system displays apparently random behaviour this can only be due to randomness within it. But there is now abundant evidence that is not true: out of even very simple systems, **chaos** can emerge.

Chaos has been an idea much discussed in recent years, and much nonsense has been talked about it. In fact, there is little agreement among researchers as to what chaos actually is. The mathematician Ian Stewart offers a nice definition:

> ... lawless behaviour governed entirely by law.

The Game of Life is a perfect example: the rules are very simple; the outcome is certainly unpredictable. Randomness need not arise from randomness, but can just as easily emerge from order.

The mathematics of chaos is generally very demanding and this course is not the place to struggle with it. In a moment I will offer a few general principles of chaos, but the best way to get some insight into chaotic systems is through a simple computer exercise.

Computer Exercise 4.4 (optional)

In this exercise, you investigate the behaviour of a very simple, and very well-known, chaotic system – *the logistic map*. If you have time, load up and complete Computer Exercise 4.4 on the course DVD.

Without going into any maths, then, we can make the following general observations about chaos:

▶ *Determinism*. This is the point I made earlier. A chaotic system obeys completely fixed rules, but produces behaviour that appears to be random.

▶ *Sensitivity to initial conditions*. The most minuscule difference in starting conditions will mean that the system state will move off on a completely different trajectory. You've already seen this kind of behaviour in the Game of Life and in the BSB.

▶ *Strange attractors*. Chaotic behaviour is obviously not convergent stability (an attractor), but neither is it periodic or quasi-periodic. In fact, the time evolution of chaotic systems is often characterised by **strange** or **chaotic attractors**. Figure 4.29 illustrates one of the most famous of these: the *Lorenz attractor*. This illustrates the trajectory through the phase space of a system generated by simple rules. As the system state winds around the attractor, it never repeats exactly the same path, but never leaves the strict bounds of the attractor.

▶ *Fractal dimension*. A line is a one-dimensional shape; a plane two-dimensional; a cube three-dimensional. Strange attractors have a *fractional* dimension, like 3/2 or 2/5. Further discussion of this will have to be left to another course.

Putting these technical points aside for a moment, chaotic behaviour is visible everywhere in the world, from patterns in the clouds to the flow of water; from

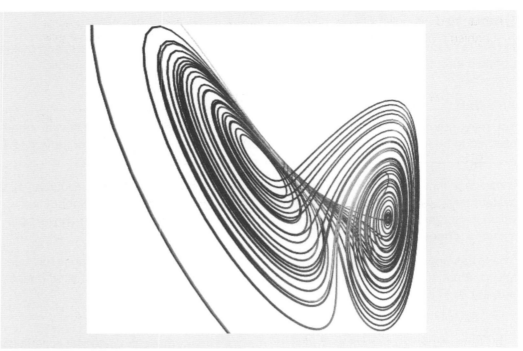

Figure 4.29   The Lorenz attractor

the behaviour of stock markets and economies to the movements of planets and galaxies.

But what has this to do with neural networks? Two points, I think – both following fairly obviously from the theme of this unit:

1   *Inputs that evolve in time.* The early part of this unit dealt with networks capable of handling time series information. But real-world systems seldom evolve in neat regular ways: most of the time we have to deal with time series that are chaotic.

2   *System states that evolve in time.* It seems immensely unlikely that real neural systems, the nervous systems of animals, behave in the kind of smooth, orderly, convergent way as the models we have looked at so far in this unit. There is just too much feedback. Highly recurrent neural networks, real or artificial, will almost certainly exhibit chaotic behaviour as they change over time. In living creatures, stability is death.

Taking the second point first, what evidence is there for it? One name stands out here: that of the American neurophysiologist, Walter Freeman. Many of Freeman's investigations have centred on the question of **olfaction** – the sense of smell. You might recall one of our case studies from Unit 1 of Block 3, the remarkable direction-finding capabilities of the lobster, which were based entirely on olfactory analysis of water-borne plumes. There are two puzzling features of olfaction:

► What mechanisms produce such a fast response to odours? Experiments with rabbits have shown that within 0.1 second of an olfactory stimulus being presented, there are neural firings across the entire region of the cortex responsible for interpreting smells, the olfactory bulb.

► Given that sometimes only a few molecules of the smell stimulus may be involved, and that the olfactory sensors are often very far apart, how is such a unified response produced?

Careful measurements with an array of 64 electrodes over the surface of the olfactory bulb convinced Freeman that a *chaotic attractor* was involved. In the absence of any odour, neurons fired all over the cortex in random patterns. On presentation of a known stimulus, neurons fired in a chaotic pattern that was similar in structure across all 64 sensors.

Freeman and his collaborators have produced a computer model of the neural mechanisms at work in olfaction. Figure 4.30 shows a simplified version of this.

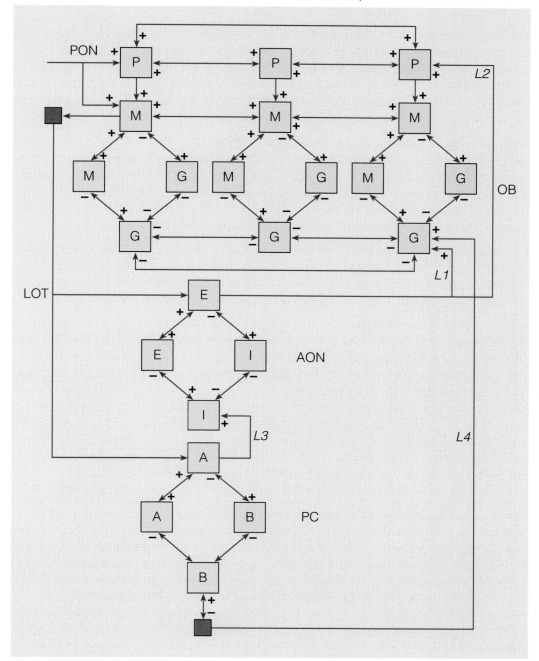

Figure 4.30   Highly simplified model of olfactory system in the rabbit

Here are its main features:

▶ Olfactory signals arrive at the bulb along the pathway labelled PON, activating the P neurons there.

▶ The P neurons excite groups of M neurons in the area marked OB, which are also stimulated by the PON pathway.

▶ There are dense recurrent excitatory connections between the M neurons and G neurons, the G cells receiving excitation from M cells, but returning inhibition. This causes their firings to oscillate at low frequency.

▶ The entire population of M and G cells in the OB region transmits activity along the LOT pathway to the AON.

▶ In the AON there are groups of E and I neurons, interconnected similarly to the M and G cells. These show the same patterns of oscillation as the M and G groups in the OB, although at a different frequency.

The interconnection of the various areas along the pathways labelled *L1* to *L4* produces a state of chaotic firing across the whole network. Simulating this on a Cray supercomputer, Freeman was able to train the network on various patterns, using a version of Hebbian learning. Thereafter the network was able to recognise, classify and generalise from new patterns presented to it. Applying a pattern shifted the activity of the whole population into a chaotic attractor that was close to periodic.

Freeman's claim is a bold and quite controversial one: the normal state of the nervous system is not stability and convergence, but *chaos*. Neurons are never at rest: they fire all the time, unceasingly, their interactions producing a basic chaotic state. Thoughts, memories and actions correspond to populations of neurons locking temporarily into transient chaotic attractors, which soon dissolve back into the background chaos. All human-engineered systems are built to avoid chaos: brains exploit it.

Can the engineers of artificial neural networks learn to accept, understand and exploit chaos too? This is still a matter of research and controversy, and the theoretical and mathematical issues become very difficult at this point. However, there have been applications in various areas, which I have just space to touch on here.

Recognition and classification. In 1991, Y. Yao, one of Freeman's collaborators, applied the olfactory model to the problem of detecting defects in small machine parts. Mixtures of parts such as ball bearings, machine screws, etc. tumbled down a chute and were scanned ultrasonically as they passed, and the resulting data was then reduced to a 64-bit vector which was presented to the olfactory model. The aim was that the system would classify parts into acceptable and defective – obviously a very difficult problem as the parts were tumbling as they moved down the chute and could thus be scanned from any angle. The result was 100% success on unacceptable components and 80% on acceptable ones (i.e. there was a 20% misclassification of acceptable parts as unacceptable. By way of comparison, a backpropagation network frequently misclassified up to 50% of unacceptable parts and 87.5% of acceptable ones!

Optimisation. There have been many attempts to exploit chaotic dynamics to solve optimisation problems such as the TSP. Most of these have been based on the Hopfield model I outlined in Section 3.5, but with amended weights and activation functions that produce chaotic attractors, and associating each attractor with a possible tour. Most of these approaches have been shown to work quite well for small problems (e.g. about ten cities), but do not scale up – you'll recall that Hopfield and Tank had the same problem. More recent research, reported by Hasegawa, Ikeguchi and Aihara (2002), combined fully recurrent networks capable of performing a conventional form of search, known as *2-opt tabu search*, with chaotic dynamics. One of these was capable of finding good solutions to TSP problems of up to 89 500 cities.

Robotic control. Mohammed Islam and Kazuyuki Murase (2005) analysed the time series structure of the sensory information flowing through three different neural controllers in an autonomous robot, as the robot navigated through various environments. The weights of the robot had been trained using a genetic algorithm (we will study these in the next block). The researchers found that all the time series had chaotic dynamics, with the robot switching between trajectories within the chaotic attractor as it faced different tasks. They also found that the controller best fitted for each task had the highest degree of chaos in its sensory flow.

Obviously I've been able to do no more than summarise these research directions here. I've provided links and references on the course website and/or the course DVD which will enable you to follow up if you have time.

5 Summary of Unit 4

The difficulty of this unit has been to condense a very complicated and wide-ranging subject into a reasonable space, and to cut down as far as possible on mathematical complexities. But the theme of the unit can be stated in one word: time. We live in a world of time, and neural networks – if they are to be useful – must live there too.

I distinguished two ways in which time affects neural systems:

▶ They may have to deal with inputs that evolve over time – time series information.

▶ The state of the network itself may evolve over time: this is especially true of recurrent systems.

To illustrate the first of these types of networks, I used the Elman system, a layered network in which context information is fed back to become part of the input at the next stage. We looked at some diverting attempts at creating music with such systems.

I then discussed the structure and typical time evolution of the second type of network, ones with fully recurrent topologies, developing some of the concepts and terminology appropriate to these kinds of dynamic system, and illustrating these with the BSB and Hopfield models. We saw how the state of such systems develops over time, and how this evolution can be used in practical applications, such as optimisation and classification.

We concluded with a necessarily brief and superficial look at the issue of chaos, which has long been recognised to be a property of fully recurrent neural networks. I suggested some concepts for thinking about chaos, and reported on some relatively recent work on its applications in neural systems.

Now look back at the learning outcomes for this unit and check these against what you think you can now do. Return to any section of the unit if you feel you need to.

Conclusion to Block 4

Block 4 conclusion

Block 4 is the longest and probably the most technically demanding block in M366. Although I've been able to do no more than present some of the groundwork to the theory and practice of neural networks, and point you in the direction of some of the research that is being done in the area, it has still been necessary to go into quite a lot of specialised detail. There was no getting away from this.

Looking back, you will recall that we've covered the following ground:

▶ pattern recognition capabilities of humans and animals;

▶ biological nervous systems and their properties;

▶ mathematical and computer models of nervous systems;

▶ layered networks, their training and applications;

▶ self-organising maps, their training and applications;

▶ recurrent networks, including dynamic systems and chaos.

In the end, though, after all the equations and the algorithms, I think it's most important to place neural networks in the context of the themes of M366. Nervous systems are a biological phenomenon, and one of the keys – perhaps *the* key – to natural intelligence. Artificial neural networks aim to replicate some of their properties: pattern recognition, classification and completion. And in neural networks, as you've seen, three of the key mechanisms of natural intelligence come together: interaction (between simple units), emergence (the ability of networks to memorise whole patterns and generalise from experience) and adaptation (the capacity to learn by the alteration of weights).

But neural networks have other applications beyond pattern recognition; and they can be made to adapt in ways other than through training. As you learned in Block 3, nature appears to have another form of adaptation, quite distinct from learning: evolution through natural selection, in which whole species adapt over aeons of time. In the next block, we're going to look into these processes more deeply, and at the end you will meet neural networks again in a quite different role.

For now, though, look back at the learning outcomes for this block and check these against what you think you can now do. Return to any part of the block if you need to.

You will find further case studies, exercises, links and other supplementary material for this block on the course DVD and on the course website.

References and further reading

Further reading

In writing this text I used many sources. The list that follows is a selection of the sources that I consider you may find helpful in reading further on this topic.

Haykin, S. (1998) *Neural Networks: A comprehensive foundation*, Englewood Cliffs, NJ, Prentice Hall.

Patterson, D.W. (1996) *Artificial Neural Networks: Theory and applications*, Singapore, Prentice Hall.

References

Chen, S., Ding, Y. and Wei, C. (2002) 'Dynamic bus arrival time prediction with artificial neural networks', *Journal of Transportation Engineering*, vol. 128, no. 5, pp. 429–438.

Eck, D. and Schmidhuber, J. (2002) 'Learning the long-term structure of the blues' in Dorronsoro, J. (ed.) *Proceedings of International Conference on Artificial Neural Networks* ICANN'02, Madrid, Springer, Berlin, pp. 284–289.

Edelman, G. (1993) *Bright Air, Brilliant Fire*, New York, Basic Books.

Elman, J.L. (1990) 'Finding structure in time', *Cognitive Science*, vol. 14, pp. 179–211.

Freeman, W.J. (1994) 'Neural networks and chaos', *Journal of Theoretical Biology*, vol. 171, pp. 13–18.

Hasegawa, M., Ikeguchi, T. and Aihara, K. (2002) 'Solving large-scale traveling salesman problems with chaotic neurodynamics', *Neural Networks*, vol. 15, pp. 271–283.

Hebb, D.O. (1946) *The Organisation of Behaviour*, New York, Wiley.

Hopfield, J.J. (1982) 'Neural networks and physical systems with emergent collective computational abilities', *Proceedings of the National Academy of Sciences of the USA*, vol. 79, pp. 2554–2558.

Hopfield, J.J. and Tank, T.W. (1985) 'Neural computation of decisions in optimization problems', *Biological Cybernetics*, vol. 52, pp. 141–152.

Islam, M.M. and Murase, K. (2005) 'Chaotic dynamics of a behaviour-based miniature mobile robot: effects of environment and control structure', *Neural Networks*, vol. 18, pp. 123–144.

Klevecz, R. (1999) 'The whole EST catalog', *Scientist*, vol. 13, no. 2, p. 22.

Kohonen, T. (2000) *Self Organizing Maps*, Berlin/London, Springer.

Kuffler, S.W., Nicholls, J.G. and Martin, R. (1984) *From Neuron to Brain: A cellular approach to the function of the nervous system*, Sunderland MA, Sinauer Associates Inc.

Lagus, K., Honkela, T., Kaski, S. and Kohonen T. (1996) 'WEBSOM – a status report', Proceedings of STeP'96 in Alander, J., Honkela, T. and Jakobsson, M. (eds) *Publications of the Finnish Artificial Intelligence Society*, pp. 73–78.

McCulloch, W.S. and Pitts, W. (1943) 'A logical calculus of the ideas immanent in nervous activity', *Bulletin of Mathematical Biophysics*, vol. 5, pp. 115–133.

Minsky, M.L. (1991) 'Logical versus analogical or symbolic versus connectionist or neat versus scruffy', *AI Magazine*, vol. 12, no. 2, pp. 34–51.

Minsky, M.L. and Papert, S.A. (1969) *Perceptrons*, Cambridge MA, MIT Press.

Mozer, M.C. (1994) 'Neural network music composition by prediction', *Connection Science*, vol. 6, pp. 247–280.

Rosenblatt, F. (1958) 'The Perceptron: a probabilistic model for information storage and organization in the brain', *Psychological Review*, vol. 65, no. 6, pp. 386–408.

Rumelhart, D.E., McClelland, J.L. and The PDP Research Group (1987) *Parallel Distributed Processing: Explorations in the microstructure of cognition: Volume 1 (Foundations), Volume 2 (Computational models of cognition and perception)*, Cambridge MA, MIT Press.

Werbos, P.J. (1990) 'Backpropagation through time: what it does and how to do it', *Proceedings of the IEEE*, vol. 78, no. 10, pp. 1550–1560.

Widrow, B. and Winter, R. (1988) 'Neural nets for adaptive filtering and adaptive pattern recognition', *Computer*, vol. 21, no. 3, pp. 25–39.

Xiang Xiao, Dow, E.R., Eberhart, R., Ben Miled, Z. and Oppelt, R.J. (2006) 'Gene clustering using self-organizing maps and particle swarm optimization', *Fifth IEEE International Workshop on High Performance Computational Biology*.

Acknowledgements

Grateful acknowledgement is made to the following sources for permission to reproduce material within this course text.

Figures

Figure 1.5(a): NASA;

Figure 1.5(b): NASA / Science Photo Library;

Figure 1.7: Copyright © 2005, the Regents of the University of Michigan;

Figure 1.8: Science Photo Library;

Figure 1.9: BCC Microimaging Corporation;

Figure 1.10: Biophoto Associates / Science Photo Library;

Figure 1.15: Professor S. Cinti / Science Photo Library;

Figure 1.17: Vincent W. Hevern, SJ, Ph.D;

Figure 2.32: Courtesy of David E. Rumelhart;

Figure 2.33: Courtesy of James McClelland;

Figure 3.8: Professor Thomas Dean, Brown University, Rhode Island, USA;

Figure 3.9: Courtesy of Markus Dahlem, Copyright © 2005 Migraine Aura Foundation;

Figure 3.14: Courtesy of Professor Teuvo Kohonen;

Figures 3.19, *3.22*, *3.23* and *3.24:* Kohonen T., 'Illustration of the Word Cluster Map', abstract from *Exploration of Very Large Databases by Self-organising Maps*, Helsinki University.

Cover image

Image used on the cover and elsewhere: Daniel H. Janzen.

Every effort has been made to contact copyright holders. If any have been inadvertently overlooked the publishers will be pleased to make the necessary arrangements at the first opportunity.

Index for Block 4

A

action potential 22, 24

activation function 36

ADALINE 64
    as adaptive filter 86

Anderson, James 194

angular distance 123

architectural graph 52

artificial neural networks 18

associative memories 87
    auto-associators 87
    hetero-associators 87

asynchronous stochastic update 198

attractors 193

axon 20

axon terminal 23

B

backpropagation through time 178
    epochwise backpropagation through time
    (EBPTT) 176
    truncated error backpropagation through time 178

BAM – see bi-directional memories 202

basin of attraction 199

batch map training 146

bi-directional memories
    bi-directional associative memory (BAM) 202

bias 46

bipolar function 81

Brain-State-in-a-Box 163, 196

C

cascade correlation networks 111

CEC – see long short-term memory 182

central nervous system 20

cerebral cortex 130

chaos 163, 205

chaotic neural networks
    chaos 205
    fractal dimension 205
    strange attractors 205

clamped activation 45

classification 12, 18

code vector 133

competitive learning 118, 134

completion 16

connectedness 89

connectionism 18

content addressability 16

content addressable memory 189

context units 169

cortical columns 130

D

data dredging 148

decision boundary 68

delta rule 76, 84
    aka Widrow–Hoff or LMS rule 77
    algorithm 83
    error space 77
    error surface 77, 79
    gradient descent 77

depolarisation 23

derivative 80

discrete time 29

dot product 55

dynamic system 163

E

EBPTT – see backpropagation through time 176

Eck, Douglas 185

Edelman, Gerald 28, 58

Elman network 163, 176

Elman, Jeffrey L 166

energy function 197

error backpropagation 108
    activation function slope 106
    algorithm 101
    batch update 108
    error minimum 107
    error surface 103
    factors affecting 108
    initial weights 105
    learning constant 105
    momentum term 106
    number of hidden units 105
    optimum architecture 104
    random presentation 107
    vanilla 103

error descent 77

error signal 74

error space 77

error surface 77

Euclidean distance 123

excitatory synapse 25

F
false attractors 199

feature detectors 90

feedforward networks 41

firing (of neuron) 23

fractal dimension 205

Freeman, Walter 206

fully recurrent network 190

G
garden path sentences 167

Gaussian function 110

gene clustering 157

generalised delta rule 95

gestalt effect 16

glial cells 21

Golgi, Camillo 19

gradient descent 76

grandmother cell 30

H
Hasegawa *et al* 208

Hebb Rule 47–48, 53, 72, 125

Hebb, Donald 30

Hebbian learning 47, 129

Hebbian synapse 30

hidden layer 41

hidden units 95

homunculi 27

Hopfield model 202
    and the TSP 202
    asynchronous stochastic update 198
    basin of attraction 199
    energy function 197
    memory constraints 200

Hopfield network 163

Hopfield, John Joseph 32

Hubel, David 127

hypercube 70

hyperplane 70

hyperpolarisation 23

I
inhibitory synapse 25

inner product 55

input space 67

ions 22

Ising spin glass model 32

Islam, Mohammed 208

K
key addressable memory 188

Kohonen, Teuvo 32, 137

L
lateral connection 42

lateral excitation and inhibition 137

lattice 118

lattice networks 42

layered recurrent networks 163, 167
    input–output model 167
    recurrent multi-layer perceptron 167
    state space model 167

learning 12

learning constant 74

learning rules 44, 47–48
Hebb Rule 48
supervised learning 48
unsupervised learning 48

learning vector quantisation 32, 146

least mean square (LMS) rule 77

lexical classes 173

linear equation 69

linear separability 69

local field 169

local minimum 102

localised potential 22

long short-term memory 163
constant error carousel (CEC) 182
memory cells 182

long-term potientiation 26

LSTM – see long short-term memory 163

LTP – see long-term potientiation 26

M
maps 26
self-organising 32

matrix 55

McClelland, Jay 93

McCollough–Pitts neuron 35

McCullough, Warren 29

Mexican hat function 139

Minsky and Papert, Perceptrons 32, 89–90, 94

Minsky, Marvin 89

momentum 106

motor strip 27

Mountcastel, Vernon 130

Mozer, Mike 182

multi-layer perceptron 111
structure 96

Murase, Kazuyuki 208

music composition and RNNs, CONCERT 182

N
natural intelligence 10, 12, 14, 29, 32, 57

neighbourhood 139

nervous system 20

neural Darwinism 28

neural firing 23

neural maps 28

neural networks 18

neural spike 23

neurocomputing 18

neuron 19–20

neurotransmitter 24

O
olfaction 206

order of perceptron 92

output function 39

overfitting 107

overtraining 107

P
Papert, Seymour 89

pareidolia 16

parity 89

PDP Papers, The 93

Perceptron 31

perceptron convergence theorem 76

perceptron geometry 70
decision boundary 68
decision hyperplane 70
hypercube 70
input space 70
linear separability 69
weight space 70

perceptron rule
algorithm 73
learning constant 74
perceptron convergence theorem 76

periodic attractors 193

peripheral nervous system 20

phase space 193

Pitts, Walter 29

plasticity 31

post-synaptic cell 25

pre-synaptic cell 24

processing element 35

Q

quasi-periodic states 193

R

radial basis function networks 110

Ramon y Cajal, Santiago 19

receptive field 127

recognition 12, 16

recurrence 32

recurrent networks 33, 42, 44, 118, 163, 167, 190

refractory period 23

reinforcement learning 48

response 12, 18

resting potential 23

retinal ganglia 126

rods and cones 126

Rosenblatt's perceptron 64

Rosenblatt, Frank 31, 214

Rumelhart, David 93

S

scalar 55

Schmidhuber, Jürgen 185

self-growing network 111

self-organisation 124

self-organising feature maps – *see* self-organising maps 137

self-organising maps 32, 137, 158
    convergence phase 144
    for optimisation 157
    in bioinformatics 158
    learning performance 145
    learning vector quantisation 147
    self-organising phase 144
    unsupervised training 143

sigma notation 53

sigmoid 39

sigmoid function
    bipolar 81
    unipolar 77

signal graph 50, 52

single-layer perceptron 93

SOFM – *see* self-organising maps 137

SOM – *see* self-organising maps 137

somatosensory strip 26

spike 23

spike train 23

state 191

state space 191

state transition 191

steepest descent 77

strange attractors 205

supervised learning 48

synapse 19, 26
    excitatory 25
    inhibitory 25

T

tessaract 70

time series 165

topographical ordering 132

topologies 39, 44
    lattice networks 42
    layered networks 41
    recurrent networks 44

training rule 72

trajectory 193

transients 193

truth table 35

U

unipolar function 77

units 35, 39

unsupervised learning 32, 48, 123

V

V1 127

validation set 107

vanilla backpropagation 103

vanishing gradients 182

vector quantisation 133

vector-matrix notation 56
    dot product 55
    matrix 55
    vector 54

visual cortex 127

visual field 126

von der Malsburg, Christoph 124

Voronoi
  cells 133
  regions 133
  tesselations 133
  vector 133

W
WEBSOM 156
  browser 155
  document encoding 151
  training 153
  word histogram 150

weight space 70

weights 35, 39

Widrow–Hoff rule 77

Wiesel, Torsten 127

winner-takes-all learning 134

word histogram 150

Y
Yao, Y 208